THE COURAGE CHALLENGE

Biblical Encouragements for Young Champions

THE COURAGE CHALLENGE

Biblical Encouragements for Young Champions

DANIEL L. SWITZER, ED. D.

Lederer Books
An imprint of
Messianic Jewish Publishers
Clarksville, MD 21029

Printed in the United States of America
Cover design by Lisa Rubin,
Messianic Jewish Publishers
Graphic Design by Yvonne Vermillion,
MagicGraphix.com

1 2020
ISBN 9781951833121

Published by:
Lederer Books
An imprint of Messianic Jewish Publishers
6120 Day Long Lane
Clarksville, MD 21029

Distributed by:
Messianic Jewish Publishers & Resources
Order line: (800) 410-7367
lederer@messianicjewish.net
www.MessianicJewish.net

This book is dedicated to my family—
my wife Silvia and our children
Anna, Caleb, Nehemiah, and Joshua. I am exceedingly grateful
for your love and encouragement along this life's journey.
The sweetness of your fellowship is one of
the greatest joys of my life.

CONTENTS

INTRODUCTION

Allow me to share my heart for this book, *The Courage Challenge: Biblical Encouragements for Young Champions.* My wife Silvia and I have run a Christian day camp for twenty-seven years, called Camp Courage. Among the fifty-some different activities that we do during a week of camp, our enduring mission has been to *encourage these children to be champions for the Lord.* The centerpiece each day of camp has been the "Courage Challenge": an inspiring message about a real Biblical person—a champion who trusted the Lord to do great exploits for God!

After we had run the camp for many years, my brother Paul encouraged me to write a book called *The Courage Challenge.* I started praying about this and gradually pulled my talks together which resulted in this book, which examines the great champions of the Bible—ordinary men and women who yielded themselves to God's purpose for their lives.

Exactly what is a champion? A champion is one who has a worthy cause, a compelling mission that is bigger than him or herself. A champion is different from a hero—a hero is someone who does a spontaneous heroic act, such as saving a baby from a burning building. Doing something heroic takes great courage. However, a champion is different; a champion gives his life for an enduring cause—one that becomes his life mission and often involves leading others. Of course, the cause of the champions of the Bible is the cause of the God of the Bible, the cause of his anointed one, Jesus.

As I went through the Bible searching out God's champions, I would ask questions such as: What made them different from others? What gave them the courage to stand for God and his Word? What motivated them to righteous action?

Now, let me share a little of my personal testimony that motivates me to this day to encourage children to be champions. As a young boy growing up in a pastor's family, I experienced serious bullying that caused great fear in my life. Out of that crucible came a personal desire to help children to become courageous. At Camp Courage, we teach the children that our natural desire when faced with fearful bullies or circumstances is the "Fight or Flight" syndrome—either we fight back or we run away. However, instead of fighting back or running away, we teach the children to *stand.*

Ephesians 6:12-13 emphasizes the need for believers to *stand* amid the battle.

> For our struggle is not against flesh and blood, but against the rulers, against the authorities, against the powers of this dark world and against the spiritual forces of evil in the heavenly realms. Therefore, put on the full armor of God, so that when the day of evil comes, you may be able to stand your ground, and after you have done everything, to stand.

Instead of running away or fighting back out of fear, we teach the children to stand and be a godly influence among their peers. We encourage them to know their position in Messiah—that they are the head and not the tail—and to lead others in the right direction. We encourage them to stand for God, to stand against negative peer pressure, and to stand up for and help the weak.

But how do we teach our children to stand in this way? This book is not only for children and young people; it's also for parents who desire to equip their children to stand for others as godly champions. As parents, we learn the following from Romans 15:4, "For everything that was written in the past was written to teach us, so that through endurance and the encouragement of the Scriptures we might have hope." All of these stories of courageous champions in the Bible provide us with real examples that help us to illustrate to our own children how they can face difficult challenges.

Parents, as you teach your children about these champions, I strongly encourage you to emphasize that the Bible is the inspired *true* Word of God. In our society, the truth of God's Word is under relentless attack. These Biblical accounts of God's champions are not just exciting "stories" of fictional characters. No, they are true accounts of true people dealing with true events in their lives. They illustrate true followers of God from which we can make true application to our lives. This is true history—Biblical history.

I encourage you to actively use the Bible to teach your children. One of our nation's founding fathers, Benjamin Rush, in giving arguments for the Bible to be used as a schoolbook for children, made this observation:

> The interesting events and characters recorded and described in the Old and New Testaments are accommodated, above all others, to seize upon all the faculties of the minds of children. The understanding, the memory, the imagination, the passions, and the moral powers are all occasionally addressed by the various incidents which are contained in those Divine books insomuch that not to be delighted with them is to be devoid of every principle of pleasure that exists in a sound mind (Barton, 54-55).

Benjamin Rush knew that these great accounts of Biblical champions are of such enjoyment that they capture the attention of children and can be used to teach them inspiring lessons.

As we teach our children, it's important to remember that these great champions in the Bible are not Superheroes. Of course, many children love the comic superheroes—characters such as Superman, Batman, Wonder Woman, and Captain America. However, here we are giving them not superheroes; rather, we are giving them real people from the Bible who learned to trust God as they faced very difficult challenges and trials. Through sharing these true Biblical accounts with our children, we are able to emphasize to our children the truth of 1 Timothy 4:12, "Don't let anyone look down on you because you are young, but set an example for the believers in speech, in life, in love, in faith and in purity." The Lord desires to use our young people to do great exploits to advance his kingdom!

How can these young people become godly champions? The common theme that you see in the lives of Biblical champions as they embraced God's call is that they understood this simple truth: that "the Lord is with you." Whether Joshua as he was about to lead the people to take the promised land, Gideon as he faced the Midianites, or the disciples as they were being commissioned by Jesus, God's encouragement over and over again to his champions are the reassuring words: "I will be with you!" And so we see through these great champions that the antidote to fear and the key to Biblical courage is a convictional focus on Messiah's presence—becoming consciously aware that God is always present!

As our children learn to count on God's presence, they will learn to walk in God's courage. In his book, *The Abolition of Man*, C. S. Lewis wrote about "men without chests," people driven by pure reason (the head) or pure emotion (the belly). In his work, "chests" referred to absolutes. In other words, people with chests are driven by character whereas people without chests are driven by the desires of their flesh or the reasoning of their minds (Lewis, Ch. 1).

Our children need to have "chests." They need to have something inside them. I would suggest that they need *godly courage!* At Camp Courage, we do this exercise in which we look into each other's eyes and declare the word "Courage!" with conviction. Our children need to have courageous character inside them that drives them forward to lead others in doing the right thing as opposed to just following the crowd. They need to have courageous "guts" inside them to stand up and lead their peers in the right direction.

After sharing about the great champions of faith in Hebrews 11, the writer of Hebrews stated the following for us in Hebrews 12:1-2:

> Therefore, since we are surrounded by such a great cloud of witnesses [who are God's champions], let us throw off everything that hinders and the sin that so easily entangles, and let us run with perseverance the race marked out for us. Let us fix our eyes on Jesus, the author and perfecter of our faith, who for the joy set before him endured the cross, scorning its shame, and sat down at the right hand of the throne of God.

Just as God's champions did, we need to encourage and train our children to fix their eyes on Messiah and count upon him as being always present!

As parents, let us encourage our children to follow the example of these Biblical champions who trusted the Lord. Let us challenge our young people to continue this relay race of faithful champions in the great cause of Messiah. Parents, one of the ways this book could be used is as a devotional for your children. One chapter could be read in the course of a week to encourage and challenge your young person. At the end of each "Courage Challenge" is an applicable Bible passage that I encourage you to have your children commit to memory. Instilling the Word of God in our children is an invaluable tool to help them stand courageously for the Lord. This book is for children, for young people, *and for their parents* who are seeking to raise up their children to become champions for God—servant leaders of godly character who give themselves for the cause of Messiah!

Dr. Daniel L. Switzer

ADAM AND EVE

Take Responsibility; Don't Pass the Blame

In Genesis chapter 3, Satan, disguised as a serpent, starts a conversation with Eve. He questions what God had said to Adam, "Did God really say, 'You must not eat from any tree in the garden'?" (Gen. 3:1). He started to raise doubts regarding God's Word. As Satan came against God's Word, Eve began to listen to his rationalizations.

Indeed, Eve added to God's Word. She said that we "must not touch it," which the Lord had not said. Satan's lies were working on her as he came against God as the rightful authority. In verse 5, he used a half-truth, which really is not a truth at all, but a lie. He said, "Your eyes will be opened," but he also said, "You will be like God." This making of man into God is an age-old lie used by Satan in the minds of people. This philosophy of life is called humanism—replacing God with man or making man his own God. In order not to be deceived by such philosophies—ideas contrary to God's Word—we need to be continually studying and growing in our understanding of God's Word. This way we will not be deceived by partial "truth"—mixing truth into what is really a falsehood.

In verse 6, we find that Adam has been with Eve for their entire conversation. (Adam should have spoken up.) Well, Adam and Eve were tempted, gave into temptation, and ate of the tree of the knowledge of good and evil. The Bible says that their eyes were opened, but sadly, their innocence was gone. At that point, they realized they were naked and tried to cover themselves.

When we sin, in our humanity we have a natural desire to try to cover it up. The Bible says that there is a deceitful quality to sin. We try to hide our sin.

For us as parents, we need to understand that our children will naturally try to hide their sin. In fact, I have observed how parents sometimes unwittingly train their children to lie to them by expressing harsh disappointment when their children do wrong. Of course, children don't want to disappoint their parents. Worse, children don't want to experience their parents' wrath—harsh yelling and punishments. This kind of parenting is not a deterrent to bad behavior as much as it can be a cause for our children lying to us in the future.

Well, the Bible tells us that Adam and Eve hid from the Lord. Sin, unconfessed, alienates us from God. A major issue impacting our youth is not just sin but *hidden* sin—unconfessed sin, hiding sin from one's parents.

Looking for Adam and Eve, God called to them, "Where are you?" (Gen. 3:9). Of course, God knew where they were. He was making a point that he was looking for them. Even when we sin, God is looking for us; he is calling out to us and desires us to return to Him because he loves us.

Adam and Eve were afraid of God, afraid of the rightful authority. Hidden sin impacts our relationship with God. Young person, when you sin, don't hide from God; repent and turn back to God quickly. When you sin, don't run away from God; instead, run *to* Him and receive God's cleansing.

God questioned Adam and Eve about what they had done. He asked them, "Who told you that you were naked? Have you eaten from the tree that I commanded you not to eat from?" (Gen. 3:11). Notice that God didn't ask them "Why did you do such a thing?" He didn't ask them *why*; he asked them a factual yes or no question.

In parenting seminars, my dad has shared how he would question my brothers and me about our behavior when a conflict had developed. We might start blaming our brother or try to give excuses for our behavior. We might stammer with "but, but, but." However, my dad would keep asking, "What did you do?" The answer to the "what" question is a confession.

Conversely, the answer to the "why" question is a reason or an excuse. My dad testifies that once we would finally answer the "what" question, often tears would come. I have seen this dynamic in my experience as well. When a child finally admits to what he has done, he often starts to cry and feels truly sorry about what he has done. Now, our task as parents is not to make our children cry, but often tears are evidence of God working on the heart, creating a heart of good soil.

The reason that it is so important that our children be truthful about what they have done is that God forgives our sins when we honestly confess them. Look at this powerful passage about walking in the truth from 1 John 1:5-9:

> This is the message we have heard from him and declare to you: God is light; in him there is no darkness at all. If we claim to have fellowship with him yet walk in the darkness, we lie and do not live by the truth. But if we walk in the light, as he is in the light, we have fellowship with one another, and the blood of Jesus, his Son, purifies us from all sin.
>
> If we claim to be without sin, we deceive ourselves and the truth is not in us. If we confess our sins, he is faithful and just and will forgive us our sins and purify us from all unrighteousness.

When our children walk in the truth through confession, they are forgiven and cleansed by Jesus' blood. In addition, they have fellowship with God and with us their parents, which is critical for our relationship with them. If our children are living in deception, we have no real relationship with them. Conversely, if we have honest relationships, we have true fellowship.

Often as parents we want to defend our children when they get into a conflict with another child. However, it is more important that our children walk in the truth about what they have done as opposed to blaming others or making excuses. For instance, a child might get into a conflict with a student at school. Even if the other student is more to blame, it's imperative that we as parents help our children to take responsibility for their part in the conflict. Doing so will help our children to grow in godly character. God calls us to focus on the sins of *our* children, not the sins of other parents' children. This attentive discipline is how we love our children—to be faithful to discipline them. And this is how our children are cleansed by Christ's blood and are covered by his grace.

When God questioned Adam, he tried to shift the blame. First, he blamed God for giving him his wife. Then he blamed his wife. He blamed what God intended for good: "It is not good for the man to be alone. I will make a helper suitable for him" (Gen. 2:18). We see here that sin affects our relationships—our marriages and our children. It causes disputes and fights. Therefore, when we sin, we must take responsibility for our wrongdoing in order to restore our relationship with God and with others.

Proverbs 16:6 says, "Through love and faithfulness sin is atoned for." If we have hurt others, sometimes the only remedy is to show consistent love and faithfulness over time. Love and faithfulness over time can heal broken relationships and bring forgiveness, healing, and restoration.

Instead of taking responsibility, Eve also sought to shift the blame. She blamed the serpent.

Well, the Lord took responsibility. He proceeded to unwind the sin and deal with the various actors in this real-life drama. It's an act of grace for God to deal with the sin in our lives. It shows his love for us. Sin is the major issue of our lives. We should be grateful for our Lord's discipline, for his forgiveness, and for his helping us to grow to maturity as believers.

First, as the rightful authority, God dealt with the serpent. He said that Eve's offspring would crush Satan. Romans 16:20 encourages us: "The God of peace will soon crush Satan under your feet. The grace of our Lord Jesus be with you." Satan, the accuser, has no authority; he can only lie to us and seek to intimidate us. However, he has no authority. Because of Messiah's legal payment for sin through his death and resurrection, Satan's accusations are no longer valid! With his death and resurrection, Satan has been thrown out of heaven, no longer to be tolerated!

Revelation 12:10-12 expresses the victory we have in Christ:

> "Then I heard a loud voice in heaven say: 'Now have come the salvation and the power and the kingdom of our God, and the authority of his Christ.

> For the accuser of our brothers, who accuses them before our God day and night, has been hurled down. They overcame him by the blood of the Lamb and by the word of their testimony; they did not love their lives so much as to shrink from death. Therefore rejoice, you heavens and you who dwell in them! But woe to the earth and the sea, because the devil has gone down to you! He is filled with fury, because he knows that his time is short."

Next, God as the rightful authority dealt with Eve. In childbearing, she would have increased labor pains. Still there would be grace—she would give birth to children and would desire her husband.

But what about the phrase "rule over you"? It's important for the lives of our family that we understand that this rulership was a consequence of sin. It wasn't God's original intention. As believers, redeemed from the curse—who follow Christ—we are to follow his example of servant leadership, not rulership. Jesus said, "You know that the rulers of the Gentiles lord it over them, and their high officials exercise authority over them. Not so with you. Instead, whoever wants to become great among you must be your servant" (Matt. 20:25-26). God calls us to be part of reversing the consequences of sin's curse through a Christ-centered marriage and home! God's intent for marriage is that of a beautiful partnership between husband and wife.

Finally, God, the rightful authority, dealt with Adam. (Adam should have taken responsibility as a servant leader in the first place.) When Adam didn't provide loving servant leadership, he abdicated his place. Because of his sin, the ground would be cursed and he would eat of the ground through "painful toil" (Gen. 3:17). But still there is grace—God would provide food to sustain life. He also provided Adam and Eve with clothing to cover their shame.

The major consequence of sin was the Fall of humanity. Young person, whenever you or your friends wonder why bad things happen, even things such as natural disasters, recognize that the fundamental reason is SIN. Romans 8:22 says that "the whole creation has been groaning as in the pains of childbirth." The creation is groaning; the ground is cursed. Instead of being "free to eat" (Gen. 2:16), we eat of the land through painful toil, a consequence of rebellion against God.

Romans 6:23 says, "For the wages of sin is death, but the gift of God is eternal life in Christ Jesus our Lord." Sin brings death, but Christ came to reverse the curse: that we would have life—indeed abundant life!

God banished Adam and Eve from the garden. He said, "He must not be allowed to . . . take also from the tree of life and eat and live forever" (Gen. 3:22). But in the fullness of time, God is restoring the tree of life. In the last book of the Bible, God declares the following: "On each side of the river stood the tree of life, bearing twelve crops of fruit, yielding its fruit every month. And the leaves of the tree are for the healing of the nations. No longer will there be any curse" (Rev. 22:2-3).

As we come to Christ, God in his grace reassures us, "No longer will there be any curse"! Through Messiah, the tree of abundant life is restored to us.

I encourage you, young person, to not walk in rebellion to the Most High God. When you sin, don't hide it, don't excuse it, and don't blame others for it. Take responsibility for what you've done before the Lord. Walk in the light of Christ and in fellowship with your parents. Submit to God's will and choose to walk in his abundant life. Then you will be well on your way to a productive life of service and fruitfulness unto the Lord!

Memory Passages

1 John 1:5-9 "This is the message we have heard from him and declare to you: God is light; in him there is no darkness at all. If we claim to have fellowship with him yet walk in the darkness, we lie and do not live by the truth. But if we walk in the light, as he is in the light, we have fellowship with one another, and the blood of Jesus, his Son, purifies us from all sin."

"If we claim to be without sin, we deceive ourselves and the truth is not in us. If we confess our sins, he is faithful and just and will forgive us our sins and purify us from all unrighteousness."

ENOCH

Walk with and Please God

The Bible speaks of a man who did not die. He simply "was no more." His name was Enoch, and he walked with the Lord so much so that one day the Lord just took him away. He did not die; he simply went to be with the Lord. We learn from Enoch our courage challenge: walk with God and please God.

Who do you try to please? Who are you concerned with impressing? Often pleasing God is a challenging task for young people because it's easy to get caught up with pleasing our peers who may not be at all interested in pleasing God. Therefore, it takes courage to please the Lord as opposed to seeking to be popular with one's peers. Enoch's life teaches us to focus on pleasing the Lord. Young person, if you live your life committed to pleasing God, you will be living the life of a courageous champion!

In Genesis chapter five, Enoch was highlighted in a genealogy listing Adam's descendants through the line of Adam's son, Seth. Enoch lived 65 years and then was the father of Methuselah, who lived 969 years, the oldest man recorded in the Bible. After Enoch had Methuselah, he lived 300 more years and had other children. Therefore, Enoch lived to the age of 365, and then God simply "took him away" (Gen. 5:24). He simply "was no more" on this earth because "Enoch walked with God" (Gen. 5:24).

Enoch's distinguishing characteristic is that he walked with and pleased God. Again, he was a descendant of Adam through Seth. Seth's and Enoch's lineage contrasts with that of Cain, who had killed his brother, Abel. Seth's line was characterized by a dependence on God as opposed to Cain's line, which was characterized by a dependence on self.

In Cain's line was born Lamech, who made an arrogant boast to his wives: "Adah and Zillah, listen to me; wives of Lamech, hear my words. I have killed a man for wounding me, a young man for injuring me. If Cain is avenged seven times, then Lamech seventy-seven times" (Gen. 4:23-24). Lamech went against God's pattern of monogamy—having one wife. Instead, Lamech took two wives for himself, an action against God's design.

Lamech also expressed sinful pride over murdering a man out of revenge. The Lord says, "Do not take revenge, my friends, but leave room for God's wrath, for it is written: 'It is mine to avenge; I will repay'" (Rom. 12:19). In other words, it's not our job to take revenge; it's the Lord's job to do what he sees fit in his justice.

However, Lamech took revenge, which is not man's purpose. He went against God's design, committing arrogant sin against God and his creation.

In contrast to the self-reliance of Cain's and Lamech's line, Seth's line was characterized by dependence on God. Some in Seth's line, such as Noah, chose to follow God. Genesis 6:9 shares how Noah was committed to the Lord: "Noah was a righteous man, blameless among the people of his time, and he walked with God." This comment about Noah is very similar to Enoch's legacy.

As Seth's and Enoch's line was introduced, Genesis 5:1 reiterates that man is distinct from the animals in that man has been made in God's likeness. The next verse states that God "created them male and female" (Gen. 5:2). God clearly states that man was created as either male or female. In our society, there have been serious consequences because of all the confusion over how we were created. Too often today people are identified as LGBTQ, with Q for "Questioning"—questioning who they are sexually. Because they don't accept how they were created, they walk in confusion.

This matter is important because it deals directly with our relationship with God as Creator. To illustrate how far our society has gone awry, when my son Caleb was filling out one of his college applications, he had *sixteen choices* from which to select for his gender! With about half of the choices, we didn't even know what they meant. In the name of tolerance, these sexual issues are being pressed upon children at such a young age in a way that creates confusion. For example, if a fifth-grade girl likes to play with the girls more than the boys, should she be told that she might be lesbian? Of course not! I know as an educator that girls want to play with girls at that age, a fact which is perfectly normal and which has nothing to do with one's sexuality. And yet, in today's sex-crazed culture, children are having these sexual identity issues crammed down their throats in such a way that it creates internal confusion. However, with God it is clear: we are created either male or female, and God already made the choice when he created us.

For parents, I pray that the Lord will give you wisdom to provide your children—even your adult children—with Biblical clarity concerning this issue. I encourage you to trust the Lord that he will give you grace and truth to communicate God's Word lovingly with your children. For your young children, help them not to be concerned about this issue; I would even advise you to seek to shield them from all of the sexual confusion. (These sexual identity issues are not age-appropriate concerns for them. If your young children have questions, answer them with factual language that is age appropriate.) Help your young children to simply grow healthy friendships with other believing children.

If you have adult children that are struggling with their sexual identity, share the Word of God with them, stay in communication with them, and encourage them to wrestle with the Lord and his Word. Help them to understand that friendship does not equate with sexuality—that adults of the same gender or of different genders can be close friends without their friendship violating the Biblical injunction that sex is reserved for a husband and a wife within a lifelong covenant of marriage. Trust the Lord and pray for your children—God's love is more powerful than this world! He will give you what you need to love your children through the process.

Genesis 5:3 tells us that Adam had a third son—Seth—who was "in his own likeness, in his own image." All human beings are created in God's image; at the same time, because of Adam's sin, we're also born like Adam with a sin nature. This nature is why we need Messiah Jesus to save us from our sin—to restore us to God's likeness and to the way God created us to be.

Of course, often children bear a distinct physical resemblance to their parents—their parents' "likeness." At the same time, we as parents need to consider what spiritual and character traits our children are gleaning from our lives. Again, Adam had Seth who was "in his own likeness, in his own image." We want our children to take on traits such as being worshipers of the Lord; obeying authority; being truthful; loving others; using wholesome and edifying words; and imitating Yeshua in their attitudes, words, and actions.

As Adam's genealogy from Seth to Enoch continued in Genesis chapter 5, the refrain "and then he died" was repeatedly mentioned. This statement is a reminder of God's judgment for the fall of man because of sin. In fact, Romans 6:23 tells us, "For the wages of sin is death, but the gift of God is eternal life in Messiah Yeshua our Lord." The ultimate punishment for sin is death, and now death was occurring over and over again in the record of humankind.

Because of the punishment of death, God the Father, out of love for his creation, made a way for us to be saved from that penalty. Thanks be to God—He *gave* his only Son Jesus to save us from that penalty of death. Again, the second half of Romans 6:23 gives us hope: ". . . but the gift of God is eternal life in Christ Jesus our Lord." John 3:16 emphasizes God's motivation of love: "For God so loved the world that he gave his one and only Son, that whoever believes in him shall not perish but have eternal life." God the Father gave us his only Son to die in our place—to take on our punishment of sin—so that we can be restored to God's image, to having a relationship with the Father, and to having new life in Messiah—abundant life on this earth and eternal life in heaven. If we turn to Yeshua and accept his sacrifice for us, we can have this kind of life as a child of God! And we can live eternally in heaven!

To review, the Bible tells us that Enoch became the father of Methuselah, who lived to be the oldest recorded human being in history at the age of 969 years old. "And after he became the father of Methuselah, Enoch walked with God 300 years and had other sons and daughters" (Gen. 5:22). About others in Adam's genealogical line, the Bible says that they "lived"; but with Enoch, the Bible says that Enoch "walked with God." Enoch didn't just live; he "walked with God."

What a great legacy! To be known for having "walked with God"! Young person, do you just want to live out your years—however long your life ends up being—and then die? Or do you want to be characterized by a walk that pleases the Lord—having a true relationship with God that compels you to be a champion?

I recall when my Aunt Bonnie went home to be with the Lord. Forty-seven years earlier, at the age of five, I was a ring bearer in her wedding. As I grew up, many times our family would celebrate Christmas and family reunions at her and her husband's farm. As she hosted extended family, prepared food, and interacted with others, she consistently showed Christ-like kindness to others. As we reflected upon her life, I was struck with the fact that she was a faithful servant of the Lord in her church since her youth, when her father—my grandfather—started that Baptist church in her hometown. At her memorial service, it was testified how she was an active servant in her church, doing such things as leading VBS, getting the young people involved in music, and caring for others. My Aunt Bonnie served in the church her father started until she went home to be with the Lord!

Genesis 5:24 reiterates the essence of Enoch's life: "Enoch walked with God; then he was no more, because God took him away." Unlike all others, Enoch didn't die! He was taken away to God's presence without experiencing death!

And now, because of Christ's substitutionary death on the cross, we can experience life with him. While we may die physically, we don't need to die spiritually. As 1 Corinthians 15:54 declares, "Death has been swallowed up in victory." Psalm 49:15 states, "But God will redeem my life from the grave; he will surely take me to himself." As followers of the Messiah, we can declare this truth with confidence! Because of Christ, we don't have to experience permanent death. Our life is redeemed from the grave; we will be taken to the Lord! As Jesus said in John 11:25-26, "I am the resurrection and the life. He who believes in me will live, even though he dies; and whoever lives and believes in me will never die." In Messiah, we too can walk with God, please God, and experience eternal life with Him!

The New Testament book of Hebrews extols Enoch for his faith: "By faith Enoch was taken from this life, so that he did not experience death; he could not be found, because God had taken him away. For before he was taken, he was commended as one who pleased God" (Heb. 11:5). In the Bible's record of faith-filled champions, Enoch was held up as one who pleased God. In fact, the writer of Hebrews used the example of Enoch's life to illustrate his definition of faith: "And without faith it is impossible to please God, because anyone who comes to him must believe that he exists and that he rewards those who earnestly seek him" (Heb. 11:6). Enoch, a man of faith who walked with God, pleased the Lord!

Young person, I challenge you to walk with and please God! What happens when you walk with someone? When you walk with that person, you get to know that person, you have a relationship with that person, and you seek to please that person. I encourage you to make it your goal to please God—focus your life on having a relationship with God's anointed one, the Messiah, in which you seek to please him! Enoch was known for walking with and pleasing God. Make it your goal to please God in your attitudes, in your thoughts, in your words, and in your actions. No matter what you do, no matter what your future may entail, make it your focus to walk with and please God.

Memory Verse

> Hebrews 11:5-6 "By faith Enoch was taken from this life, so that he did not experience death; he could not be found, because God had taken him away. For before he was taken, he was commended as one who pleased God. And without faith it is impossible to please God, because anyone who comes to him must believe that he exists and that he rewards those who earnestly seek him."

NOAH

Learn to Work, Wait, and Endure Obediently and Patiently

We've all heard the story about Noah, the ark, and the flood. But have you ever wondered about Noah's preparation—all the years it took to construct the ark? Have you ever considered all the ridicule that he had to endure? Noah's courage challenge required him to work, wait, and endure obediently and patiently.

The story of Noah teaches us about sin and its destructive effects. Sin is violating God's commands; put concisely, it's doing wrong. Left unchecked, sin brings destruction to one's life and one's relationships. The account of Noah helps us to understand that God judges righteously those who sin and who fail to turn to Christ for salvation.

Genesis 6:4 speaks of the ancient Nephilim. Although the Nephilim were considered heroes in the world's eyes, the Hebrew word *Nephilim* means "fallen ones." From God's perspective, these men were not heroes but fallen because of their rampant sin. Because man's wickedness had become exceedingly great, God sent his judgment. Men had given themselves to violent sin in such a way that caused destruction.

These people embraced wickedness and rebelled against God. They sinned in such a terrible way that it hurt others. People were mean to others and even profited from causing others' harm. God, the just Judge, knew that he had to judge their sin.

Genesis 6:11 says, "Now the earth was corrupt in God's sight and was full of violence." The Hebrew word for "violence" is *hamas*, which has to do with purposeful wrongs to hurt and destroy others. Again, sin left unchecked and unrepented of results in God's judgment.

Genesis 6:6-7 tells us the following: "The Lord was grieved that he had made man on the earth, and his heart was filled with pain. So the Lord said, 'I will wipe mankind, whom I have created, from the face of the earth . . . for I am grieved that I have made them.'" God is grieved not only when we sin but also when we choose to continue in our sin and consequently bring destruction to the people in our lives. However, if we turn back to him, he is overjoyed, forgives us, and cleanses us from all unrighteousness (1 John 1:9).

Amid the rampant sin, the Bible says that Noah found favor with God. Noah was not sinless; no one is. However, the Bible tells us that Noah was blameless.

Noah was humble instead of arrogant. Noah walked with God. He was chosen by God to be different.

There is a difference between being faultless and blameless. No one is faultless. We all have faults. However, it's possible to be blameless before the Lord. When we sin, if we turn to God and confess that sin humbly, the Lord forgives us and then the blame stops. We become, in effect, blameless. The key for us is to humbly acknowledge the truth of our sin before the Lord. That's what confession is—it's telling the truth about our sin. If we turn back to the Lord and humbly confess our sin, the Bible tells us he will forgive us. Then we become blameless. The blame stops.

Back to the fascinating story of Noah and the Great Flood. Different ancient cultures refer to a great flood in their history. As young people, you need to be equipped to stand on the authority of God's Word when college professors scoff at you for believing the Biblical accounts of men such as Noah and Jonah.

Because of the wickedness of man and the violence filling the earth, God decided to judge man through sending a great flood. But the Lord instructed Noah to build an ark to protect him, his wife, and his sons and their wives. Amid God's judgment of evil, the ark was designed to be a large vessel to carry Noah, his family, and the animals safely through the flood.

Indeed, the ark is symbolic of our receiving salvation from the judgment of sin. The Bible teaches, "For the wages of sin is death, but the gift of God is eternal life in Christ Jesus our Lord" (Rom. 6:23). The great news is that Jesus took our judgment! He died in our place. Jesus Christ is like an ark which saves us from the judgment of the flood.

By providing the means of the ark, God established a covenant of protection with Noah. And that life-giving protection extended to Noah's family.

The Bible teaches that there is a covenantal blessing that extends to the children of godly parents. While each child must come to the Lord for salvation, there is a covenant of protection and blessing toward our children that emphasizes the importance of our parental responsibility toward them. Malachi 2:15 shares the following: "Has not the Lord made them [husband and wife] one? In flesh and spirit they are his. And why one? Because he was seeking godly offspring." God is seeking to raise up champions for him through the marriage of godly parents.

God instructed Moses to bring into the ark two "of every *kind* of animal" (Gen. 6:20, italics added). This action supports Genesis 1:24: "And God said, 'Let the land produce living creatures according to their kinds: livestock, creatures that move along the ground, and wild animals, each according to its kind.' And it was so." The emphasis is on "according to its kind."

This Biblical understanding of animals created according to their *kinds* is in direct contradiction to the teaching of evolution. Throughout natural history, there has been variation, or adaptation, within a species. However, we don't have evidence of one *kind* of species changing into another *kind* of species. This is another area in which our young people need to be equipped—to not fall prey to the atheistic teaching of evolution with its corresponding philosophy of humanism, where man is worshiped and the idea of God is scoffed at.

Noah built the ark exactly according to God's specifications. He followed all of God's instructions. He was marked by obedience: he worked, waited, and endured obediently and patiently. While God judges those living in unrepentant sin, he saves those who turn and respond to him in obedience and faith.

Can you imagine the ridicule Noah must have had to endure? Wickedness prevailed in that society, but Noah chose to live righteously before God. Imagine what it was like for wicked men to taunt him mercilessly? I can hear the taunts now: "Where's the water, Noah? What are you going to do with this big boat, Noah? You're building an ark where there is no water, Noah! How's it going to float, Noah? Oh, there's Noah! Still working on his ark!"

It took a long time for Noah to build the ark—perhaps 100 years! Enduring ridicule, Noah went through a crucible of trusting God for years. He believed the Lord when there was no outward manifestation of God's promise.

In Genesis 7:1, God instructed Noah, "Go into the ark, you and your whole family, because I have found you righteous in this generation." God found Noah righteous in his generation! In 2 Peter 2:5, Noah was called "a preacher of righteousness." The challenge for you, young person, is to be a leader of righteousness in your generation. Live for Christ, be a godly example, and share Christ with your peers.

Hebrews 11:7 says, "By faith Noah, when warned about things not yet seen, in holy fear built an ark to save his family. By his faith he condemned the world and became heir of the righteousness that comes by faith." While the wicked did not choose to believe in God, Noah lived by faith. Because he trusted God, Noah was declared righteous.

1 Peter 3 shares the message that we need to take from the life of Noah: "It is better, if it is God's will, to suffer for doing good than for doing evil" (1 Pet. 3:17). If we suffer, like Noah, for doing good, it's better than joining our lot with those who are doing evil like the Nephilim of Noah's day.

The passage continues to use the symbolism of Noah's ark to illustrate the salvation of Jesus Christ:

> For Christ died for sins once for all, the righteous for the unrighteous, to bring you to God. He was put to death in the body but made alive by the Spirit, through whom also he went and preached to the spirits in prison who disobeyed long ago when God waited patiently in the days of Noah while the ark was being built. In it only a few people, eight in all, were saved through water, and this water symbolizes baptism that now saves

> you also—not the removal of dirt from the body but the pledge of a good conscience toward God. It saves you by the resurrection of Jesus Christ, who has gone into heaven and is at God's right hand—with angels, authorities and powers in submission to him (1 Pet. 3:18-22).

Noah's ark is symbolic of salvation. The Lord provides an ark—an ark named Jesus Christ—to save us today! God is patient; he wants all to come to repentance and turn to him! He lovingly desires us to find his Ark—Jesus Christ—who can safely bring us through the flood of God's judgment for sin to the security of salvation! Romans 2:4 speaks of the riches of God's kindness and patience: "God's kindness leads you to repentance." Young person, God calls us to repent from sin and turn to Christ—to have a loving, personal relationship with the Lord!

God vindicated Noah's patient and trustful obedience. He saved Noah and his family from the flood—his judgment for sin! Noah was a champion of faith. Noah had to work, wait, and endure obediently and patiently until the promise of the flood came and his ark would be necessary as a means of salvation from the judgment of sin. He was declared righteous by faith, a faith that was demonstrated by his obedience!

When we learn the implications of Noah's life, we not only understand that God has provided salvation from sin's judgment through Jesus Christ, but also become compelled to share the Lord with others. Knowing the destruction caused by sin—hurt relationships and eternal judgment—we become motivated to share the good news of salvation through Jesus Christ. I encourage you, young person, to share Christ with your friends, with your family, and with everyone the Lord brings into your life!

Memory Verse

> Hebrews 11:7 "By faith Noah, when warned about things not yet seen, in holy fear built an ark to save his family. By his faith he condemned the world and became heir of the righteousness that comes by faith."

MOSES' PARENTS

Have Faith for Your Children

Parents have a universal desire for their children: They desire the best for their children. Whether Christian or not, parents are motivated to provide their children with a better life. Throughout our nation's history, immigrants coming to the United States have been motivated to work for something fundamental: a better life for their children. This incentive remains the same today.

Similarly, for us who have given our lives and our children for the Lord's purposes, the same motivation applies spiritually. God desires us as parents to live in such a way that our children will stand on our shoulders—that they will go further in the Lord in advancing his kingdom! I want to challenge us as parents to be motivated not so much that our children will gain the so-called "American Dream," but that our children will give their lives to be the Lord's champions!

The irony of God's Kingdom is that we go up by giving up; as we lose our life, we gain our life. Jesus made this point in Matthew 10:39 "Whoever finds his life will lose it, and whoever loses his life for my sake will find it." Let's look at this principle in the life of Moses, but not just in Moses—in Moses' parents!

Hebrews 11:23 emphasizes the faith of Moses' parents: "By faith Moses' parents hid him for three months after he was born, because they saw he was no ordinary child, and they were not afraid of the king's edict." In Hebrews' great hall of faith, Moses is remembered. But who's commended here? Not just Moses, but Moses' parents! It's not Moses' faith that is extolled, but his parents' faith.

The Egyptian king's edict was that all Israelite males were to be killed at birth—they were to be thrown into the Nile River to be drowned. But Moses "was no ordinary child." His parents knew that God had a special plan for his life. But in order to reach his destiny, Moses would have to go through many twists and turns. Moses even committed murder! Think of it—What if your son committed murder? You would more than likely think that your son's life and your parenting had been a failure.

However, God's destiny would still be fulfilled in Moses. After murdering an Egyptian who was striking a fellow Israelite, Moses fled Egypt and spent many years in the desert. In fact, it wasn't until Moses was eighty years old that God's destiny started to be fulfilled in his life. God honored Moses' parents' faith and used Moses to lead his people out of slavery. Moses became one of the greatest leaders in the history of the world.

In addition, Acts 7:38 emphasizes how God used Moses to bring his Word to us: "He received living words to pass on to us." Recall that Moses' parents had faith for Moses when he was just a babe. But it wasn't until Moses was eighty years old that God's purposes would come to fruition in his life.

Parents, my encouragement to you is to persevere as you seek to influence your children, even your adult children. It may not be until much later in life when God's purposes start to be fulfilled in your child! One thing we all know: our growth—and our children's growth—is not finished when we turn 18. Although your relationship with your children changes from training to influence when they reach adulthood, the process continues. It's all about ***Relationship***—continue that influence through loving and godly relationship!

Acts 7:22 says that "Moses was educated in all the wisdom of the Egyptians and was *powerful in speech and action*" (italics added). Moses received a great education, and he became an outstanding writer. In fact, God entrusted him with his inspired Word. (It's thought that Moses wrote the first five books of the Old Testament.) And yet, Moses had to go through years of training in the desert. After living a lifestyle of luxury in Egypt, Moses made his abode in the Midian Desert.

In the Bible, the desert is symbolic of a dry time, of trials, of waiting, of suffering, of persecution. For someone who was "powerful in speech and action," Moses went through desert experiences to the extent that when God called him, he possessed no more self-confidence and definitely did not see himself as eloquent. Instead of being "powerful in speech and action," Moses called himself "slow of speech and tongue" (Exodus 4:10). At that point, Moses lacked self-confidence; he had been stripped of self, which is actually a good characteristic for a champion of God.

Although Moses had received an outstanding education and was a gifted person, he had to go through training in order to be stripped of all self. This *desert training* equipped him to be God's servant.

As parents, we love to see our children express their gifts. Gifts such as athleticism, singing, and humor bring us joy. We have faith for our children to be gifted, such as Moses who had been "powerful in speech and action." But more importantly, in order for our children to become champions for God, we need to have faith that God will instill his character in them as we partner with God in the training of our children. From a Biblical standpoint, we come to understand that God uses desert experiences in our children's lives in order to grow godliness in them.

Sometimes that process is hard for us as parents. It's hard for us to see our children go through desert-type experiences: dry times, depressed times, trials, even suffering and persecution. However, just as Christ's strong disciple Peter had to be stripped of self so that God could use him, that same process applies to us. Possessing much self-confidence, Peter boasted to Jesus, "I will lay down my life for you" (John 14:37). When Jesus was arrested, Peter took a sword to cut off the ear of the high priest's servant. But then just as Jesus predicted, Peter denied knowing Jesus three times before the rooster crowed. Later, after Jesus rose from the dead, he restored Peter, asking him, "Do you love me?" After asking Peter this question three times, Jesus commissioned him to "feed my sheep" and to "follow me!" (John 21:17-19).

Just as Peter had to go through that process of being sifted of self, so too we and our young people have to go through that same excruciating process. Quite frankly, we and our children can sometimes be full of ourselves, seemingly denying God by our actions, just as Peter did. Sometimes we don't seem to be those "others-focused champions" that God is calling us to be. Sometimes, we need to go through some desert experiences in order to be stripped of self. In order to be a champion for the Lord, we need to come to that point of needing God.

When God called me as a young man to teach and encourage young people in their walk with the Lord, I had no self-confidence whatsoever. In fact, I was barely surviving. Because of my struggle I could barely face the future—life seemed so hard! I could barely make it through the day. And yes, there was a point in time in which God called and I responded; however, my journey through the desert continued for years!

What is the process that has to take place in our young people's lives? The process is that of *God changing self-confidence to Christ-consciousness!* When we become champions for God, he changes self-confidence to Christ-consciousness! Instead of confidence in ourselves, we become more and more conscious of Christ and his presence. Over and over in Scripture, when God called forth his champions, he promised that he would be with them. This is the process of coming forth in God.

Hebrews 11:24-25 shares Moses' faith-filled decision as a young man: "By faith Moses, when he had grown up, refused to be known as the son of Pharaoh's daughter. He chose to be mistreated along with the people of God rather than to enjoy the pleasures of sin for a short time." Moses made a decision as a young man to identify with God's people.

We often ask our children what they want to be when they grow up. More significant faith-instilling questions are the following: "What do you think the Lord is calling you to? What is his direction for your life? What kind of person is he making you to be? What character is he working in you? How is he preparing you to serve him?" As parents, we have to ask ourselves, "What are our true desires for our children and do they reflect God's priorities?" The decisions our young people are making for their future reflect their true values.

I recall one of my students writing about his future mansion in Miami—that was his ultimate desire. As parents, what do you want for your child? The "American Dream"? (The "Egyptian Dream"?) Do you want the good things that this life has to offer for your child, the things of this world, materialistic things?

Do you want your young person to grow up to be a professional football player? Or do you want your child to be raised up to be a Moses, a champion who was willing for God to use him for a great task?

Moses had the "Egyptian Dream"—all the pleasures of this world. Moses had it all! He was in line to take the throne of Egypt! However, rather than embracing this worldly inheritance, Moses instead chose to identify with slaves! He identified with the Lord and his people, a people enslaved in Egypt. Moses "chose to be mistreated along with the people of God rather than to enjoy the pleasures of sin for a short time" (Heb. 11:25). Moses chose to shun the things of this world—he sold all for Christ!

Moses "regarded disgrace for the sake of Christ as of greater value than the treasures of Egypt, because he was looking ahead to his reward" (Heb. 11:26). He considered it of greater value to experience Christ's disgrace than to enjoy worldly pleasures.

As a parent, are you willing to train up your child to experience disgrace for the cause of Christ? What a goal! How's that for faith for our children? To raise our children to be willing to live a life of disgrace: to stand up and be counted for the Lord, to stand for God's people, to help others even while being criticized, and to serve those who sometimes don't want the service, such as the Israelites in their grumbling! Our young people coming forth in God is about their learning to take up their cross and follow Christ.

If our young people are going to serve God and his purposes, they will need to learn to identify with Christ who had to anticipate the cross. This quality means learning to endure not only the cross but also the time leading up to the cross. That's where our young people learn to utterly depend on Christ!

Moses looked ahead to his reward instead of having his reward now. "By faith he left Egypt, not fearing the king's anger; he persevered because he saw him who is invisible" (Heb. 11:27). Moses left Egypt, the luxury of Egypt, and the good times of Egypt. He persevered because he trusted an invisible God.

When we have God-given faith for our children, we seek to pray and train for their values to be changed from the values of this world to the values of God's Kingdom. For our young people, this kind of faith impacts their important decisions and their daily choices. It affects life-altering priorities related to their future: their God and his Kingdom; their calling, including college and work choices; and their relationships, including their life mate.

Parents, my heartfelt encouragement is that you honor God as you train your child—in the big things and in the little things. Of course, our "little" decisions communicate important values to our children. I encourage you to trust the Lord for your child's future. Honor him. Show your children that you are going to lead your family in honoring Him. If you dishonor the Lord before your children, that communicates a powerful message to them. Conversely, if you honor the Lord before your children, that leaves them a lasting example and legacy.

What kind of legacy do you desire to leave for your children? More important than a material inheritance, leave your children a Christian inheritance—a spiritual inheritance that honors the Lord. This inheritance is far more important than that of worldly wealth. It's far more important than worldly status.

Ultimately values make an impact. The values that our children embrace will impact their lives. I encourage you to train, exhort, communicate, and relate with your children in such a way that they take their values from the Bible, from Christ. That's the faith we need to have for our children—faith that impacts both their values and their decisions!

Moses "saw him who is invisible." He had a relationship with the invisible Christ. Exodus 33:11 reveals to us the following: "The Lord would speak to Moses face to face, as a man speaks with his friend." What a relationship Moses had with the Lord! Parents, encourage your young people to see the invisible—the invisible God—and to have a relationship with Christ! A true relationship with Christ will impact their values and change their decisions!

Hebrews 11:1-2 counsels us, "Now faith is being sure of what we hope for and certain of what we do not see. This is what the ancients were commended for." Parents, this is how we receive God's commendation! Have faith for your children: pray in faith, communicate in faith, and live before your children in faith!

As disciples of Christ, we're called to live by faith, to walk in faith. When it comes to our children, we need to "see to it." We need to train in faith, inculcate values in faith, discipline in faith, encourage in faith, and call forth our children to be champions in faith!

Jeremiah 29:11 shares God's great plans for Israel even when they were in captivity: "For I know the plans I have for you. . . plans to prosper you and not to harm you, plans to give you hope and a future." After that verse, the passage goes on to say how we find the Lord and his plans: "Then you will call upon me and come and pray to me, and I will listen to you. You will seek me and find me when you seek me with all your heart!" (Jer. 29:12-13). Our young people will find God—and His plans for them—when out of a heart of surrender, they call on God and seek Him with all their heart!

How do we please God as their parents? Hebrews 11:6 states definitively, "And without faith it is impossible to please God, because anyone who comes to him must believe that he exists and that he rewards those who earnestly seek him." That's how we please God! Have a trusting, loving relationship with the Lord! We're called to sell everything for Christ! We're called to trust God and to honor him before our children.

Moses' parents serve as a great example for us. Parents, be examples of honoring the Lord before your young people! If we're going to raise up our children to be champions for the Lord, we as parents need to be hot for the Lord, not cold or lukewarm! We have to be on-fire for Christ—worshiping him with all our heart! We need to have a relationship with God that impacts our values, a relationship that makes us different from the world!

And then we need to have a faith-filled relationship with our young people! The same message that we're seeking to live, we need to communicate to our children: Trust God—Trust his Word—Trust his values—Honor him. Trust the Lord in such a way that you surrender your life to him! Love the Lord! Live a life that glorifies the Lord!

As our young people seek God with all of their heart, he will reveal his promised land to them—his purpose for their lives! In surrendering to God's plans, they become champions. Parents, this is the kind of faith God calls us to have for our children!

Memory Verse

> Hebrews 11:26-27 "He regarded disgrace for the sake of Christ as of greater value than the treasures of Egypt, because he was looking ahead to his reward. By faith he left Egypt, not fearing the king's anger; he persevered because he saw him who is invisible."

MOSES

Walk Humbly with Your God

At Camp Courage and Living Grace Christian School, we continually call, challenge, and seek to equip the children to be leaders—leaders in righteousness, servant leaders for God's Kingdom, champions with the cause of Christ. We emphasize the traits that they need to embrace in order to be these kinds of leaders. One such trait is that of humility.

Moses was one of the greatest leaders of all time, and he was marked by humility: "Now Moses was a very humble man, more humble than anyone else on the face of the earth" (Num. 12:3). From Moses we learn that in order to be a champion for the Lord, we must embrace humility and be willing to endure criticism. We learn that we need to walk humbly with our God.

Moses accomplished great things as a leader. Under the inspiration of the Holy Spirit, Moses wrote the first Bible, which was the first five books of the Old Testament. Of course, he was used by God to lead his people out of Egyptian bondage, out of slavery. However, as he continued to lead God's people through the desert toward the promised land, Moses received much criticism. As a leader, Moses received criticism from his enemies, including Pharaoh; from God's people, whom he led out of bondage; and from his very own family. He was criticized from all angles. It was imperative for Moses to be equipped with humility.

What happens when someone insults you? Out of pride, do you seek to get back at them and return insult for insult? Moses didn't respond to others' cuts that way; rather, he learned to stay humble. Refusing to walk in pride, he did not retaliate and seek to hurt others. Why was he able to endure that intense criticism without quitting? The secret lies in his humble relationship with the Lord. Moses walked with God; he kept his eyes fixed on God. He sought God's face; he walked in the light of God's presence! Moses walked humbly with his God.

However, Moses wasn't always marked by humility. God worked that humility in him through various trials over the course of his life. He had to learn to walk in humility from the crucible of experience. This training prepared him for the great task of his life.

We know from the Bible that Egypt's Pharaoh was concerned that the Israelite slaves were becoming too numerous and that they might join their enemies; therefore, he ordered that all of the Israelite baby boys be thrown into the Nile River to die. Well, after Moses was born, his mother placed him in a basket in the reeds along the bank of the Nile. When none other than Pharaoh's daughter went down to the Nile to bathe, she saw him and had compassion on him. Then Moses' older sister, who had been watching from a distance, asked Pharaoh's daughter if she wanted her to get one of the midwives to nurse Moses. Of course, Moses' sister got Moses' mother to care for him; but when Moses became older, his mother took him to Pharaoh's daughter to be her son. So Moses grew up in the luxury of the Egyptian Pharaoh's royal court with all of Pharaoh's wealth.

After Moses grew to become a man, he went to see his people at hard labor. When he saw an Egyptian beating a Hebrew slave, Moses killed the Egyptian. When the Pharaoh heard of Moses' action, he attempted to kill Moses; but Moses fled to Midian, a dry and solitary desert.

After having lived in the luxury of Pharaoh's court, Moses now made his abode in the desert. He married the daughter of a Midian priest named Zipporah, and they had a son which Moses named Gershom. Upon Gershom's birth, Moses said, "I have become an alien in a foreign land" (Exodus 2:23). Moses had to leave the land of his birth and make a new home in a foreign land.

Moses lived in the desert for many years. Embracing a much different existence from that of the luxury of Pharaoh's palace, Moses became a shepherd, tending his father-in-law Jethro's flock. One day, when Moses had taken the sheep "to the far side of the desert," he came to the mountain of the Lord at Horeb. There he saw a burning bush. However, the bush would not burn up; it just kept burning. As Moses approached the burning bush, God called to Moses. Moses feared God, and he humbled himself by taking off his sandals and hiding his face.

During that encounter, God called Moses to lead his people out of slavery to the Egyptians. However, Moses was not easily convinced to take on this role. He did everything he could to dissuade the Lord. One of Moses' arguments had to do with his speaking ability. He said, "O Lord, I have never been eloquent, neither in the past nor since you have spoken to your servant. I am slow of speech and tongue" (Exod. 4:10).

However, God continued to challenge Moses: "Who gave man his mouth? Who makes him deaf or mute? Who gives him sight or makes him blind? Is it not I, the Lord? Now go; I will help you speak and will teach you what to say" (Exod. 4:11-12).

When Moses continued to argue with the Lord, God became angry with him. However, God agreed to have Moses' brother Aaron go with him and speak for him. Although Moses was resistant to his assignment, he ultimately accepted God's challenge with Aaron's help.

Young person, when God calls you, he will equip you with what you need. He will work in you the motivation, character, and skills to do the task he is giving you. Yes, we do need to be humble, but it's possible to take humility to a negative extreme. In the name of humility, don't act as if you can't do anything or that you have nothing to offer. Don't allow fear to keep you from embracing God's purpose for you. Rather, allow the Lord to grow his wholesome confidence in you. That confidence is born out of your relationship with the Lord!

When Moses returned to Egypt to lead the people out of Egyptian bondage, he received criticism from all sides. When he initially went to Pharaoh to request that he allow God's people to go on a three-day trip to offer sacrifices to God, Pharaoh refused and criticized Moses and his God. Pharaoh bellowed, "Moses and Aaron, why are you taking the people away from their labor? Get back to your work!" (Exod. 5:4). To punish Moses and the Israelites, Pharaoh immediately ordered the slave drivers to not supply the slaves with straw to make the bricks—they had to get their own straw and still be responsible to make the same number of bricks. Pharaoh made the work harder on the Israelites.

After the Israelite foremen appealed to Pharaoh to not take such harsh action, Pharaoh called them lazy and refused their appeal. The Israelite foremen then proceeded to blame Moses and Aaron: "May the Lord look upon you and judge you! You have made us a stench to Pharaoh and his officials and have put a sword in their hand to kill us" (Exod. 5:21). At this point, Moses must have felt intense pressure; he was in the middle of receiving opposition from both Pharaoh and God's people. He was being inundated by criticism from all sides. After Moses cried out to God directly, God reassured him; God reminded him of his promise to free his people from Egyptian slavery.

Young person, when following God doesn't seem to be yielding the results you want, don't use the argument that "it's not working." Stay in obedience. It's okay to cry out to God and even to question him. But stay in relationship and obedience to the Lord while you are doing so. Sometimes the only reassurance and commendation you will receive is the Lord's voice. And that's all you need. Simply seek to be steadfast in pleasing the Lord through obedience.

God used Moses to bring the ten plagues upon Egypt. Because Pharaoh's heart was very hard against God and his people, he continued to refuse to allow the Israelites to leave Egypt. Finally, after the tenth plague—the death of the firstborn—Pharaoh let the Israelites go! With this plague, the angel of Death passed over the Israelite homes that had the blood of the lamb on the doorframes, but he killed the Egyptians' firstborns, including Pharaoh's child. In his intense grief, Pharaoh finally let the Israelites go!

Moses led God's people out of Egypt, out of slavery. They made it as far as the sea, but then the Israelites saw the Egyptians racing after them. There the Israelites cried out against Moses and questioned him repeatedly: "Was it because there were no graves in Egypt that you brought us to the desert to die? What have you done to us by bringing us out of Egypt? Didn't we say to you in Egypt, 'Leave us alone; let us serve the Egyptians'? It would have been better for us to serve the Egyptians than to die in the desert!" (Exod. 14:11-12). Moses answered the Israelites by calling them to stand in faith and to see the Lord's deliverance.

Young person, sometimes you as a leader will be questioned and criticized by the very people you are trying to help. You may not even know how to answer all of their questions. Sometimes you may feel caught in the middle between the people and the Lord. However, as God's champion you still need to encourage them even amid their criticism.

Moreover, you must be willing to receive the Lord's correction. The Lord questioned Moses, "Why are you crying out to me?" (Exod. 14:15). Then the Lord gave Moses instructions for leading the people through the sea on dry ground before the waters would come back and destroy the Egyptian army as they chased the Israelites. Through all of the conflict, the Lord won a great victory through Moses!

However, the Israelites' gratitude for God's miraculous deliverance was short-lived. They continued their complaining ways. The people that Moses had led out of slavery and through a miraculous deliverance from the pursuing Egyptian army grumbled to him about not having food and water. They said that they wanted to go back to Egypt—to slavery! The Bible says that they argued against Moses and demanded that he give them water for their thirst. Moses responded by saying, "Why do you quarrel with me? Why do you put the Lord to the test?" (Exod. 17:2). The Bible says that "they grumbled against Moses" (Exod. 17:3).

To "grumble against" God's leader really is to grumble against the Lord. In the final analysis, the people were rebelling against God, who is in control of our lives. The people grumbled and complained about their food—manna and quail provided by God—and about water. The people grumbled against Moses instead of going to God with their complaints. This action was in direct contrast to how Moses communicated with God. In effect, the people grumbled about God whereas Moses went directly to God with his concerns. This distinction is instructive for us. When we appeal directly to the Lord as opposed to grumbling and gossiping with others, God responds directly to us as well! He answers our prayers!

Moses cried out directly to God many times. One such prayer is illustrated in Numbers 11:10-13:

> Moses heard the people of every family wailing, each at the entrance to his tent. The Lord became exceedingly angry, and Moses was troubled. He asked the Lord, "Why have you brought this trouble on your servant? What have I done to displease you that you put the burden of all these people on me? Did I conceive all these people? Did I give them birth? Why do you tell me to carry them in my arms, as a nurse carries an infant, to the land you promised on oath to their forefathers? Where can I get meat for all these people?"

In all of Moses' questions, we see that he had a confident relationship with God; from experience, Moses knew that he could bare his heart to God and be received.

Through Moses' relationship with the Lord, we learn that God responds and answers when we go directly to him with our questions and concerns as opposed to grumbling about our life and circumstances to others. Rather than grumble against God, we should trust God through our circumstances. Through our trials, we should trust God for faith, hope, and love as well as righteousness, joy, and peace even while he continues to make us into the people he's calling us to be.

Referring to the Israelites, the Apostle Paul gives us this warning: "Do not grumble, as some of them did—and were killed by the destroying angel" (1 Cor. 10:10). We need to recognize that it's a very serious matter to grumble and complain. Again, it's okay to cry out to God and even to question him. But while you are doing so, stay in obedient relationship to him.

In fact, later when the Israelites built an idol in the form of a golden calf, those involved had to be destroyed for this abomination. The people criticized Moses for taking so long with the Lord: "When the people saw that Moses was so long in coming down from the mountain, they gathered around Aaron and said, 'Come, make us gods who will go before us. As for this fellow Moses who brought us up out of Egypt, we don't know what has happened to him'" (Exod. 32:1). What a complaint! Here they are calling Moses "this fellow" for taking a long time on the mountain of the Lord and show no sense of gratitude to him or to God! They were determined to worship an idol made of human hands! After they made the idolatrous golden calf, they arrogantly proclaimed, "These are your gods, O Israel, who brought you up out of Egypt" (Exod. 32:4). When Moses did come down the mountain, God used him to discipline the people involved in this grievous sin.

Young person, as you grow into leadership—as a parent, as a teacher, or even as a pastor—there will be times in which you will be called to bring discipline to others. Even as you seek to handle this responsibility lovingly and redemptively, sometimes that process will not be very pleasant. As you're seeking to help others in a conflict or to bring God's Word to a certain situation, you might be blamed in the process. That is part of God's working in your life. God calls you to be a strong leader that can handle hard issues, all for the sake of his Kingdom.

Moses' relationship with God was such that God used him to establish his covenant with Israel—his law. He had such a close relationship with the Lord that after being in God's presence, his face would be radiant! His face would glow to such an extent that he would use a veil to cover his face! Indeed, Moses walked in the glorious light of God's presence!

The Apostle Paul clearly shares that God's radiant light can be in our lives as well: "But whenever anyone turns to the Lord, the veil is taken away. Now the Lord is the Spirit, and where the Spirit of the Lord is, there is freedom. And we, who with unveiled faces all reflect the Lord's glory, are being transformed into his likeness with ever-increasing glory, which comes from the Lord, who is the Spirit" (2 Cor. 3:16-18). When we walk with the Lord, we truly shine!

Still, even though God clearly had ordained Moses to be his servant, Moses continued to receive criticism. His own siblings attacked him. His brother Aaron and his sister Miriam started talking against Moses. They used the fact that Moses married a foreigner to criticize him, but they really were simply envious of his close relationship with the Lord. In their gossip, they asked, "Has the Lord spoken only through Moses? . . . Hasn't he also spoken through us?" (Num. 12:2).

However, God defended Moses before Aaron and Miriam: "When a prophet of the Lord is among you, I reveal myself to him in visions, I speak to him in dreams. But this is not true of my servant Moses; he is faithful in all my house. With him I speak face to face, clearly and not in riddles; he sees the form of the Lord. Why then were you not afraid to speak against my servant Moses?" (Num. 12:6-8).

Young person, as you seek to follow God and be a servant leader for him, realize that you will be criticized. When you are closely following God, expect to be attacked. But don't fall into the trap of getting defensive. Trust the Lord that he will defend you. Exodus 15:2 encourages us that God will be our defense: "The Lord is my strength and my defense; he has become my salvation. He is my God, and I will praise him." Romans 12:19 calls us to refrain from being revengeful: "Do not take revenge, my dear friends, but leave room for God's wrath, for it is written: 'It is mine to avenge; I will repay,' says the Lord." Remember that God will vindicate you. You don't have to seek to defend yourself.

However, like all of us, Moses was fallible. He was subject to the same emotions, limitations, and temptations that we all face. As we have clearly seen, Moses had to endure much grumbling and complaining from the Israelites. In Numbers chapter 20, the people again rose up in opposition to Moses and Aaron. Arguing against Moses, they said, "If only we had died when our brothers fell dead before the Lord! Why did you bring the Lord's community into this desert, that we and our livestock should die here? Why did you bring us up out of Egypt to this terrible place? It has no grain or figs, grapevines or pomegranates. And there is no water to drink!" (Num. 20:3-5).

To provide the people with water, God told Moses to "speak to that rock before their eyes and it will pour out its water" (Num. 20:8). However, Moses was fed up with their complaining. Instead of speaking to the rock, Moses struck the rock twice. Because of his rash action, the Lord punished Moses: "Because you did not trust in me enough to honor me as holy in the sight of the Israelites, you will not bring this community into the land I give them" (Num. 20:12). Because of his action, Moses' punishment would be that he would not lead God's people into the promised land.

However, even though Moses never entered the promised land, he received God's commendation in history. In the Hebrews hall of champions, this is what is said of this great man of God: "By faith Moses, when he had grown up, refused to be known as the son of Pharaoh's daughter. He chose to be mistreated along with the people of God rather than to enjoy the pleasures of sin for a short time. He regarded disgrace for the sake of Christ as of greater value than the treasures of Egypt, because he was looking ahead to his reward. By faith he left Egypt, not fearing the king's anger; he persevered because he saw him who is invisible" (Heb. 11:24-27). In faith, Moses gave up his life for the cause of the Lord!

Young person, I encourage you to learn from the life of Moses. We learn from Moses the secret of walking humbly with our God. Proverbs 18:12 says that pride comes before a fall "but humility comes before honor." With pride, one's focus is on oneself. Pride doesn't enable us to endure others' criticisms and can cause us to react to others in a way that could cause our downfall. In contrast, with humility, one's focus is on Jesus Christ who enables us to help others even through their criticisms. Christ's humility enables us to endure through the trials of opposition. We learn this secret from the life of Moses, who walked humbly with God.

Memory Passage

1 Peter 5:2-5 "Be shepherds of God's flock that is under your care, serving as overseers—not because you must, but because you are willing, as God wants you to be; not greedy for money, but eager to serve; not lording it over those entrusted to you, but being examples to the flock. And when the Chief Shepherd appears, you will receive the crown of glory that will never fade away. . . . All of you, clothe yourselves with humility toward one another, because, 'God opposes the proud but gives grace to the humble.'"

ABRAHAM AND ISAAC

Young People and Parents, Have a Faith-filled Relationship with One Another

When Abraham was without any children, he was told by God that he would become the father of many nations. Because he believed God, he was declared righteous. He took God at his Word! Abraham walked by faith, not by sight! When God told him to move to a place he knew nothing about, he obeyed and went. When he was told that his descendants would be as numerous as the sand on the seashore and as the stars in the sky, he believed God. Although his wife Sarah was barren (not able to have children), he believed God that he would be the father of many nations. In fact, it wasn't until Abraham was one hundred years old and his wife was ninety years old, that she gave birth to their son Isaac. But then God tested Abraham in such a way that tested not only his faith in God but also his relationship with his son Isaac.

In Abraham's relationship with his son Isaac, we see a bond of trust. As parents, our goal should be to have a faith-filled relationship with our young people. As young people, your goal should be to have a trusting relationship with your parents! The courage challenge for us all is to have a faith-filled relationship with one another! As parents, God calls us to walk by faith in our interactions with our children and to help them to come to faith in Christ. As young people, one of the quickest ways for you to walk into your promised land—your destiny—is to obey and honor your parents.

By obeying your parents with a great attitude, you will be walking in a straight path to your promised land. The Bible confirms this truth. Ephesians 6:1-3 says, "Children, obey your parents in the Lord, for this is right. 'Honor your father and mother'—which is the first commandment with a promise—'that it may go well with you and that you may enjoy long life on the earth.'" This promise is based on one of the commandments in Deuteronomy 5:16: "Honor your father and your mother, as the Lord your God has commanded you, so that you may live long and that it may go well with you in the land the Lord your God is giving you." The land referenced is your promised land! I don't know of anyone who wants to have a sad, miserable, and short life. The way you are blessed to have a fruitful and rewarding life is to obey and honor your parents from your heart.

For parents, the passage in Ephesians continues with the following guidance: "Fathers, do not exasperate your children; instead, bring them up in the training and instruction of the Lord" (Eph. 6:4). For us parents, we're to embrace the faith-filled process of bringing up our children to follow the Lord. In order to do so, we need to cultivate a strong relationship with our young people. The key word is *relationship*. We need to have a close, loving relationship with our young people.

In Genesis 22, we see a vivid example of this kind of relationship. The relationship between Abraham and Isaac shows the power of a trusting relationship of a father and his son.

As we tell the story of Abraham and Isaac, it's important to understand that as Christians we will face tests. Our faith will be tested! What are tests like? We may have different views of tests, perhaps depending on how our schooling has gone. In Genesis 22:1, we read that Abraham faced a momentous test: "Some time later God tested Abraham." When God called Abraham, Abraham responded with the heart of a servant: "Here I am" (Gen. 22:1). God proceeded to tell Abraham the following: "Take your son, your only son, Isaac, whom you love, and go to the region of Moriah. Sacrifice him there as a burnt offering on one of the mountains I will tell you about" (Gen. 22:2).

Now it's important to understand that God's command to Abraham was a test—God had no intention of killing Isaac. However, God wanted to test Abraham's faith. With God, tests are not for the purpose of failing the test but for the purpose of rising to the challenge of the test. In the process of rising to the test's challenge, we grow in our relationship with the Lord. Our faith in God is strengthened!

When Abraham was tested in this way, it's also important to understand that Isaac was a teenager. Genesis 22 starts out by saying, "Some time later." The previous chapter emphasizes that "Abraham stayed in the land of the Philistines for a long time" (Gen. 21:34). Isaac was becoming a young man by now.

What is your most valued treasure? I think we can safely say that for Abraham, his most valued treasure was his son Isaac. We can see God's emphasis here on Abraham's loving relationship with his only son Isaac, calling him "your son, your only son, Isaac, whom you love." Knowing that Abraham loved his only son Isaac dearly, God chose to test Abraham's faith.

In fact, Abraham's love for his son Isaac speaks of Father God's love for his son Jesus. John 3:16 says, "For God so loved the world that he gave his one and only Son, that whoever believes in him shall not perish but have eternal life." When Father God sent his only son to die on the cross in our place, he passed the test! It proved that God's love for us is real!

For Abraham, Isaac was the basis of his life. God's promise to Abraham would come through Isaac. This command to sacrifice his son was the ultimate test of Abraham's faith!

Genesis 22:3 says that "early the next morning," Abraham prepared to leave. What must that night have been like for Abraham? I wonder if he was able to sleep at all. "Early the next morning Abraham got up and saddled his donkey. He took with him two of his servants and his son Isaac. When he had cut enough wood for the burnt offering, he set out for the place God had told him about" (Gen. 22:3). Even though this was a terrible thing Abraham was being told to do, Abraham responded with faithful obedience.

Abraham, Isaac, his servants, and his donkey went on a forty-eight mile trip to the region of Moriah. When they had traveled to where they could see the appointed place in the distance, Abraham told his servants, "Stay here with the donkey while I and the boy go over there. We will worship and then we will come back to you" (Gen. 22:5).

Now Abraham was hiking with just Isaac—just the two of them. It's notable that Abraham told his servants that "we will come back to you"; he emphasized that "*we* will worship and then *we* will come back to you" (Gen. 22:5, italics added). Abraham was a man of faith in God. Hebrews 11:19 explains Abraham's thinking this way: "Abraham reasoned that God could raise the dead, and figuratively speaking, he did receive Isaac back from death."

Abraham "reasoned" in faith. Previously God had told him that the promise would come through Isaac—the son of the promise. Abraham believed God. He wasn't sure how it would happen, but he knew that the promise of being a father of many nations would come through Isaac! Therefore, Abraham reasoned that once he sacrificed Isaac, God could raise Isaac from the dead. Abraham had faith that as he obeyed God, God's promise to him would come true.

Genesis 22:6 describes Abraham and Isaac as they started out together on that final hike: "Abraham took the wood for the burnt offering and placed it on his son Isaac, and he himself carried the fire and the knife." Abraham placed the load of wood on youthful Isaac, and Isaac carried the rest of the necessary materials for the burnt offering.

I wonder what that walk must have been like for Abraham and Isaac. As they started on their hike, perhaps there was an uneasy silence hanging in the air. Perhaps Isaac detected consternation in his father's heart—that his dad's mind was preoccupied. The Bible poignantly describes their walking together: "As the two of them went on together, Isaac spoke up and said to his father Abraham, 'Father?'

'Yes, my son?' Abraham replied.

'The fire and wood are here,' Isaac said, 'but where is the lamb for the burnt offering?'

Abraham answered, 'God himself will provide the lamb for the burnt offering, my son.' And the two of them went on together" (Gen. 22:6-8).

What a picture of the father and son relationship! In this exchange between Abraham and Isaac, the statements "the two of them went on together" are the bookends to their dialogue. These verses emphasize that Abraham and his son Isaac walked together, emphasizing a trusting relationship. Abraham was able to tell his son confidently that "the Lord will provide." It was a statement of faith; he expressed confidence that God would provide.

Parents and young people, it is important that you cultivate a trusting relationship with one another. When I was a teenager driving a friend, I was stopped by a policeman for speeding. The officer had mercy on me and didn't give me a ticket. I told my friend that I would have to tell my dad. But my friend questioned why I would tell my dad—my dad would never have to know! But I knew I couldn't hide this matter from my dad. After telling my dad what I had done, he told me to slow down with my driving. He didn't react angrily to my action.

Young people, it's important that you share what is going on in your life with your parents; don't hide things from them. They may get a little angry; but in the long run, it's the best thing for you to have an open, honest, and trusting relationship with your parents.

Of course, Abraham's test was of a magnitude that we will probably never face. However, we all face tests, including tests of our faith in God. How might we experience tests? Perhaps you have not yet experienced some kind of provision. Perhaps you're sharing Christ with someone and it doesn't seem to be getting through. Perhaps you have not received some desired breakthrough. Perhaps you've made a recent commitment to the Lord and all you've experienced since making that commitment is an increase in trials. God calls you to walk by faith, not by sight. God may be testing you. Will you stay faithful to him? Will you stay faithful to share Christ with others? Will you submit your desires to God's will for you? Will you stay faithful to worship with God's people? Will you continue to obey God's Word even when it seems God is not providing your desired breakthrough on your timetable?

There is a saying: the TEST will result in a TESTimony! If we rise to the test, if we stay faithful to God, if we give up our will and submit to his will, he will provide the breakthrough in his timing!

When Abraham and Isaac arrived to their destination, we see the climax of Abraham's test. Abraham began to make the altar. I have often wondered how that must have taken place. Here Isaac is watching his father make the altar, arranging the wood. Then Abraham tied up his son. Isaac was a youth whereas Abraham was over one hundred years old; surely Isaac could have escaped his father's grasp and run away. However, there was such a trusting relationship between the two of them, that no such conflict ensued. The Bible simply says that Abraham "bound his son Isaac and laid him on the altar, on top of the wood" (Gen. 22:9). Isaac willingly participated with this sacrifice. He trusted his father.

Abraham trusted God, and Isaac trusted Abraham and by extension God. When Abraham had bound and placed Isaac on the altar and then was about to slay his son with the knife, the angel of the Lord stopped him: "Abraham! Abraham!" (Gen. 22:11).

As the angel of the Lord urgently called his name, Abraham must have felt an incredible sense of relief! He again responded to the Lord with the heart of a servant: "Here I am" (Gen. 22:11).

The angel said to Abraham, "Do not lay a hand on the boy. . . . Do not do anything to him. Now I know that you fear God, because you have not withheld from me your son, your only son" (Gen. 22:12). Abraham had passed the test!

The test of Abraham's faith as well as the test of our faith is that of obedience based on trust in God. James 2:21-24 emphasizes how our actions prove our faith: "Was not our ancestor Abraham considered righteous for what he did when he offered his son Isaac on the altar? You see that his faith and his actions were working together, and his faith was made complete by what he did. And the scripture was fulfilled that says, 'Abraham believed God, and it was credited to him as righteousness,' and he was called God's friend. You see that a person is justified by what he does and not by faith alone."

Abraham's faith was proved by his actions. Actions show the obedience of faith. Faced with a harrowing trial, we may be shaking inside—that's fine as long as our actions show our faith. The fruit of our life is the evidence of our faith. It's not enough to say, "I believe" without the actions that prove our faith.

Abraham believed God as evidenced by his obedience. That faith in God made him righteous, and he was called "God's friend" (James 2:23). Regarding friendship, Jesus made this statement:

> Greater love has no one than this, that he lay down his life for his friends. You are my friends if you do what I command. I no longer call you servants, because a servant does not know his master's business. Instead, I have called you friends, for everything that I learned from my Father I have made known to you. You did not choose me, but I chose you and appointed you to go and bear fruit—fruit that will last. Then the Father will give you whatever you ask in my name. This is my command: Love each other. (John 15:13-17)

As the ultimate substitutionary sacrifice, Jesus laid down his life for us. He is our true friend!

Returning to the story of Abraham and Isaac, God indeed provided a substitute for Isaac. When Abraham looked up from this harrowing experience, he saw a ram, a male lamb. God provided a lamb that would be the sacrifice "instead of his son" (Gen. 22:13). This event is the first time in the Bible that we see the principle of a substitutionary sacrifice—one sacrificed in place of another. Again, the provision of a substitutionary sacrifice points to Christ, who became the substitute for us on the cross. Jesus said of his own life: "For even the Son of Man did not come to be served, but to serve, and to give his life as a ransom for many" (Mark 10:45). Jesus gave his life for us!

Indeed, Jesus gave his life to save us from our sins, which can lead to death and destruction. John exclaimed of Jesus: "Look, the Lamb of God, who takes away the sin of the world!" (John 1:29). When we come to Christ and accept his death on the cross for us, he takes away our sin. He saves our life from sin! What a work! He becomes our substitute, taking our penalty on himself. Christ is the sacrificial Lamb given by God the Father to die in our place. He took our punishment!

After God provided the lamb, Abraham called that place "The Lord Will Provide" (Gen. 22:14). This statement means that the Lord "will see to it." Whatever matter you're dealing with, God will take care of it. When we go through a challenging test, we learn anew to commit every matter into God's hands and truly trust him to take care of it. He'll see to it!

Abraham passed the test! God reiterated his promise to Abraham: "Because you have done this and have not withheld your son, your only son, I will surely bless you and make your descendants as numerous as the stars in the sky and as the sand on the seashore. Your descendants will take possession of the cities of their enemies, and through your offspring all nations on earth will be blessed, because you have obeyed me" (Gen. 22:16-18). Abraham passed the ultimate test; he had trusted God to the ultimate degree!

Through it all, Abraham and Isaac showed not only faith in God but also a faith-filled relationship with one another. Abraham showed his faith in God by his obedience. Isaac showed his trust of his father. They had a relationship between one another that should inspire us as parents and young people. Abraham was a friend of God; because he was a friend of God, he was able to develop a close friendship with his adolescent son. And because of his obedience, all nations have been blessed!

Young person, this wonderful anecdote of Abraham and his son Isaac is a true story. It's a message of God's redeeming grace. God the Father spared Abraham's son Isaac, but God gave up his only son Jesus for us. God passed the test of love for you and for me!

1 John 4:9 emphasizes the point: "This is how God showed his love among us: He sent his *one and only* Son into the world that we might live through him" (italics added). In Isaac's willingness to die and be the sacrifice, we see a picture of Christ. In addition, the substitute lamb that God provided in place of Isaac is illustrative of Christ, the Lamb of God. Christ is the completely pure, unblemished Lamb provided for us. God provided a substitute for Isaac—the lamb. God gave the perfect substitute for us—his Son Jesus Christ.

1 Peter 1:18-19 emphasizes the Lamb's payment for our sin: "For you know that it was not with perishable things such as silver or gold that you were redeemed from the empty way of life handed down to you from your forefathers, but with the precious blood of Christ, a lamb without blemish or defect."

Like Abraham, let's pass the test of faith and be called a friend of God! As parents and young people, let's have a faith-filled relationship with one another. Parents, work at your relationship with your young people. Young people, make it your highest priority to have a close friendship with your parents. It's your pathway to your promised land!

Memory Passage

Genesis 22:6-8 "As the two of them went on together, Isaac spoke up and said to his father Abraham, 'Father?'

'Yes, my son?' Abraham replied.

'The fire and wood are here,' Isaac said, 'but where is the lamb for the burnt offering?'

Abraham answered, 'God himself will provide the lamb for the burnt offering, my son.' And the two of them went on together" (Gen. 22:6-8).

JACOB AND ESAU

Learn to Love Your Brothers and Sisters

Sibling rivalry is a very serious issue among brothers and sisters. Proverbs 17:17 says, "A friend loves at all times, but a brother is born for adversity." The challenge for you today is to be a "best friend" to your brother or your sister! It goes against the grain, which means it's not easy to do, but God can work this miracle in your heart.

In Genesis 25 there were twin boys in the womb of Isaac's wife Rebekah: Esau and Jacob. The Bible says that these boys were jostling each other in the womb. It was as if they were wrestling each other—jockeying for position even in their mother's womb. They had already begun that intense competition so characteristic among siblings.

Esau's body was red and very hairy compared to Jacob's smooth skin. Esau was born first with Jacob coming right behind as he grasped Esau's heel. From their very beginnings, it seemed as if Esau and Jacob were adversaries.

As they grew up, Esau became a skillful hunter comfortable working in the open country, while Jacob was a quiet man staying among the tents. Their father, who had a taste for wild game, loved Esau. However, Rebekah, their mother, loved Jacob.

Genesis 25:29-34 relates a key event in these brothers' lives:

> Once when Jacob was cooking some stew, Esau came in from the open country, famished. He said to Jacob, "Quick, let me have some of that red stew! I'm famished!" . . .
>
> Jacob replied, "First sell me your birthright."
>
> "Look, I am about to die," Esau said. "What good is the birthright to me?"
>
> But Jacob said, "Swear to me first." So he swore an oath to him, selling his birthright to Jacob.
>
> Then Jacob gave Esau some bread and some lentil stew. He ate and drank, and then got up and left.
>
> So Esau despised his birthright.

Esau sold the long-term blessing of his birthright for the short-term desire for food. This passage points out the need for young people to not sell their destiny for the pleasures of this world. Young person, I encourage you to remember that God has a special plan for your life and to trust him for your future blessing. Don't give up your destiny for the short-term pleasures of this world.

After the boys had grown older, their father Isaac was getting ready to die and wanted to bless Esau his firstborn before he died. He told Esau to go to the open country to hunt some wild game and then to prepare him a nice meal. Then Isaac would pronounce his blessing on Esau.

However, Rebekah was eavesdropping on their conversation. She proceeded to help Jacob to trick his father into giving him his blessing. They came up with a scheme to prepare the meal for Isaac. Jacob, whose name means "he deceives," deceived his father.

After Jacob had successfully deceived Isaac into giving him his blessing, Esau arrived home from hunting. Esau was ready to receive his dad's blessing; however, Isaac shuddered when he realized that he had been deceived by Jacob. Of course, Esau was distraught that he missed out on the blessing. As a result of this conflict between the two brothers, Esau developed a grudge against Jacob. Genesis 27:41 says, "Esau held a grudge against Jacob because of the blessing his father had given him. He said to himself, 'The days of mourning for my father are near; then I will kill my brother Jacob.'" Esau's grudge led him to hate his brother.

Young person, have you ever held a grudge against your brother or sister? Jesus spoke of the seriousness of hatred in Matthew 5:21-22: "You have heard that it was said to the people long ago, 'Do not murder, and anyone who murders will be subject to judgment. But I tell you that anyone who is angry with his brother will be subject to judgment." Jesus was saying that the heart issue of hatred was the root of murder. We may not consider murdering our brother or sister; however, we need to be sure to not let anger develop into a grudge or even hatred toward our siblings. Rather, we need to be sure to reconcile and forgive one another. Jesus said, "Therefore, if you are offering your gift at the altar and there remember that your brother has something against you, leave your gift there in front of the altar. First go and be reconciled to your brother; then come and offer your gift" (Matt. 5:23-24).

Jacob and Esau left home, grew up, became married, had children, and led their own families. However, they had never reconciled. They still had unresolved issues between them. Over time, fear of Esau grew in Jacob's heart. At one point, Jacob sent a messenger to Esau seeking his favor.

For those of you who are older siblings, you need to know that your younger brothers and sisters greatly desire your favor; they greatly desire for you to like them. You may not be aware of it, but they really look up to you!

Well, the messenger came back to Jacob and said, "We went to your brother Esau, and now he is coming to meet you, and four hundred men are with him" (Gen. 32:6) When Jacob heard that Esau was coming with all of these men, he was filled with fear.

Young people, I want to strongly encourage you to resolve issues with your siblings when you are young. If you fail to do so, they will develop into strongholds of fear in your life. Jacob prayed, "Save me, I pray, from the hand of my brother Esau, for I am afraid he will come and attack me, and also the mothers with their children" (Gen. 32:11). Young person, make it your goal to be best friends with your siblings today!

Well, Jacob sent large gifts of herds of animals ahead of him to pacify Esau! Preparing to meet Esau, he sent his family and his possessions across a ford on the river Jabbok. He himself stayed that night on the other side of the river. Jacob, who had wrestled with Esau starting in the womb, that night wrestled with God. As they wrestled, here is the exchange between them:

> When the man saw that he could not overpower him, he touched the socket of Jacob's hip so that his hip was wrenched as he wrestled with the man. Then the man said, "Let me go, for it is daybreak."
>
> But Jacob replied, "I will not let you go unless you bless me."
>
> The man asked him, "What is your name?"
>
> "Jacob," he answered.
>
> Then the man said, "Your name will no longer be Jacob, but Israel, because you have struggled with God and with men and have overcome."
>
> Jacob said, "Please tell me your name."
>
> But he replied, "Why do you ask my name?" Then he blessed him there.
>
> So Jacob called the place Peniel, saying, "It is because I saw God face to face, and yet my life was spared." (Gen. 32:25-30)

The Bible says that Jacob was limping after he wrestled with God. Young person, instead of fighting with your siblings and your parents, I encourage you to wrestle with God. As you go through life, you may end up with a "limp," a condition in your life that causes you hardship. When the Apostle Paul was faced with a debilitating thorn in his flesh, he appealed to God three times for it to be removed. God answered in this way: "My grace is sufficient for you; for my strength is made perfect in weakness" (2 Cor. 12:9). I encourage you to remember that a spiritual thorn—or a limp—may cause you to depend on God.

Young person, I encourage you to wrestle with God. Get your breakthrough with God in order to have the breakthrough with your sibling. Jacob got the breakthrough with God before he received the breakthrough with his brother. Jacob had to wrestle with God and get the breakthrough with him in order to be able to reconcile with his brother Esau. Instead of fighting with your brothers, or even your parents, wrestle with God. Whatever issue you have, young person, don't make it an issue with your parents or teachers. Go to God, go to His Word, wrestle with God, and work it out with Him. Ask God, get your answer from Him, and you will be blessed!

God changed Jacob's name to Israel, meaning "He struggles with God." As a result of wrestling with God, Jacob was fundamentally changed. He was no longer marked by deceit. Instead he was now marked by being an overcomer. 1 John 2:14 says, "I write to you, young men, because you are strong, and the word of God lives in you, and you have overcome the evil one." Jacob—now named Israel—had become an overcomer!

What happened when Jacob and Esau finally met? After wrestling with God, Jacob met Esau. Instead of hiding behind his family, Jacob now traveled ahead of his family as a godly leader. He humbly bowed seven times as he approached Esau. Genesis 33:4 describes their reconciliation: "But Esau ran to meet Jacob and embraced him; he threw his arms around his neck and kissed him. And they wept." Jacob and Esau had reconciled!

Young people, I encourage you to reconcile with your brothers and sisters. Seek to be best friends with your siblings. Learn to love your brothers and sisters *now* while you are young!

Memory Verse

> Genesis 32:28 "Then the man said, 'Your name will no longer be Jacob, but Israel, because you have struggled with God and with men and have overcome.'"

JOSEPH

Persevere through Disappointment

Joseph grew up as the youngest of Jacob's many sons. Born in his father's old age, Joseph became Jacob's favorite son. When Jacob gave Joseph a colorful robe, he demonstrated this favoritism toward Joseph. Because their father preferred Joseph, his brothers developed a hatred toward him. As he grew up, Joseph started taking care of his father's sheep along with his brothers. When he was seventeen years old, Joseph shared a bad report about his brothers to his father. Because of these circumstances, Joseph and his brothers did not get along. His brothers treated him badly.

The Lord began to speak to Joseph in his dreams. These dreams indicated that one day Joseph's brothers and parents would bow down to him. In his naivete, Joseph shared his dreams with his brothers, who didn't like hearing about them. Jacob rebuked Joseph but took notice of what Joseph was sharing. However, the jealousy of Joseph's brothers was aroused all the more against him.

Young person, Proverbs 17:17 says, "A friend loves at all times, but a brother is born for adversity." It's the natural way of things for siblings to get into conflicts. Often brothers and sisters argue and fight with one another. However, I want to encourage you to seek to love your brothers and sisters. Make it your purpose to be kind and loving to your siblings. Seek to be their friend.

Unfortunately, Joseph had to endure the hateful jealousy of his brothers. One day, Jacob sent Joseph on a trip to check on his brothers as they were watching over the flocks. When his brothers saw Joseph coming in the distance, they schemed to kill him. However, the oldest of the brothers, Reuben, tried to rescue Joseph. Reuben was only partially successful though. After Joseph's brothers had thrown him into a cistern, they decided to sell him into slavery.

Now Joseph was headed to a foreign land—Egypt. After growing up with his father's favor, Joseph was now being forcibly cut off from his father. Removed from his family, he was headed to an unknown land to be a slave.

After they sold Joseph into slavery, his brothers took his ornamented robe and dipped it into goat's blood. When they returned home, they showed it to their father as evidence of Joseph's death. Of course, Jacob was heartbroken; he could not be consoled from his terrible grief of losing his favorite son.

As Joseph arrived in Egypt, he was sold to Pharaoh's captain of the guard, a man named Potiphar. While surely Joseph was terribly disappointed at this turn of events, he decided to honor the Lord, even as a slave. He was faithful to his master Potiphar. He was so responsible in his duties that he gained Potiphar's favor, and

Potiphar put him in charge of everything in his house. Genesis 39:2-4 illustrates that the Lord was with Joseph and gave him favor: "The Lord was with Joseph and he prospered, and he lived in the house of his Egyptian master. When his master saw that the Lord was with him and that the Lord gave him success in everything he did, Joseph found favor in his eyes and became his attendant. Potiphar put him in charge of his household, and he entrusted to his care everything he owned." Potiphar put Joseph in charge of all he owned. As a result, Potiphar was blessed: "From the time he put him in charge of his household and of all that he owned, the Lord blessed the household of the Egyptian because of Joseph" (Gen. 39:5).

Now Joseph was a handsome man, and over the course of time Potiphar's wife took notice of him. She made tempting advances to him. But Joseph sought to honor both Potiphar and the Lord. He said to her, "How then could I do such a wicked thing and sin against God?" (Gen. 39:9). Joseph knew that giving in to her enticements would be doing wrong not only against Potiphar but also against God.

Young person, ultimately our sin is against God. When we sin and continue in that sin, we have the potential to hurt the people in our lives. Sin can destroy relationships. However, in the final analysis, we are sinning against God. Only Christ can save us from our sin. Christ came to pay the penalty for our sin on the cross. If we repent of our sin and turn to Christ in faith, he forgives us, cleanses us, and saves us. He redeems our life from the destructive effects of sin!

Well, Joseph resisted the advances of Potiphar's wife, but one day he was caught alone with her in the house. When she grabbed his clothes, he ran away. However, she used the cloak she had snatched from Joseph to make a false accusation against him. After Potiphar's wife had tried to seduce Joseph to give into temptation, she falsely accused him to her husband. In anger, Potiphar had Joseph thrown into prison: "When his master heard the story his wife told him, saying, 'This is how your slave treated me,' he burned with anger. Joseph's master took him and put him in prison, the place where the king's prisoners were confined" (Gen. 39:19-20).

The Bible doesn't tell us exactly whom Potiphar was angry with. (I wonder if Potiphar was really angry with his wife and not with Joseph whom he had come to respect.) Anyway, Joseph had to be removed from Potiphar's house. After being a slave, Joseph was now suffering the indignity of being a prisoner.

What a disappointment! Here Joseph had done the right thing. He had not given in to Potiphar's wife. Now when his wife lied to Potiphar, Potiphar had Joseph thrown into prison.

However, after this terrible disappointment, Joseph continued to persevere. What a trial he had to endure! Through his suffering, Joseph continued to honor the Lord. As a prisoner, the Lord was with Joseph! Knowing that God was with him gave Joseph the encouragement he needed to persevere and to give his best every day. While in prison, Joseph continued to live for the Lord—to help and serve others—no matter his circumstances. After being in prison for a period of time, Joseph gained the favor of the prison warden: "But while Joseph was there in the prison, the Lord was with him; he showed him kindness and granted him favor in the eyes of the prison warden" (Gen. 39:20-21).

Have you ever experienced something unjust? Perhaps your teacher accused you of something you didn't do? Well, Joseph dealt with a very serious unjust accusation. He was put into prison for something he didn't do. Joseph had achieved a certain status—he was responsible for the household of Potiphar, a respected official. Now he was thrown into prison. But he didn't get an attitude. He continued to honor the Lord.

Young person, sometimes we experience unfair situations in life. You might be unfairly relegated to a lower position. You may be working in a job in which you are doing your best and seeking to do what is right. But then another person—someone you know isn't working as hard but has gained the boss's favor—gets the promotion; and *you* don't get recognized for *your* work. If that happens to you, remember the experience of Joseph.

As Joseph persevered in prison and stayed faithful to the Lord, eventually an incredible development occurred. The prison warden made Joseph the manager of the entire prison, including all the prisoners! "So the warden put Joseph in charge of all those held in the prison, and he was made responsible for all that was done there. The warden paid no attention to anything under Joseph's care, because the Lord was with Joseph and gave him success in whatever he did" (Gen. 39:22-23). Joseph—as a prisoner—was overseeing the prison! What trust the prison warden had in Joseph! A prisoner was taking care of the prisoners! Wow! The Lord was certainly with Joseph through his troubles.

Young person, Joseph is a great example of the principle that he who is faithful in small things will be faithful in larger things. In Jesus' Parable of the Talents, he said, "Well done, good and faithful servant! You have been faithful with a few things; I will put you in charge of many things" (Matt. 25:23). If you want to be great in God's kingdom, remember to seek to please God in everything that you do. God is watching how you're living and being responsible for the small things in life. When it seems that no one is watching—when it seems that you're only serving in obscurity, remember that the Lord sees. Promotion is from the Lord. He is the one person who sees all of your life—not your boss, not your teachers, not even your parents. As you are faithful with whatever God gives you to do through your parents, teachers, pastors, coaches, and supervisors, God will eventually reward you with larger responsibilities. It's the Lord who will ultimately promote you. Always remember, promotion is from the Lord, the one person who sees all things!

As he took care of the prisoners, one morning Joseph noticed that the faces of two of them—Pharaoh's cupbearer and baker—were downcast. (Pharaoh had put them in prison after they had angered him.) When Joseph asked the cupbearer and the baker why they were sad, they answered, "We both had dreams, but there is no one to interpret them" (Gen. 40:8).

As a servant of the Lord, Joseph gave honor to God: "Do not interpretations belong to God? Tell me your dreams" (Gen. 40:8). Joseph proceeded to interpret their dreams: in three days, the cupbearer would be restored to his position, but the baker would be killed. Joseph asked the cupbearer to remember him: "But when all goes well with you, remember me and show me kindness; mention me to Pharaoh and get me out of this prison. For I was forcibly carried off from the land of the Hebrews, and even here I have done nothing to deserve being put in a dungeon" (Gen. 40:14-15).

However, Joseph had to endure continuing disappointment. Once the cupbearer was restored to his position by Pharaoh, the cupbearer forgot all about Joseph. Joseph was left in prison. Serving an unjust prison sentence, Joseph continued to suffer for two more years.

Young person, sometimes you may be treated in an unjust manner that lasts for a long time. Continue to persevere through that season. Honor the Lord and be faithful to him. Like Joseph, help and serve others. The Lord will see your life and eventually reward you for your perseverance.

One night Pharaoh, the king of Egypt, had two dreams. He was disturbed by his dreams and thought that they had an important meaning. However, none of his people could interpret them. Finally, the cupbearer remembered Joseph in prison and told Pharaoh of Joseph's ability to interpret dreams.

Pharaoh sent for Joseph. After being cleaned up, Joseph was brought before the king of Egypt. The Pharaoh told Joseph that he had heard of his ability to interpret dreams. As he had done in the past, Joseph responded by giving God glory: "I cannot do it, but God will give Pharaoh the answer he desires" (Gen. 41:16).

Young person, we learn from Joseph a very important life lesson. Whether in poor circumstances or lofty ones, the Lord is with you to serve others. Whether with other prisoners, coworkers, your boss, or people in powerful positions, the Lord is with you to help others.

Well, Pharaoh told Joseph his dreams of seven fat cows being eaten up by seven skinny ugly cows and of seven full heads of grain being eaten up by seven thin heads of grain. Joseph interpreted Pharaoh's dreams which had the same meaning: Egypt would have seven years of abundance followed by seven years of famine. The seven years of famine would be so extreme that all of the years of abundance would be swallowed up. Joseph emphasized to Pharaoh, "The abundance in the land will not be remembered, because the famine that follows it will be so severe" (Gen. 41:31).

After interpreting the dreams, Joseph gave Pharaoh a plan for saving the food in the years of abundance in preparation for the years of famine:

> And now let Pharaoh look for a discerning and wise man and put him in charge of the land of Egypt. Let Pharaoh appoint commissioners over the land to take a fifth of the harvest of Egypt during the seven years of abundance. They should collect all the food of these good years that are coming and store up the grain under the authority of Pharaoh, to be kept in the cities for food. This food should be held in reserve for the country, to be used during the seven years of famine that will come upon Egypt, so that the country may not be ruined by the famine. (Gen. 41:33-36)

After consulting with his officials, Pharaoh put Joseph in charge of all Egypt: "Since God has made all this known to you, there is no one so discerning and wise as you. You shall be in charge of my palace, and all my people are to submit to your orders. Only with respect to the throne will I be greater than you" (Gen. 41:39-40). What a turn of events! At thirty years of age, Joseph was now responsible to lead Egypt! From being sold into slavery to being put in charge of Potiphar's house to being put in charge of the prison, Joseph was now being made responsible for all of Egypt. Joseph's task would be to lead the country in preparation for a terrible famine. Joseph made a life of being a servant—first to Potiphar and then to the prison warden and lastly to the king of Egypt. Through it all, Joseph was ultimately serving the Lord and his purposes!

No matter his circumstances, Joseph served in such a way to make the person he was serving successful. First he made Potiphar successful, then the prison warden, and finally the king of Egypt. Joseph made a career of helping his boss be successful. Young person, this is a great formula for success. Seek to make your supervisor successful. As you do so, you will surely grow in influence and be given larger and larger responsibilities. Who knows? Before you know it, perhaps you will be the one in charge!

Joseph persevered through thirteen years of repeated disappointments. He was faithful through many difficult trials. Throughout all these hardships, God was preparing him for a very important purpose. God used Joseph to help feed people not only from Egypt but also from other countries hit hard by the famine: "When the famine had spread over the whole country, Joseph opened the storehouses and sold grain to the Egyptians, for the famine was severe throughout Egypt. And all the countries came to Egypt to buy grain from Joseph, because the famine was severe in all the world" (Gen. 41:56-57).

When the famine hit Joseph's homeland, Joseph's father Jacob sent his brothers to get food from Egypt. That was how Joseph was finally reunited with his family. Through all of Joseph's trials, God had a plan; he was preparing Joseph for his life purpose.

When Joseph's brothers came to Egypt to get food, of course they didn't realize that they were dealing with their brother Joseph. When Joseph finally revealed his true identity to his brothers, they were shocked as well as very scared.

However, Joseph reassured them with a strong statement of God's sovereign purpose through everything:

> Then Joseph said to his brothers, "Come close to me." When they had done so, he said, "I am your brother Joseph, the one you sold into Egypt! And now, do not be distressed and do not be angry with yourselves for selling me here, because it was to save lives that God sent me ahead of you. For two years now there has been famine in the land, and for the next five years there will not be plowing and reaping. But God sent me ahead of you to preserve for you a remnant on earth and to save your lives by a great deliverance." (Gen. 45:4-7)

Joseph was telling his brothers that God had a purpose all along. God even had a purpose through his brothers' jealousy and their selling him into slavery. Joseph was telling his brothers that he was not angry with them, that he had forgiven them, and that God had used even their bad actions for his good purpose.

Joseph's perspective teaches us. When people do something bad to us, realize that the Lord can turn it around for his good purpose. Romans 8:28 says, "And we know that in all things God works for the good of those who love him, who have been called according to his purpose." As disciples committed to God's purpose, we can be confident that the Lord will use all things for our good.

The Lord was working all along through Joseph's and others' prophetic dreams: Joseph's two dreams that he shared with his family as a youth, the two dreams that he interpreted for the cupbearer and the baker in prison, and finally Pharaoh's two dreams. When Joseph interpreted Pharaoh's dreams, that led to the fulfillment of Joseph's initial two dreams. Through all of the disappointments and even through the sin of his brothers, God had a purpose!

Young person, when you are enduring life's disappointments, remember that the Lord has a purpose for them. God desires that you honor him through those trials, that you stay faithful to him, and that you serve others. As you are faithful in the small things, including what seems to be unimportant, God sees your faithfulness. Eventually he will prepare you for larger and larger responsibilities. Who knows? Perhaps you will one day lead a nation through a difficult and challenging time. Remember that the Lord is with you to achieve his great purpose!

Memory Passage

> Romans 5:3-5 "Not only so, but we also rejoice in our sufferings, because we know that suffering produces perseverance; perseverance, character; and character, hope. And hope does not disappoint us, because God has poured out his love into our hearts by the Holy Spirit, whom he has given us."

AARON, MOSES, AND THE GOLDEN CALF

Be a Leader Who Takes Responsibility without Excuses, Blame Shifting, or Lies

In Exodus 32, we have the story of how Aaron, Moses' assistant, appeased the people of Israel and allowed them to make an idol, a golden calf. We find from Exodus 31:18 that during this time, God was giving Moses "the two tablets of the testimony," God's covenant with Israel—two copies of what are known as The Ten Commandments.

While waiting for Moses on Mount Sinai, the people grew idle and restless. Because of their lack of purpose, there was opportunity for wrongdoing. Gathering around Aaron, the leaders pressured him: "Come, make us gods who will go before us. As for this fellow Moses who brought us up out of Egypt, we don't know what has happened to him" (Exod. 32:1). Their ingratitude to "this fellow Moses" was ironic. The Lord had declared in the preamble to The Ten Commandments the following: "I am the Lord your God, who brought you out of Egypt, out of the land of slavery" (Exod. 20:2). In other words, instead of being grateful to and worshiping the one true God who had brought them out of slavery, the people were clamoring for an idol!

Godly leaders must learn to stand up against ungodly pressure. Instead, Aaron yielded to the pressure. He reacted by saying, "Take off the gold earrings that your wives, your sons and your daughters are wearing, and bring them to me" (Exod. 32:2). Demonstrating weakness, Aaron led the people in creating an idol: "He took what they handed him and made it into an idol cast in the shape of a calf, fashioning it with a tool" (Exod. 32:4). Then they worshiped the golden calf, saying, "These are your gods, O Israel, who brought you up out of Egypt" (Exod. 32:4). Seeking to replace God with an idol, the Israelites gave credit to this man-made golden calf for bringing them out of slavery to Egypt.

Young person, every belief system that tries to replace the one true creator God will set up an idol to take God's place. Be on the lookout for those who espouse ideologies that are contrary to Biblical truth. If you think Biblically, you will be able to recognize the idol that is being set up against God. People will try to take an ungodly belief system and make it into a god, seeking to replace the one true God. This action is the epitome of rebellion. Rebellion is coming against the rightful authority; of course God is the most high authority. Rebellion is placing anything above God. When one creates an idol or practices idolatry, that person is walking in rebellion. It's a violation of the second commandment:

> You shall not make for yourself an idol in the form of anything in heaven above or on the earth beneath or in the waters below. You shall not bow down to them or worship them; for I, the Lord your God, am a jealous God, punishing the children for the sin of the fathers to the third and fourth generation of those who hate me, but showing love to a thousand generations of those who love me and keep my commandments. (Exod. 20:4-6)

Aaron recognized the idolatry taking place and made a weak attempt to rectify the situation. He announced that the next day there would be a festival to the Lord. However, after they made sacrificial offerings, the people engaged in revelry, giving themselves to sinful acts. The Apostle Paul describes in 1 Corinthians 10:6-13 what they did and what we should learn from their actions:

> Now these things occurred as examples to keep us from setting our hearts on evil things as they did. Do not be idolaters, as some of them were; as it is written: "The people sat down to eat and drink and got up to indulge in pagan revelry." We should not commit sexual immorality, as some of them did—and in one day twenty-three thousand of them died. We should not test the Lord, as some of them did—and were killed by snakes. And do not grumble, as some of them did—and were killed by the destroying angel.
>
> These things happened to them as examples and were written down as warnings for us, on whom the fulfillment of the ages has come. So, if you think you are standing firm, be careful that you don't fall! No temptation has seized you except what is common to man. And God is faithful; he will not let you be tempted beyond what you can bear. But when you are tempted, he will also provide a way out so that you can stand up under it.

These events serve as a warning to us to not set up an idol against the one true God. An idol is anything that replaces God in our lives. Often idolatry—pagan worship—resulted in sexual promiscuity—sexual wrongdoing. In fact, in the news over and over again, with ungodly religions, cults, ideologies, and distortions of true Christianity, we see sexual deviations from God's plan for marriage: that of one husband and one wife for a lifetime of committed love.

While Moses was still on the mountain, the Lord spoke to him about the people's rebellious sinfulness. God called them "a stiff-necked people" (Exod. 32:9). Having a stiff neck means that a person is unwilling to bow his neck. It's a person that is unsubmitted and unresponsive to authority. Stubborn and prideful, that individual is walking in rebellion.

The Lord declared to Moses: "Now leave me alone so that my anger may burn against them and that I may destroy them. Then I will make you into a great nation" (Exod. 32:10). The Lord's anger was such that he was going to destroy his people, but Moses appealed to God to not destroy them based on God's works on their behalf and his promises toward them. The Lord listened to Moses and relented.

Moses made his way back to the camp with his attendant Joshua, who had accompanied Moses some of the way up the mountain. On their way back down the mountain, they discussed the noise in the camp. When Moses drew near to the camp and saw the sinful revelry, in anger he threw the two tablets with the Ten Commandments, breaking them in the process. This action of breaking the tablets graphically communicated to the people that they were guilty of breaking their covenant with God.

In contrast to Aaron who had declared a festival, Moses took strong leadership. He rebuked and disciplined the people: "He took the calf they had made and burned it in the fire; then he ground it to powder, scattered it on the water and made the Israelites drink it" (Exod. 32:20).

However, then Moses made a mistake. Biblical leaders are fallible, and Moses was no exception. He was a human just like us. Instead of asking Aaron directly what he had done as a leader, he gave Aaron the opportunity to give an excuse for his actions and even to lie about what he had done. He asked Aaron, "What did these people do to you, that you led them into such great sin?" (Exod. 32:21).

Aaron responded with a very convoluted answer:

> Do not be angry, my lord. . . . You know how prone these people are to evil. They said to me, "Make us gods who will go before us. As for this fellow Moses who brought us up out of Egypt, we don't know what has happened to him." So I told them, "Whoever has any gold jewelry, take it off." Then they gave me the gold, and I threw it into the fire, and out came this calf! (Exod. 32:22-24)

Aaron made excuses, alluding to the people's inclination to do evil. He sought to shift the blame to the people as well as to Moses, because of his absence. Finally, Aaron ultimately lied. Instead of admitting that he had fashioned the golden calf idol with a tool, he said that he threw all the gold into the fire "and out came this calf!" Aaron sounded like Adam when Adam blamed Eve and the serpent when

God confronted Adam for his sin. A weak leader, Aaron did not take responsibility for his actions.

Young person, you will not be perfect. Aaron wasn't perfect in this matter and neither was Moses, who gave Aaron the opportunity to make excuses when Moses confronted him. When you are confronted by your parents or a teacher about a matter, it's important to take full responsibility for what you have done. Instead of making excuses, shifting the blame to someone else, or even worse, lying about the matter, confess fully to what you've done. The reason this action is important is that truth telling is how you are forgiven. You see, when you admit the truth about what you've done, that's confession. This truth of how we are forgiven is explained in 1 John 1:8-10: "If we claim to be without sin, we deceive ourselves and the truth is not in us. If we confess our sins, he is faithful and just and will forgive us our sins and purify us from all unrighteousness. If we claim we have not sinned, we make him out to be a liar and his word has no place in our lives."

For us as parents, we need to be careful not to do what Moses did. Instead of asking our children *why* they did something—in effect giving them the opportunity to give an excuse, we should ask them, "*What* did you do?" The answer to that question is a confession, which is necessary for forgiveness. Then we can look into our child's eyes and fully communicate forgiveness to our children! It's important that our children walk in truth, responsibility, and forgiveness for their actions, not in deception!

My dad relates a story about disciplining my brothers and me. My brothers and I would be blaming each other: "But he did such and such." However, my dad would persist in asking us, "*What* did *you* do? *What* did *you* do?" When we finally confessed to the truth of *what* we did in the conflict, we would often start crying and be repentant. While our goal is not to make our children cry, I encourage parents not to seek a reason for our children's wrongdoing, even though we may feel a personal need to find some good explanation for our children's sin. When our children answer to *what* they have done, they are confessing to the truth of their actions. Then we can communicate forgiveness to our children.

It's important to focus on our children's growth in godly character by helping them to take responsibility for their actions. Look to their future. Keep your eyes on the goal: your child's growth in godly character. Although we may need to explore the heart behind our children's actions, we should be careful that we are not inadvertently giving our children an excuse for their actions by asking them *why* they did something as opposed to *what* they did. The reason for wrongdoing is the sin nature, plain and simple; and we need to help our children to learn to take responsibility for their actions without excuses, blame shifting, or even lying.

As a principal, I have seen that lying has become an epidemic among children. Aaron's response to Moses' question is reminiscent of some of the responses I receive in my office when disciplining children. I've observed that sometimes parents inadvertently train their children to lie to them by harshly responding to their children's actions: "How could you do such a thing? You're a terrible person!" Even worse, in the misguided name of patience, parents may tolerate wrong behavior and attitudes until they lose their temper and slap their children. Instead of these kinds of harsh reactions to our children's misbehavior, we need to take the time to calmly help our children to take responsibility for their sin through admonishment, to forgive them once they have confessed, and then to issue an appropriate discipline (Fugate, 204-205). This process consistently applied will yield good fruit in our children's lives.

My dad taught me the following principle for life: "When caught in a fault, acknowledge the fault; once you acknowledge the fault, the blame stops." Although we will never be faultless, we can be blameless. We become blameless by quickly confessing our wrongdoing. If we lie, blame shift, or give excuses for our actions, the blame will keep coming our way. Rather, if we quickly confess our wrongdoing, the blame will stop and we become "blameless."

Psalm 19:12-13 shares how we can walk in this blameless way: "Who can discern his error? Forgive my hidden faults. Keep your servant also from willful sins; may they not rule over me. Then will I be blameless, innocent of great transgression." In the continuum of sin, we all have errors and hidden faults. Sometimes we want to keep our faults hidden, even from ourselves, because if we admit to them and continue to do them, then they are no longer hidden faults but "willful sins." If we give ourselves to sinning willfully, then those sins may begin to rule us and become our master; at that point, we are in danger of "great transgression." However, if we learn to take responsibility for our sin without blame shifting, excuses, or lies, then we become blameless. And the sin won't become our master.

Let's get back to our story. Aaron was to be punished by God for his actions, but Moses prayed for Aaron to be saved from God's wrath: "And the Lord was angry enough with Aaron to destroy him, but at that time I prayed for Aaron too" (Deut. 9:20).

Aaron had allowed the people to get out of control and run wild. Proverbs 29:18 says, "Where there is no revelation, the people cast off restraint; but blessed is he who keeps the law." The revelation is the Word of God. When people decide to rebel against the principles of God's Word, they cast off restraint and lack self-control. When individuals decide not to obey and worship the one true God, they lose all sense of what is right and refuse to restrain their sinful impulses. They start doing whatever they want to do as opposed to what God declares to be right.

When Moses saw that Aaron had allowed the people to get out of control and run wild, he provided strong leadership. He called for them to make a choice: "Whoever is for the Lord, come to me" (Exod. 32:26). Similarly, Jesus himself calls us to make a decision: "No one can serve two masters. Either he will hate the one and love the other, or he will be devoted to the one and despise the other. You cannot serve both God and Money" (Matt. 6:24).

Those who chose not to follow the one true God had to suffer the consequences of giving themselves to uncontrolled sinfulness. Moses appealed to the Lord on behalf of the people. He even took responsibility himself for the people; even though he had no part in their sin, Moses was willing to die if God chose to proceed with destroying the people. Moses appealed to God: "But now, please forgive their sin—but if not, then blot me out of the book you have written" (Exod. 32:32). God denied Moses' request, but Moses' willingness to die in this way speaks of Christ, who offers himself to us as the mediator for our sin.

Those who remain in rebellion, who are stiff-necked and stubborn, and who don't repent of their sin will ultimately be destroyed. But if we turn to our mediator Christ in repentance, bend our neck, humble ourselves, and confess our sin, we will be forgiven and saved! And just as God kept his promises to the nation of Israel, he will keep his promise to us. Jesus declared, "There is rejoicing in the presence of the angels of God over one sinner who repents" (Luke 15:10).

I encourage you, young person, to be a strong leader who doesn't surrender to ungodly pressure. At the same time, make it a principle of your life to take responsibility for your actions. Instead of giving excuses, shifting the blame, or even lying about your actions, in repentance confess your sin quickly and be forgiven! When you do so, you are considered blameless before God! And the *Lord* will be your salvation and your defense!

Memory Verse

Proverbs 25:26 "Like a muddied spring or a polluted well is a righteous man who gives way to the wicked."

CALEB AND JOSHUA

Take the Promised Land

What is God's Promised Land for your life? All of us in Christ have a promised land; it's the destiny—the plans—that God has for you. Jeremiah 29:11 is a great verse reminding us of this truth: "'For I know the plans I have for you,' declares the Lord, 'plans to prosper you and not to harm you, plans to give you hope and a future.'" God has a plan for your life—that's your promised land!

In God's Word we can look at the story of the Israelites to gain principles for walking into God's promised land for our lives. Always remember: The promised land in your life has to do with others. We're called to be others-focused champions!

The Bible shares the great story of Moses sending out the twelve spies to explore the promised land. All twelve spies admitted that the land was a good land, but ten spies shrank back and spread a bad report, even a deceptive one, to discourage the people. Two spies—Caleb and Joshua—shared a positive report. They had the attitude of Philippians 4:13: "I can do all things through Christ who strengthens me." They believed that God would lead them in overcoming all obstacles to take the promised land. They had a we-can-do-it attitude!

In Numbers 13, Moses instructed the twelve spies, one from each tribe of Israel, to explore the promised land. He commissioned the spies to find out what kind of people were living in the land and whether the land was a fruitful one.

The first principle for taking the promised land is to *identify your promised land.* As part of our relationship with the Lord, we need to explore prayerfully God's promised land for us. In prayer—communicating with God—we need to count the cost and set definitive God-ordained goals.

I recall when I was a young teacher. I had had some success teaching high school English and coaching varsity basketball and soccer. However, the Lord led me to a different school, one that was a kindergarten through eighth grade school that didn't have an athletics program. I was tempted to see this change as a step back in my calling, but the Lord led me in prayer to set a goal: to become principal of that school within three years. Within a year I was associate principal and in two years principal. In prayer, the Lord led me to set a goal—to see the promised land for my life.

In order to take the promised land for your life, you need to ask the Lord what *his goal* is for your life; you need to prayerfully seek him for direction. Proverbs 3:6 instructs us, "In all your ways acknowledge him, and he will make your paths straight." Psalm 37:5 encourages us, "Commit your way to him; trust in him and he will do this: He will make your righteousness shine like the dawn, the justice of your cause like the noonday sun." As you seek the Lord with all your heart—as you walk in a prayerful relationship with him, he will make your promised land clear.

After the twelve spies returned from exploring the promised land, they gave Moses and Aaron their report. They all agreed that the promised land was a good one—a fruitful land. However, ten of the spies emphasized the negative; they emphasized the obstacles, namely the enemies in the land. They highlighted the descendants of Anak. (Anakites were large people causing fear.)

It's a great thing to know that God has a promised land for your life—to know that He has a plan for you. When you come to that prayerful realization, that is a great victory! Once you know that God has a plan for you, there are other important principles to walk out in order to realize your destiny—one focused on the Lord and on others.

A second principle in taking your promised land is to *realize that there will be opposition*. Once you have identified God's promised land, you will have two choices before you. Those two choices are *faith or fear*.

As the spies gave their report to Moses and Aaron, two spies—Caleb and Joshua—made a convictional decision based on faith as opposed to fear. Caleb declared, "We can certainly do it!" (Num. 13:30).

One of the best pieces of advice I ever received came from a mentor of mine; in fact, this mentor was the school principal that equipped me when I was an associate principal. His counsel was the following: *Make decisions out of faith. Analyze the process of your decision making: Make decisions out of faith instead of fear.*

Similarly, I challenge you to make decisions with a perspective of pleasing God as opposed to pleasing man. Realize that there will be opposition when taking your promised land. People may talk negatively about the Lord's calling for you. They may even spread bad reports about you.

In Numbers 13:31-33, the ten spies spread a bad report, even a deceptive one: "We can't attack those people; they are stronger than we are. . . . The land we explored devours those living in it. All the people we saw there are of great size. We saw the Nephilim there (the descendants of Anak come from the Nephilim). We seemed like grasshoppers in our own eyes, and we looked the same to them."

The ten spies were now calling the Anakites Nephilim. Back in Genesis 6 when God brought the judgment of the flood because of man's evil doing, the Bible speaks of the Nephilim.

Although the Nephilim were giants of great physical strength, they were really like any other men. The Hebrew for Nephilim means "Fallen ones." In God's eyes, the Nephilim were not great; rather, they were fallen because of their wickedness.

By saying "we saw the Nephilim there," ten of the spies were exaggerating the Anakites' size for the purpose of creating fear. Now these Israelites were doers of evil themselves. When they said, "We seemed like grasshoppers in our own eyes," (Num. 13:33) they were belittling God by belittling themselves who were God's creation!

In taking the promised land for your life, it's important that you view yourself as a great creation of your Creator God—that you not belittle yourself to view yourself as a "grasshopper." You need to see yourself as a child of God. You need to see yourself as a growing young man or woman of God. You are becoming God's champion and taking the promised land! You are serving a great God with a great purpose!

In fact, it's evil to speak wrongly of yourself and your destiny—your promised land! It's evil to speak wrongly of the God who created you, to speak wrongly of Creator God!

I encourage you, young person, to fix your eyes on Christ—not on all your enemies and obstacles. Have the overcoming perspective of Caleb: "We can certainly do it!" (Num. 13:30). When you have faith in God, you become characterized by a certain boldness.

Unfortunately, the Israelites did not take up Caleb's challenge to be champions. They committed a terrible sin, one that works directly against our taking the promised land. What did they do? They grumbled, and in their grumbling they rebelled against the Lord and his purpose for them. In fact, the entire community talked about stoning Joshua and Caleb.

Because of their convictional faith about taking the promised land, Joshua and Caleb were the only ones who would later take the promised land. What is the principle that we can glean here for taking the promised land? *Please the Lord—seek to please the Lord as opposed to seeking to please people. Keep your eyes on Christ. Seek His commendation.*

Conversely, if you want to take the promised land, don't be a grumbler. 1 Corinthians 10:9-10 warns us, "We should not test the Lord, as some of them did—and were killed by snakes. And do not grumble, as some of them did—and were killed by the destroying angel."

Grumbling and complaining will work directly against your taking the promised land.

Philippians 2:12-13 emphasizes the need for obedience in taking our promised land: "Therefore, my dear friends, as you have always obeyed—not only in my presence, but now much more in my absence—continue to work out your salvation with fear and trembling, for it is God who works in you to will and to act according to his good purpose."

Who is the one person that sees all things? God! What is the most direct route to your Promised Land? Obedience. *The straightest line to your promised land is that of obedience.* Obedience—faithful obedience—shows your faith and will bring you into your promised land.

Philippians 2:14-15 goes on to emphasize obedience without grumbling: "Do everything without complaining or arguing, so that you may become blameless and pure, children of God without fault in a crooked and depraved generation in which you shine like stars in the universe."

Young people, do you want to know how to shine? Do you want to know how to shine in such a way that others will notice? Do you want to know how to bring positive favor to your life? *Do everything without grumbling and arguing.* Obey your parents the first time with a cheerful attitude and without grumbling. Do that and you will be well on your way to your destiny—your promised land.

Coming into God's promised land is not a selfish pursuit; it's a serving pursuit. When you enter your promised land, you are coming into a place of serving God and serving others.

Do you want to know how to come into God's promised land? Whatever God, your parents, your teachers, your coaches, your pastor, or your employer calls you to do—no matter how big or small—do it obediently, faithfully, wholeheartedly, and cheerfully.

The Bible teaches that if you are faithful in small things, you will be faithful with larger things. In the Parable of the Talents, Jesus emphasized, "Well done, good and faithful servant! You have been faithful with a few things; I will put you in charge of many things. Come and share your master's happiness!" (Matt. 25:21). Remember this principle of taking the promised land: God is the one person who sees everything—He is the one person who sees whether we are truly being faithful. He sees what no one else sees. He sees your faithfulness. If you are faithful in one area, he may promote you in another area. He sees all! Promotion is from the Lord. As you are faithful in what you're given to do, you will be walking in a straight line to your promised land.

Finding God's promised land for your life is not about you. It's about others and the Lord using you to pour out your life for his service. Philippians 2:17 says, "But even if I am being poured out like a drink offering on the sacrifice and service coming from your faith, I am glad and rejoice with all of you." Finding God's destiny for you has to do with giving your life away for the cause of Christ—a great work indeed!

In taking your promised land, you need to be willing to wait patiently in your spirit while taking active steps of faith. Time is no object to the Lord. In fact, because of the disobedience of the ten spies and the Israelite community, that whole generation had to die in the desert before the next generation could take the promised land. God forgave the Israelites, but they still had to receive the disciplinary consequences of their actions. They missed their opportunity to take the promised land.

In our lives, there will be key points in time—opportunities to seize—in which we need to take our promised land! Ephesians 5:15-17 warns us: "Be very careful, then, how you live—not as unwise but as wise, making the most of every opportunity, because the days are evil. Therefore do not be foolish, but understand what the Lord's will is." That's God's promised land for you—the Lord's will! Make the most of every opportunity; don't be foolish; understand his will!

Because of their rebellion expressed through their grumbling, the Israelites were not allowed to take the promised land. They had to wait forty years, one year for each of the days the spies explored the land, until all of that generation, except for Caleb and Joshua, died in the desert.

Sin—rebelling against God—has its effect. What's the effect? The effect is missing your promised land—selling yourself short of God's best for you. I encourage both young people and parents to honor the Lord, take the long view, and trust him and his ways for your life, family, and children—your future and their future!

Sometimes in life we come to the point where we honestly express, "I can't do it." We don't say this out of rebellion, but out of a sincere sense of difficulty. What is hard for you? I recall that after starting to go to a Christian school in the sixth grade and struggling academically, I expressed to my dad, "Well, maybe I'm not cut out for Christian schools!"

Later as a young man, after having a long season of personal hardship, I came to a point of surrender. In effect, I shared with the Lord: "You see me; you see how weak I am. But if you can do something with my life, here I am." That week the Lord did a wonderful work in my life: he revealed his promised land to me, calling me to teach and encourage young people in their walk with the Lord!

When we come to a place of weakness, saying in effect "I can't do it," that's an opportunity for the Lord. At that point we simply need to surrender to the Lord. After that great verse in Jeremiah 29:11 in which God says, "I know the plans I have for you," there's the truth of Jeremiah 29:12-13: "Then you will call upon me and come and pray to me, and I will listen to you. You will seek me and find me when you seek me with all your heart."

That's surrender: Calling on the Lord—seeking him with all your heart! God wants your heart. He wants to help you, but you need to allow Jesus to help you by calling out to him in prayer and walking with him until he reveals his plans for you. He helps you by helping you to get your eyes off yourself and your weakness and getting your eyes upon Christ! As Philippians 4:13 reminds us, "I can do all things through Christ who strengthens me."

Of course, a generation later, Joshua led God's people to take the promised land. Forty-five years after they had spied out the land, Caleb received his promised land, his mountain, his "hill country" (Joshua 14:12). Caleb said to Joshua, "Now then, just as the Lord promised, he has kept me alive for forty-five years since the time he said this to Moses, while Israel moved about in the desert. So here I am today, eighty-five years old! I am still as strong today as the day Moses sent me out; I'm just as vigorous to go out to battle now as I was then. Now give me this hill country that the Lord promised me that day" (Joshua 14:10-12). After waiting all those years, Caleb now took his promised land!

It doesn't matter if you're eighteen years old or eighty-five years old, God can still bring you into your promised land! I encourage you to take your promised land—the plans God has for you!

Memory Verse

Numbers 14:24 "But because my servant Caleb has a different spirit and follows me wholeheartedly, I will bring him into the land he went to, and his descendants will inherit it."

JOSHUA

Get Ready to Take the Promised Land

One of the greatest leaders of all time was Moses. Moses led God's people out of Egyptian slavery. The Lord accomplished amazing miracles and great victories through Moses. But in the course of time, this revered leader of the Israelites died. After Moses died, there could have been a very serious leadership gap. The people could have become disillusioned. In fact, we often see in the Bible that when God's chosen leader died, the people fell into sin and floundered without godly leadership. A new leader was needed—a strong leader who would lead God's people to take the promised land.

To meet this leadership challenge, God called Moses' assistant Joshua. As God called Joshua, the Lord referred to Moses as "my servant" (Joshua 1:2). Moses had been an example to Joshua of a faithful servant of the Lord. In fact, being the Lord's servant is a major part of taking God's promised land in our lives. Taking the promised land is not a selfish endeavor; rather, it is a serving endeavor.

The Lord described the promised land for Joshua. He would lead the people in crossing the Jordan River to take the promised land: "From the desert to Lebanon, and from the great river, the Euphrates—all the Hittite country—to the Great Sea on the west" (Joshua 1:4). By describing the promised land of Canaan, God gave Joshua a vision. By God's grace, the Lord would work in Joshua to bring the people into the promised land. It's the same with us. By God's grace, the Lord works in us to identify—to envision—our promised land, and then he leads us by the Holy Spirit to take that land!

Through communicating with God in prayer, we need to envision God's promised land for us. What is your promised land? What is God calling you to? What is your goal in life? What is your destiny? God knows your promised land and wants you to identify it. Through prayer, God helps you to see your promised land and gives you the inspiration to accomplish it!

In Joshua 1:5, the Lord gave Joshua the inspiration for his mission: "No one will be able to stand up against you all the days of your life. As I was with Moses, so I will be with you; I will never leave you nor forsake you." Romans 8:31 encourages us, "If God is for us, who can be against us?" When you know that God is with you, that knowledge gives you the necessary confidence to take your promised land. The victory resides in the Lord! Christ in you will bring the promise to fulfillment.

When God called Joshua, he commanded him to be courageous: "Be strong and courageous, because you will lead these people to inherit the land I swore to their forefathers to give them" (Joshua 1:6). Because it was the Lord's commissioning, God would give Joshua everything he needed. 2 Corinthians 12:10 declares, "For when I am weak, then I am strong." At times, we may feel too weak to rise up to God's call, but God turns our weakness into Christ's strength! God equips us with everything we need to take the promised land!

Then the Lord gave Joshua important instructions for success: "Be strong and very courageous. Be careful to obey all the law my servant Moses gave you; do not turn from it to the right or to the left, that you may be successful wherever you go. Do not let this Book of the Law depart from your mouth; meditate on it day and night, so that you may be careful to do everything written in it. Then you will be prosperous and successful" (Joshua 1:7-8). How does true lasting success come? What is our responsibility? How do we actually take the promised land in our lives? *We take it by studying, learning, knowing, and following God's Word!* We may not get the short-term results right away but following God's Word with all of our heart yields the long-term results—actually reaching God's promised land for our lives.

In other words, apart from God and his Word, there is no guarantee that we will achieve our promised land. In order to realize God's plans for our life, we need to walk with God. We do so by putting his Word into practice. We have to obey God's Word.

This need to obey God's Word is vividly illustrated in Deuteronomy chapter 8. If you are going to *walk into* the promised land for your life, you have to *walk out* the principles of God's Word. Deuteronomy 8:1-2 explains, "Be careful to follow every command I am giving you today, so that you may live and increase and may enter and possess the land that the Lord promised on oath to your forefathers. Remember how the Lord your God led you all the way in the desert these forty years, to humble you and to test you in order to know what was in your heart, whether or not you would keep his commands." Note that this passage says that the Lord humbled and tested his people. The word for *test* in Hebrew is *nasah*[BR1]; it's a test to prove out the character in a person—to bring forth positive character. This "test" causes one to rise up as a person. It's the same connotation expressed in Genesis 22:1 when God "tested" Abraham's faith by telling him to sacrifice his only son Isaac, through whom would come the promise: "Some time later God tested Abraham." God tests us to prove our faith commitment.

Then God shared a major purpose for our trials: "He humbled you, causing you to hunger and then feeding you with manna, which neither you nor your fathers had known, to teach you that man does not live on bread alone but on every word that comes from the mouth of the Lord" (Deut. 8:3). Our trials teach us to depend on God's Word for our very sustenance. They help us to learn to walk according to his Word.

Related to the purpose of trials is that God uses our trials to discipline us: "Know then in your heart that as a man disciplines his son, so the Lord your God disciplines you" (Deut. 8:5). Receiving discipline is part of our being able to take the promised land in our lives. God needs to build his character in us in order for us to be able to take the promised land. Through disciplinary trials, we learn to depend on God as opposed to depending on ourselves.

When we persevere through the disciplinary trials and continue to walk out God's Word, he ultimately brings us into the promised land. However, once we taste the joy of walking in his plans for us, we need to be sure not to forget our God: "When you have eaten and are satisfied, praise the Lord your God for the good land he has given you" (Deut. 8:10). We need to remember to thank God and give him glory for bringing us into the promised land!

Young person, when God's plans start to come to fruition in your life, don't forget him; and don't forget the heart lessons that he has taught you through the character-building process. Stay in that place of honoring him. Deuteronomy 8:11 admonishes us, "Be careful that you do not forget the Lord your God, failing to observe his commands, his laws and his decrees that I am giving you this day."

When you come into the land of God's promises for you, the temptation will be for you to forget to honor the Lord and somehow give yourself the credit. As Deuteronomy 8:17-18 says, "You may say to yourself, 'My power and the strength of my hands have produced this wealth for me.' But remember the Lord your God, for it is he who gives you the ability to produce wealth, and so confirms his covenant, which he swore to your forefathers, as it is today." Always remember to honor the Lord. Give him glory. Remember the Lord! It's God who gives us our ability, our gifts, our motivation, and even our desire to accomplish great things!

This passage is a strong reminder that in order to take the promised land, we need to obey God and his Word. "If you ever forget the Lord your God and follow other gods and worship and bow down to them, I testify against you today that you will surely be destroyed. Like the nations the Lord destroyed before you, so you will be destroyed for not obeying the Lord your God" (Deut. 8:19-20).

This admonishment to live according to God's Word and to honor him was embraced by our champion Joshua. As Joshua faced his mission in life, God gave him a direct command: "Have I not commanded you? Be strong and courageous. Do not be terrified; do not be discouraged, for the Lord your God will be with you wherever you go" (Joshua 1:9). This is the key verse of Joshua's call to take the promised land. The important thing to understand here is that God *commanded* Joshua to be strong and courageous! It was not an option for him! And for us as Christians taking the promised land, we really have no choice. God calls us forward into the promised land. If we are going to be obedient Christians, the only way is the path forward; we can't go back and we can't waffle in indecision. We have to decisively follow God. It's the only way to be a true disciple of Christ. It takes courage to obey God.

And one other point about courage: it takes courage because there are risks involved in giving God our full obedience. There could be a downside if we fail. Therefore, Christians who are fully committed and obedient to following God's will for their lives become characterized by godly strength and Christ-like courage. We're called to "be strong and courageous!"

After receiving his call from God, Joshua did not hesitate; he took action. "So Joshua ordered the officers of the people: 'Go through the camp and tell the people, "Get your supplies ready. Three days from now you will cross the Jordan here to go in and take possession of the land the Lord your God is giving you for your own"'" (Joshua 1:10-11). When you choose to follow God with all your heart, this decision gives you a certain authority—a moral authority. The following principle of authority becomes operational in your life: in order to walk in authority, one must first be under authority. Because Joshua was fully obedient to the Lord and to Moses when he was Moses' assistant, when it came time for Joshua to lead the people, he was able to do so with full convictional confidence.

Joshua called the people to get ready! They had to get ready to take the promised land. And so for us as well! We need to prepare ourselves by fully obeying God and the authorities God has placed in our lives.

In order to take the promised land, you must walk in this kind of obedience. Joshua reminded certain Israeli tribes of Moses' command and of the corresponding rest that they would experience: "Remember the command that Moses the servant of the Lord gave you: 'The Lord your God is giving you rest and has granted you this land'" (Joshua 1:13). When we take the promised land, there is a certain sense of "rest" that comes into our lives as opposed to striving in our own strength. We rest in God's provision as we wholeheartedly obey him.

Joshua also ordered those same tribes to remember that we have to work together in teamwork in order to take the promised land: "All your fighting men, fully armed, must cross over ahead of your brothers. You are to help your brothers until the Lord gives them rest, as he has done for you, and until they too have taken possession of the land that the Lord your God is giving them. After that, you may go back and occupy your own land" (Joshua 1:14-15). Taking the promised land is not a man-made, selfish pursuit; rather, it is a God-ordained, others-focused pursuit. We work with others in teamwork to accomplish the promised land in our lives. There are no lone warriors in God's Kingdom—we work with others in teamwork.

In Joshua 1:16-17, the people responded in obedience: "Whatever you have commanded us we will do, and wherever you send us we will go. Just as we fully obeyed Moses, so we will obey you. Only may the Lord your God be with you as he was with Moses." As the people recognized that Joshua was fully obeying God, they willingly obeyed Joshua.

Young person, in order to get ready to take God's promised land in your life, it is critical to focus on three areas. First, you must focus on obeying authority. God has authorized three institutions in our lives: our family, our church, and our government. Of course, it's critical that you obey your parents. Colossians 3:20 says, "Children, obey your parents in all things, for this is well pleasing to the Lord." In the Ten Commandments given to Moses by God, the fifth one commands the following: "Honor your father and your mother, as the Lord your God has commanded you, so that you may live long and that it may go well with you in the land the Lord your God is giving you" (Deut. 5:16). That command of honoring our parents comes with the corresponding promise of enjoying "the land the Lord your God is giving you"—that's your promised land! As you learn to cheerfully honor and obey your parents, you will have no problem with obeying and working with your teachers, your church leaders, and the governing authorities. In the process, you will be walking in a direct path to your promised land!

Second, you need to develop your relationship with the Lord. You need to know that God is with you! Again, Joshua 1:9 emphasizes the need for you to focus on Christ's presence: "Have I not commanded you? Be strong and courageous. Do not be terrified; do not be discouraged, *for the Lord your God will be with you wherever you go*" (Joshua 1:9, italics added). The enemy will seek to cause you to be fearful about taking the promised land. However, the secret to conquering fear is to focus on Christ's presence with you. Be with the Lord, walk in his presence, and talk with him! Being a friend of Jesus will equip you with godly confidence. In the process, you will increasingly gain clarity regarding Christ's plan—his promised land—for your life.

Third, in order to prepare yourself to take the promised land in your life, become an excellent student. The Bible says to study to show yourself approved unto God (2 Tim. 2:15). You need *to study*. You need to equip yourself with excellent study habits. A student knows how to learn. In order for you to become a champion for God, you need to become an excellent student of God's Word! In the calling of Joshua, we see how important it was for him to study God's Word and not to turn from it "to the right or to the left" (Joshua 1:7). In order for you to take the promised land, you need to study God's Word. You need to grow in being a disciplined student. This advance in your life will enable you to prosper in God's direction for your life, both in college and in the work field.

Young person, as you learn to walk in obedience to your parents, to the authorities God has placed in your life, and to God's Word, you will be walking on a direct, straight-line path to the Lord's promised land in your life! The Lord promises to be *with you* as you embrace your call. He will give you the strength and the courage you need! I challenge you to live this great adventure of taking the promised land!

Memory Verses

Colossians 3:20 "Children, obey your parents in all things, for this is well pleasing to the Lord."

Deuteronomy 5:16 "Honor your father and your mother, as the Lord your God has commanded you, so that you may live long and that it may go well with you in the land the Lord your God is giving you."

GIDEON

Don't Think of Yourself as a Small Person; Think of Your God Who Is a Big God

As a grown man, I'm a big guy—six feet four inches. However, when I was a child, I felt very small. When I was in elementary school, I was a weak person. I was a "PK"—a *pastor's kid* who was unmercifully picked on and threatened with bodily harm. I lived in much fear in my elementary years—particularly in grades two through four. When I got off the bus, I would have to make like a running back to cut through and around those trying to beat me up. As I grew older, I still didn't have much confidence. However, right before my second year of college, God called me to my life purpose. That year I learned to get my eyes off the smallness of who I was and on the bigness of who God is! I no longer thought of myself as a *small person*; I began to focus on God who is a *big God!*

In Judges chapters six and seven, we see how God made that change in the life of Gideon. Gideon thought of himself as a small person from a weak family. However, God raised Gideon up to deliver his people the Israelites from the oppression of the Midianites.

Israel had done evil in God's eyes. Because of their wickedness, God allowed the Israelites to be oppressed by the Midianites. Israel had to endure a terrible situation. Afraid of their enemies, the Israelites lived in hideaways. At harvest time, the Midianites would invade Israel by storming through the land on their camels to plunder the Israelites. The Israelites' crops were often destroyed by the Midianites and other nations. Of course, this destruction of their crops impoverished Israel severely.

The Bible says that these peoples—the Midianites, the Amalekites, and other Eastern peoples—would come on the land like locusts. Judges 6:5 says the following of these peoples: "They came up with their livestock and their tents like swarms of locusts. It was impossible to count the men and their camels; they invaded the land to ravage it." With their seemingly countless numbers, these peoples would literally overwhelm the Israelites.

Because of this terrible oppression by Midian, Israel eventually called out to God to deliver them. God sent a prophet to rebuke Israel for walking away from his ways, for not listening to him, and for not remembering what he had previously done to deliver them from oppression. The prophet rebuked them for forgetting how God had brought them out of Egyptian bondage and into the promised land. And he rebuked them for worshiping pagan gods—giving themselves to idolatry.

The Israelites needed to repent and turn back to God. Young person, repentance is how we come to God. If we've turned away from God, repentance is how we start to renew our relationship with God again. We're called to live lives of repentance. Repentance is turning around and going in the opposite direction; it is a 180-degree turn. When we sin by disobeying God, we need to turn back to God. How do we turn back to God? We start by praying in effect, "Lord, I repent." Then we need to confess our sins before the Lord and receive his forgiveness. That is how we are restored to relationship with God.

Into this environment of oppression, an angel of the Lord appeared to Gideon one day while he was threshing wheat under a large oak tree. Out of fear, Gideon was hiding from the Midianites. He was doing work in a concealed manner so that the Midianites would not destroy his crop. As Gideon was working in this hideaway, the angel greeted him with these words: "The Lord is with you, mighty warrior" (Judges 6:12).

However, Gideon certainly didn't view himself as a "mighty warrior." He countered the angel by saying that it didn't seem to him that the Israelites had God with them because of the Midianites' oppression. Very hesitant, Gideon was unconvinced of the Lord's presence with them. And he surely didn't see himself as a "mighty warrior."

Young person, sometimes you too may be hesitant to believe that God can use you. No matter what you presently think of yourself, God *can* use you! If you are willing, he will build you up to be a champion for him!

However, as with the Israelites in their oppression, if we live in sin, we won't receive God's help. Still, God waits for us to repent. He waits for us to turn away from sin and turn back to him. He wants us to desire his help because he is eager to support us.

The Lord commissioned Gideon to his task: "Go in the strength you have and save Israel out of Midian's hand. Am I not sending you?" (Judges 6:14). God wanted to use Gideon to deliver Israel from Midian. He was being sent by the Lord. This is what God will do with you if you're willing to be his servant.

Gideon wanted to be God's servant. However, he had to be convinced that God was truly with him. Out of his own sense of weakness and insecurity, Gideon argued with God regarding God's plans for him. He said, "But Lord, how can I save Israel? My clan is the weakest in Manasseh, and I am the least in my family" (Judges 6:15). Gideon saw himself as a small person from a weak family.

Young person, no matter your family, no matter your background, no matter your station in life, God wants to use you!

In response to Gideon's doubts, God again said that he would be with Gideon and that Gideon would defeat the Midianites. He responded to Gideon's arguments by encouraging him with these words: "I will be with you, and you will strike down all the Midianites together" (Judges 6:16). This statement—"I will be with you"—is used by God over and over in the Bible when he has called his champions to do great exploits! It's what the Lord says to you if you have received him as Lord and Savior and are willing to be used for his cause! He says, "I will be with you!"

However, Gideon remained unconvinced that he would "strike down all the Midianites" (Judges 6:16). It seemed to be an impossible task that Israel would be delivered from a people so large that they seemed to be countless swarms of locusts. However, even though the odds may seem to be insurmountable, God can do all things! He can do his work through you! He says I will accomplish victorious exploits through you!

Still unsure, Gideon asked God for a sign that this was really God. Meanwhile, Gideon prepared a meal for the angel. The angel gave these instructions regarding the food: "Take the meat and the unleavened bread, place them on this rock, and pour out the broth" (Judges 6:20). Gideon obeyed the angel's instructions and placed the food on the rock. Lo and behold, when the Lord's angel touched the food with his staff, fire came from the rock and the food was consumed! Then the angel disappeared.

After realizing that he had been dealing with God's angel, Gideon thought he would die. But God assured Gideon that he would not die: "Peace! Do not be afraid. You are not going to die" (Judges 6:23). Gideon proceeded to build an altar and named it "The Lord is Peace" (Judges 6:24).

In Gideon's commission to deliver the Israelites, how did the Lord direct Gideon to start leading his people? The Lord had Gideon begin by taking responsibility for his own family's sins. He took his father's bull, which was sacred to his community's pagan religion, and dealt with his own family first. This taking of the bull signaled a turning from false gods and an embracing of the one true God.

Young person, the Bible says that if we're going to lead God's people, we must lead our own family first. 1 Timothy 3:4-5 says the following about spiritual leaders: "He must manage his own family well and see that his children obey him with proper respect. (If anyone does not know how to manage his own family, how can he take care of God's church?)."

After taking the bull, Gideon and his servants demolished his father's altar to the Baal idol and the Asherah pole next to it. In its place, they constructed a righteous altar to the Lord. However, out of fear of his family and neighbors, Gideon performed this task during the night.

The next morning when the men of the town discovered that Gideon had destroyed these pagan idols, they said that Gideon must be put to death. As one can see, these Israelites were so staunchly committed to their idolatry that they intended to kill Gideon!

However, amid the crowd clamoring for his son's death, Gideon's father Joash spoke up and defended him: "Are you going to plead Baal's cause? Are you trying to save him? Whoever fights for him shall be put to death by morning! If Baal really is a god, he can defend himself when someone breaks down his altar" (Judges 6:31). Of course, the import of Joash's words is that no idol can defend itself—having no power, an idol is just an object made by man!

With his father's support, Gideon gained some standing as a leader. Through the empowerment of the Holy Spirit, Gideon blew the trumpet. The people of the community could now see that God was with Gideon! Gideon's playing of the trumpet was Spirit-inspired! With the playing of the trumpet, Gideon's townspeople, the Abiezrites, who just recently had sought to kill Gideon for destroying their idols, now chose to follow Gideon! What a turnaround!

Young person, we learn from Gideon's experience that when we take a righteous stand for the Lord, often others will follow. When we stand for God courageously, we gain people to our cause. That's what happened with Gideon.

Well, even though Gideon could now see that God was with him and inspiring him, he still needed more reassurance. In order to be sure that God was calling him to defeat the Midianites, he asked God for two more signs. He asked God the following: "If you will save Israel by my hand as you have promised—look, I will place a wool fleece on the threshing floor. If there is dew only on the fleece and all the ground is dry, then I will know that you will save Israel by my hand, as you said" (Judges 6:36-37). God confirmed Gideon's request with the fleece.

Then Gideon asked God for one last sign. He asked that God would not be angry with him for asking for a similar request in reverse. He said, "This time make the fleece dry and the ground covered with dew" (Judges 6:39). Again, God answered Gideon's request, giving Gideon assurance that God was with him and that he had called him to be his champion to save Israel from Midian.

Young person, just as God was patient with Gideon as he wrestled with God's call for him, God will be patient with you as well. Don't condemn Gideon for asking for multiple signs that God was with him. Gideon had shown obedience; at the same time, he was a man who desired reassurance. As you seek God with all your heart, he will confirm his presence and purpose in your life as well.

Against the overwhelming numbers of Midian, the Israelites had much smaller numbers. However, the Lord wanted Gideon and the Israelites—as well as their enemies—to know that it was God and God alone who would achieve this great victory! Therefore, the Lord proceeded to drastically reduce the numbers of the Israelite army.

Directing Gideon, God said, "You have too many men for me to deliver Midian into their hands. In order that Israel may not boast against me that her own strength has saved her, announce now to the people, 'Anyone who trembles with fear may turn back and leave Mount Gilead'" (Judges 7:2-3). Those submitting to fear would be a hindrance to the Israelite army; the Lord wanted courageous warriors that would encourage each other in their cause. Through this action, the Lord trimmed Israel's military from 32,000 soldiers to just 10,000.

However, the Lord told Gideon that he still had too many soldiers! Remember that the Midianites were like "swarms of locusts," too numerous to count; but now the Lord was severely limiting Israel's army! The Lord told Gideon to take the remaining soldiers "down to the water, and I will sift them for you there" (Judges 7:4). The Lord would choose those who were ready to be his servants!

At the water, God gave Gideon these instructions: "Separate those who lap the water with their tongues like a dog from those who kneel down to drink" (Judges 7:5). The Bible tells us that three hundred soldiers used their hands to lap the water to their mouths, but the vast majority of the soldiers lapped the water like a dog with their mouths in the water. Through this mechanism, God chose three hundred soldiers who demonstrated their readiness to be his servants.

The three hundred chosen soldiers lapped the water with their heads up. They showed that they were ever prepared for battle. They had "heads on a swivel." In other words, their heads—with their eyes—were ever looking around, alert to the enemy! They were eager to serve God; they were ready to be the Lord's champions!

Now only three hundred soldiers were left with Gideon to go up against an army with numbers "like swarms of locusts." And this is the main point of the story: *With God all things are possible*. It may look as if the odds against us are insurmountable, but if God is on our side, all things are possible! As Deuteronomy 32:30-31 declares, even one person with God is an advantage: "How could one man chase a thousand, or two put ten thousand to flight, unless their Rock had sold them, unless the Lord had given them up? For their rock is not like our Rock, as even our enemies concede." The great leader Joshua, used by God to take the promised land, emphasized the importance of loving God: "One of you routs a thousand, because the Lord your God fights for you, just as he promised. So be very careful to love the Lord your God" (Joshua 23:10-11). The key to being a champion for God is loving him with all your heart!

Even though Gideon didn't ask for it this time, the Lord gave Gideon another positive sign as he prepared to face the Midianites. As Gideon anticipated the battle, the Lord gave Gideon this encouraging word in the middle of the night: "Get up, go down against the camp, because I am going to give it into your hands. If you are afraid to attack, go down to the camp with your servant Purah and listen to what they are saying. Afterward, you will be encouraged to attack the camp" (Judges 7:9-11).

Young person, as you prepare to be the Lord's servant, God will encourage you. When I was a young man persevering through much doubt, the Lord provided me with a Christian friend who encouraged me with this word: "Be encouraged. You're my child. You're on the right path." This word gave me courage to keep persevering in the fight of faith!

Gideon and his servant Purah went to spy on their enemies. As they crept closer to the Midianites' camp, Gideon overheard a man's dream: "I had a dream . . . . A round loaf of barley bread came tumbling into the Midianite camp. It struck the tent with such force that the tent overturned and collapsed" (Judges 7:13).

As Gideon and Purah overheard this conversation, the man's friend replied, "This can be nothing other than the sword of Gideon son of Joash, the Israelite. God has given the Midianites and the whole camp into his hands" (Judges 7:14).

How did Gideon respond to hearing this encouraging dream? Greatly bolstered by the dream's interpretation, Gideon praised the Lord. Gathering his soldiers together, Gideon called them to action: "Get up! The Lord has given the Midianite camp into your hands" (Judges 7:15). A changed man, Gideon was now a confident champion leading his soldiers into battle!

Young person, God is with us on this journey! He will encourage us as we accept his call to be his champions!

Gideon divided his men into three groups. He gave them trumpets and jars containing torches. Taking leadership, Gideon charged his fellow soldiers with these words: "Watch me. Follow my lead. When I get to the edge of the camp, do exactly as I do. When I and all who are with me blow our trumpets, then from all around the camp blow yours and shout, 'For the Lord and for Gideon'" (Judges 7:17-18). We see in Gideon's leadership the important principle of leading by example. Followers watch their leader closely to see what to do.

Gideon led his men to attack the Midianite camp at night after their enemies had gone to sleep. The three divisions jarred their enemies awake with the loud noise of trumpets and crashing jars. With the torches in their left hands and the trumpets in their right hands, Gideon's soldiers yelled, "A sword for the Lord and for Gideon!" (Judges 7:20).

Being harshly awakened from their sleeping stupor, the Midianites ran out of fear. When Gideon's three hundred men sounded the trumpets, the Midianites turned on each other and started killing each other. Then they fled their camp.

Helping Gideon, the other tribes of Israel gave chase to capture the Midianites. That day Gideon led the Israelites to achieve a great victory!

Young person, in order to be God's champion, you need to know that the Lord is with you! Are you confident that God is with you? Are you confident that you have a personal relationship with the Lord? The Lord's angel said to Gideon, "The

Lord is with you, mighty warrior!" (Judges 6:12). If you have received Jesus as your Lord and Savior, you know that God is with you. If you respond to his call, you can be a champion for the Lord by focusing on his presence! In order to be a champion for the Lord, you need to walk with God; you need to have a loving relationship with him.

At present, you may think of yourself as a weak person; but if you know that God is with you, everything changes! Instead of being that person that is picked on, you can be that person that stands up for others. Instead of being bullied, you can be the bully stopper! Not by fighting back, but by standing firm! The battle is the Lord's! Learn to stand for the Lord and see his victory! As you learn to walk in God's strength as opposed to your own strength, you will become a mighty warrior for his kingdom!

There is only one way to know that the Lord is with you: by receiving Jesus as Lord and Savior. John 1:12 says, "Yet to all who received him, to those who believed in his name, he gave the right to become children of God." If you have never come to Christ, I encourage you to talk with your parents, your pastor, or a Christian teacher today. You come to Jesus by turning from the way of sin and receiving him as your Lord and Savior. Romans 10:9 says, "If you confess with your mouth, 'Jesus is Lord,' and believe in your heart that God raised him from the dead, you will be saved." If you believe in your heart that Jesus died for your sin and rose from the dead, I encourage you to pray to receive Jesus as your Lord and Savior. As you do so, thank him for coming into your life and making you his child. When you do so, you will become a new person—one inhabited by God himself! Then you will know that "the Lord is with you, mighty warrior!" Then you can become a champion for the Lord!

Memory Verse

Judges 6:12 "When the angel of the Lord appeared to Gideon, he said, 'The Lord is with you, mighty warrior.'"

RUTH AND BOAZ

Show Kindness and Reap Kindness

Let me give you some background to the story of Ruth and Boaz. It's a great love narrative, one illustrating God's redeeming kindness! First, I have to tell you about Elimelech and his wife Naomi. Their story is that of a normal, everyday family who sought to please God in a time of moral degradation in society. Elimelech and Naomi were Israelites, God's people. Because of God's judgment of Israel's terrible unfaithfulness through a famine, Elimelech and Naomi moved to Moab with their two sons Mahlon and Kilion. You see, the nation of Israel was practicing idolatry—idol worship. This story instructs us today: even though many have turned away from God, we can be different and live for Christ.

After they moved to Moab, Naomi's husband died. After marrying Moabite women and living in Moab for ten years, Naomi's sons also died. Now Naomi had no children. Of course, Naomi was heartbroken at this turn of events for her family.

After hearing that the Lord had helped her people by providing food, Naomi prepared to go back to her homeland of Judah, but she urged her two daughters-in-law to stay in their home of Moab. However, one of her daughters-in-law, Ruth, made a courageous decision to identify with Naomi and her people—God's people. Ruth expressed her heart to Naomi: "Don't urge me to leave you or to turn back from you. Where you go I will go, and where you stay I will stay. Your people will be my people and your God my God. Where you die I will die, and there I will be buried. May the Lord deal with me, be it ever so severely, if anything but death separates you and me" (Ruth 1:16-17). Ruth showed outstanding kindness toward her mother-in-law. When Naomi saw that she could not dissuade Ruth from her courageous and kind commitment, she relented and allowed Ruth to return with her to her hometown of Bethlehem.

However, as she returned to Bethlehem, Naomi told the women there of her bitterness: "Call me Mara [meaning bitter], because the Almighty has made my life very bitter. I went away full, but the Lord has brought me back empty. Why call me Naomi? The Lord has afflicted me; the Almighty has brought misfortune upon me" (Ruth 1:20-21). When Naomi left her homeland, she had a "full" family—a husband and two sons. Now she was returning home "empty," without her husband and sons.

As Ruth settled into her new homeland with Naomi, Ruth did not assume that she would just be taken care of. After the death of her own husband, she did not slide into self-pity and depression. Rather, she showed godly character by getting right to work to help provide for Naomi and herself. She went out into the fields to glean grain behind those bringing in the harvest. (The nation of Israel had a law allowing the poor to glean the leftovers from the harvesters.)

Ruth 2:3 reveals to us God's favor toward Ruth: "As it turned out, she found herself working in a field belonging to Boaz." To repeat, the passage says, "As it turned out." This clause shows that God was working on their behalf. God was working behind the scenes to provide for Naomi and Ruth; indeed, God would provide for them in more ways than one!

In fact, the man owning the field—Boaz—happened to be Naomi's relative. The name Boaz means "in him is strength." Indeed, our society needs strong men with true godly strength, men of real kindness expressed through their actions. Boaz was that kind of godly man, a man of real strength.

When Boaz came to the field, he greeted his workers with kindness: "The Lord be with you!" They responded with enthusiasm: "The Lord bless you!" (Ruth 2:4). Boaz showed himself to be an encouraging leader, even by his greeting. He greeted his workers first and with enthusiasm. Giving a hearty greeting is a great way to encourage others.

Young person, I want to encourage you to show kindness by greeting others cheerfully. Make it a friendly competition to greet others first—in other words, greet others before they greet you! Who do you see in the morning? Your parents, your brothers and sisters, your neighbors, the people at the bus stop, your teachers, and your classmates. Make it your goal to greet them kindly first. Doing so helps you to walk in a kind, grateful attitude as opposed to a complaining, grumbling attitude expressed by sentiments such as the following: "I don't want to get out of bed; I don't want to go to school; I'm tired." Rather, God wants us to wake up and greet others cheerfully!

Boaz started inquiring about Ruth; he was told that she was a "Moabitess," a foreigner. He was told that she had come back with Naomi. In addition, he was told about her work ethic: "She went into the field and has worked steadily from morning till now, except for a short rest in the shelter" (Ruth 2:7).

Boaz showed kindness to Ruth by providing her with care and protection. Because of moral degradation, there was much immorality; often women would be treated wrongly. Boaz made it a point to tell the men not to touch Ruth. And he gave godly and kind instruction to Ruth: "My daughter, listen to me. Don't go and glean in another field and don't go away from here. Stay here with my servant girls. Watch the field where the men are harvesting and follow along after the girls. I have told the men not to touch you. And whenever you are thirsty, go and get a drink from the water jars the men have filled" (Ruth 2:8-9). Boaz was protecting Ruth and showing care for her; he was taking Ruth under his wing.

At the same time, Ruth showed godly character herself. She showed respect toward authority, toward Boaz. She had demonstrated commitment and loyalty to Naomi. Because of Ruth's identifying with Naomi, her people, and her God, Boaz said to her: "May the Lord repay you for what you have done. May you be richly rewarded by the Lord, the God of Israel, under whose wings you have come to take refuge" (Ruth 2:12). Young people, that is where you want to be—under God's wings. What does it mean to be "under God's wings"? Being under his wings is being under his protection, provision, and blessing. As you honor God and live for the Lord, you will come under his wings with all of his blessings!

Moreover, Ruth had the character of servanthood. She referred to herself as "your servant" (Ruth 2:13). In addition to kindness, Ruth showed modesty and gratitude, qualities that brought her favor. These are excellent traits to cultivate, young person. Sincere kindness, humility, servanthood, and thankfulness will bring favor to your life!

Well, Boaz definitely showed favor toward Ruth and blessed her with provision. Instead of giving her just what had fallen from the gleaning, Boaz instructed his workers to provide more for Ruth: "Even if she gathers among the sheaves, don't embarrass her. Rather, pull out some stalks for her from the bundles and leave them for her to pick up, and don't rebuke her" (Ruth 2:15-16). Boaz showed kindness to Ruth by looking after her; he made sure she was both protected and provided for. Of course, his kindness toward Ruth was also showing kindness to Naomi.

Young person, acts such as these are the way to show kindness toward others. Instead of being self-focused, we should be others-focused by seeking to bless others. God wants us to grow in caring for others.

Under Boaz's care, Ruth prospered on her first day of work! She gathered an ephah of grain—about forty pounds—a very large amount! When Ruth returned home, Naomi realized that Ruth had been blessed with a great day's work. They had been blessed by God's provision! By this development, Naomi gained hope! She realized someone was helping them: "Where did you glean today? Where did you work? Blessed be the man who took notice of you!" (Ruth 2:19).

When Ruth told Naomi of Boaz, Naomi replied, "The Lord bless him! . . . He has not stopped showing his kindness to the living and the dead. . . . That man is our close relative; he is one of our kinsman-redeemers" (Ruth 2:20). Naomi started to gain hope that God was looking out for them! She recognized that God's hand was at work!

You see, young person, you will be blessed when you are kind to others. If you are good to others, you will eventually reap good in return. Ruth was kind to Naomi, and Boaz was kind to Ruth. Boaz's kindness to Ruth extended to Naomi as well. Of course, God was superintending all these interactions and looking out for both Naomi and Ruth. Psalm 145:14-19 is expressive of how the Lord lifted up Naomi and Ruth from the depths of despair:

> The Lord upholds all those who fall and lifts up all who are bowed down.
> The eyes of all look to you, and you give them their food at the proper time.

> You open your hand and satisfy the desires of every living thing. The Lord is righteous in all his ways and loving toward all he has made. The Lord is near to all who call on him, to all who call on him in truth. He fulfills the desires of those who fear him; he hears their cry and saves them.

Naomi shared with Ruth that Boaz was one of Naomi's kinsman-redeemers. A kinsman-redeemer was a close relative. In addition, a kinsman-redeemer could choose to be responsible to protect and to provide for needy extended family members. Well, it wasn't just a coincidence that Boaz was a relative of Naomi's husband Elimelech. As we can see, Boaz started providing for and protecting both Naomi and Ruth out of the principle of redemptive kindness; significantly, he did so before choosing to take on the legal responsibility of being a kinsman-redeemer.

Young men, Boaz was a godly man, the kind of man that we should seek to emulate. And young ladies, Ruth is the kind of lady that you should emulate. The story of Ruth and Boaz is a beautiful story of kindness reaping more kindness and eventually blooming into great love.

In fact, Boaz, as the kinsman-redeemer, ended up marrying Ruth. Boaz and Ruth had a son named Obed, who was the father of Jesse, who was the father of David. Of course, David became king of Israel. And through David's line eventually came King Jesus, through whom we have salvation!

Young people, I encourage you to be like Ruth and Boaz. Be someone who considers others above yourself. Resolve to be one in whom others can find refuge, shelter, protection, care, and provision! Even when it's hard, show kindness to others through friendly actions; eventually you will reap that same kindness!

The story of Naomi, Ruth, and Boaz speaks of our Lord. Jesus is the ultimate kinsman-redeemer. He redeems our life from emptiness, from lack of hope, from despair, and from death. Just as Boaz helped Ruth and Naomi in their despair, Jesus helps us. He redeems our life and gives us hope! Trust the Lord as your kinsman-redeemer today!

Memory Verses

> Ruth 1:16, "But Ruth replied, 'Don't urge me to leave you or to turn back from you. Where you go I will go, and where you stay I will stay. Your people will be my people and your God my God.'"
>
> Ruth 2:4 "Just then Boaz arrived from Bethlehem and greeted the harvesters, 'The Lord be with you!'
>
> 'The Lord bless you!' They called back."
>
> Ruth 2:12 "May the Lord repay you for what you have done. May you be richly rewarded by the Lord, the God of Israel, under whose wings you have come to take refuge."

HANNAH

Cry Out to the Lord; He Hears You and Will Answer You

Early in our marriage, my wife Silvia developed a condition called endometriosis, which hinders a woman from bearing children. A prayer warrior gave me a Biblical word to pray over her. I recall being on my face many times, as I cried out to God to open my wife's womb. In time, the Lord did open my wife's womb and gave us our firstborn named Anna! Now we have four children. God heard our prayers; we cried out to him, and he answered!

In 1 Samuel 1, the Bible tells the story of a special lady named Hannah, which means "Grace." This lady was married to a godly man named Elkanah. Year after year, this God-honoring family went to sacrifice to the Lord at a festival—probably the Feast of Tabernacles, which celebrates God's care and provision.

Because Hannah was not able to bear children, the Bible says that her rival provoked her—she would ridicule her. (It was a disgrace in Israel to be unable to bear children.) Hannah's condition and this unkind treatment caused Hannah to be distraught.

Her husband Elkanah asked her, "Hannah, why are you weeping? Why don't you eat? Why are you downhearted? Don't I mean more to you than ten sons?" (1 Sam. 1:8). Elkanah was really asking, "Why is your heart bad?"

What is a bad heart? A bad heart is one that develops resentment and bitterness because of hurt. Roots of bitterness can develop against those that cause the hurt. However, if you're going to serve the Lord as his champion, you must keep your heart free of bitterness. You need to keep a good-soil heart—a soft heart toward the Lord and others.

But how do we do that? 1 Samuel 1:10 says, "In bitterness of soul Hannah wept much and prayed to the Lord." As a child cries out to her parent, Hannah cried out to the Lord with a sense of dependence and outright need.

How do we keep a good-soil heart that keeps us from getting bitter? We need to cry out to God. I encourage you, young person, to learn to cry out to the Lord—with whatever you're going through. Whatever hardship, hurt, or need you're experiencing, use it to grow closer to the Lord. Have a close, personal relationship with the Lord in which God is your all and all! He is there and he hears you!

When I'm feeling consternation in my heart, I like to go running to a creek near our home called Great Seneca Creek. In this secluded place, I feel like I'm out by myself with no one around. I cry out, "Lord!" I pour out my heart to him. By the time I'm finished with my run, the Lord's peace returns to my soul.

Hannah made the following vow to the Lord: "O Lord Almighty, if you will only look upon your servant's misery and remember me, and not forget your servant but give her a son, then I will give him to the Lord for all the days of his life" (1 Sam. 1:11). Hannah promised the Lord that if God answered her prayer and gave her a son, she would give him to the Lord for his service.

This vow is significant for a number of reasons. First, Hannah recognized that children are a gift from the Lord. Parents, children are a gift; they are not of our own creation. They are created by God and given as a gift to us!

Secondly, Hannah was willing to give the child back to the Lord. Parents, are you willing to give your child to the Lord for his service?

Thirdly, Hannah referred to herself as God's servant, which is a statement of surrender. She was not bribing God; she was calling out to God with total surrender to him. I encourage you to understand that calling out to God involves all-surrender to him! It requires total commitment of everything to him, including our children.

In crying out to the Lord, Hannah asked him to "look upon" her anguish, to "remember" her, and to "not forget" her. Hannah was counting on the Lord to pay attention to her!

Be assured, young person, that the Lord is paying attention to you! Psalm 8:4 says, "What is man that you are mindful of him, the son of man that you care for him?" God is attentive to us!

Hannah proceeded to continue pouring her heart out to the Lord. She prayed earnestly and silently. Eli the priest saw her lips moving without her voice being heard. He then made a mistake and rebuked her for what he perceived to be drunkenness. The Priest Eli thought Hannah was drunk!

You know what, young person. Sometimes leaders, ministers, teachers, and even parents, misjudge situations and make mistakes. Eli's time was one of moral decay—people would even be drunk in the temple! There was such a state of moral degradation in society that people would even be drunk in the house of the Lord. Can you imagine people coming to church drunk?

What would we do as God's loving, compassionate people?

When Eli misjudged her for being drunk, Hannah didn't get angry. Hannah made a humble appeal to Eli: "Not so, my lord, I am a woman who is deeply troubled. I have not been drinking wine or beer; I was pouring out my soul to the Lord. Do not take your servant for a wicked woman; I have been praying here out of my great anguish and grief" (1 Sam. 1:15-16). Hannah appealed to Eli to not judge her as a wicked woman. She explained that she was praying and crying out to the Lord.

Young person, Psalm 62:8 is a great verse to remember when your heart is troubled: "Trust in him at all times, O people; pour out your hearts to him, for God is our refuge."

Parent, Lamentations 2:18-19 is an important passage to remember when you need to pray for your young people: "The hearts of the people cry out to the Lord. O wall of the Daughter of Zion, let your tears flow like a river day and night; give yourself no relief, your eyes no rest. Arise, cry out in the night, as the watches of the night begin; pour out your heart like water in the presence of the Lord. *Lift up your hands to him for the lives of your children*, who faint from hunger at the head of every street" (italics added).

Even when we sin, especially when we sin, we need to cry out to God! The Bible says, "For his anger lasts only a moment, but his favor lasts a lifetime; weeping may remain for a night, but rejoicing comes in the morning. . . . To you, O Lord, I called; to the Lord I cried for mercy; 'What gain is there in my destruction, in my going down into the pit? Will the dust praise you? Will it proclaim your faithfulness? Hear, O Lord, and be merciful to me; O Lord, be my help'" (Psalm 30:5, 8-10). When you sin, the enemy Satan might say that God doesn't want anything to do with you; when Satan whispers that thought in your mind, remember that it is a lie from the ultimate liar. Cry out to God. Repent and turn back to him! Luke 6:21 says, "Blessed are you who weep now, for you will laugh." Acts 3:19 encourages us, "Repent, then, and turn to God, so that your sins may be wiped out, that times of refreshing may come from the Lord."

After Hannah explained to Eli that she was crying out to God, Eli assured her and encouraged her of God's intention to answer her prayer. Hannah proceeded to break her prayerful fast and ate food. The Bible says that her face was lifted up. God had encouraged her.

Sure enough, in God's timing, Hannah gave birth to a boy. Hannah named him Samuel "because I asked the Lord for him" (1 Sam. 1:20). The name of Samuel is similar to the Hebrew word for "heard of God." Indeed, Hannah was heard of God!

Young person, you are *heard of God*! I encourage you to cry out to God—He hears you!

Hannah's husband Elkanah supported his wife in fulfilling her vow to the Lord—she gave Samuel to the Lord to serve the Lord all the days of his life! Her son Samuel became a great leader—a champion in Israel! He even anointed Israel's first two kings: King Saul and King David.

Parents, I encourage you to cry out to God for your family—for your children.

Young people, I challenge you to cry out to God regarding your future and regarding the things you don't understand. Don't let your heart get bitter. Don't allow yourself to have a bad heart. Take the bitterness of your heart and cry out to God! Learn to go to God with anything on your heart. He will hear, he will answer, and be assured—He will meet the need of your heart!

Memory Verse

1 Samuel 1:10 "In bitterness of soul Hannah wept much and prayed to the Lord."

SAMUEL

Hear the Voice of the Lord

As we learned in the last chapter, Hannah was heard by God. God heard her cry for a child and answered her. That child was Samuel. Samuel grew up in God's house and became characterized as one who heard God's voice.

As children of God, we can learn to hear the voice of the Lord. Jesus said of his children: "My sheep listen to my voice; I know them, and they follow me" (John 10:27). As a child of God, you are a sheep of the good Shepherd, and you can learn to recognize his voice. God's Word can be revealed to you!

The boy Samuel was one who had to learn to recognize the voice of God. He learned to hear God's voice at a young age. He is an example of a child through whom God worked.

The Bible is clear that the Lord works through children. Psalm 8:2 says, "From the lips of children and infants you have ordained praise because of your enemies, to silence the foe and the avenger." The Lord has ordained praise from the lips of children and infants! When our children are praising the Lord, the enemy is literally silenced! No matter what is going on in our lives, when we see our children praising God, the enemy's lies and condemnations are silenced.

In Matthew 18:3-4, Jesus extolled the humble nature of children: "I tell you the truth, unless you change and become like little children, you will never enter the kingdom of heaven. Therefore, whoever humbles himself like this child is the greatest in the kingdom of heaven." The boy Samuel in the Bible was humble, which meant he was teachable and receptive to the Lord's Word. He was an attentive listener.

In Matthew 11:25 Jesus said, "I praise you, Father, Lord of heaven and earth, because you have hidden these things from the wise and learned, and revealed them to little children. Yes, Father, for this was your good pleasure." It is our Father God's good pleasure to reveal the principles of his Word to children. And we find that the Lord revealed his Word to Samuel who learned to listen to God's voice.

Indeed, the quality of listening is very important to learning. I recall teaching my first-grade daughter Anna an important concept as her basketball coach. It was the importance of having a "swivel head" while playing defense to keep her eye both on the person she was defending and on the ball. Well, in the game, when I saw that Anna was doing exactly what I had taught her, I was overjoyed. I saw that she had listened and learned! The skill of listening is very important to being a great student!

Samuel was born to Hannah, who had not been able to have a child. Distraught because of this circumstance, Hannah cried out to the Lord for a child. When God answered her prayer and Samuel was born to Hannah, she dedicated him to the Lord. As he grew up, Samuel learned the importance of listening to his elders, and ultimately, the importance of listening to the Lord!

1 Samuel 2:11 says that "the boy ministered before the Lord under Eli the priest." Samuel grew up in God's presence. However, while Samuel was serving under the priest, Eli's sons were walking in rebellion against God, doing evil and sinning against the Lord. Eli rebuked his sons but took no action to discipline them. However, "The boy Samuel continued to grow in stature and in favor with the Lord and with men" (1 Sam. 2:26).

Now a man of God went to Eli to tell him that he was honoring his sons more than God. Eli's sons were fattening themselves with the choice parts of the Israelites' offerings. They were more concerned for their stomachs than for the Lord. This man told Eli the Lord's declaration: "Those who honor me I will honor, but those who despise me will be disdained" (1 Sam. 2:30). The man of God said that Eli's family line would be cut off.

Because Eli took no action to discipline his sons and restrain them from their evil doing, eventually the Lord took action against Eli's sons. As parents, we need to take action to discipline our children for wrongdoing. It is an evidence of our love when we take disciplinary action that will help our children to grow in godly character. Proverbs 3:11-12 encourages us: "My son, do not despise the Lord's discipline and do not resent his rebuke, because the Lord disciplines those he loves, as a father the son he delights in." When we discipline our children, it helps them to learn godly character and to avoid worse consequences later on in their lives. Hebrews 12:10 says, "Our fathers disciplined us for a little while as they thought best; but God disciplines us for our good, that we may share in his holiness. No discipline seems pleasant at the time, but painful. Later on, however, it produces a harvest of righteousness and peace for those who have been trained by it." Rightfully applied, discipline is the expression of loving parents who are focused on their children's growth in godly character.

1 Samuel 3:1 tells us, "In those days the word of the Lord was rare; there were not many visions." Eli's eyes were such that he could hardly see; his near physical blindness was accompanied by his near spiritual blindness to the things of God. However, "The lamp of God had not yet gone out, and Samuel was lying down in the temple of the Lord, where the ark of God was" (1 Sam. 3:3). Samuel had positioned himself in the temple where God's ark was. This was significant—he had placed himself in God's very presence!

"Then the Lord called Samuel." Samuel responded with, "Here I am" (1 Sam. 3:4). This response indicated Samuel's readiness and availability to serve. For young people, that is the message that you want to communicate to your parents and to your teachers: "Here I am"!

Samuel ran to Eli and told him, "Here I am; you called me" (1 Sam. 3:5). But Eli said he did not call him and to go back and lie down. Then the Lord called Samuel a second time. Again Samuel presented himself to Eli. Eli told Samuel the same thing. (Eli didn't have a very close relationship with the Lord to understand what was happening.) When the Lord called Samuel a third time and Samuel again went to Eli, Eli now understood what was happening. "So Eli told Samuel, 'Go and lie down, and if he calls you, say, "Speak, Lord, for your servant is listening"'" (1 Sam. 3:9).

As young people, it's very important to learn to listen. We need to listen to our parents' voices as well as to our teachers' voices. That's how we learn. Most importantly, we need to learn to listen with our hearts to the voice of the Lord!

When the Lord called Samuel the fourth time, it was with a sense of urgency: "Samuel! Samuel!" (1 Sam. 3:10).

Samuel responded, "Speak, for your servant is listening" (1 Sam. 3:10). The Lord proceeded to tell Samuel a very serious message: that Eli's sons had been contemptible with their willful sin and rebellion; and that Eli had failed to restrain them.

Parents, we have a serious responsibility to discipline and restrain our children. Proverbs 19:18 counsels us, "Discipline your son, for in that there is hope; do not be a willing party to his death." I encourage parents to be diligent to help their children walk on the narrow path that leads to life as opposed to the wide path that leads to destruction (Matt. 7:13-14). We accomplish this goal through our encouraging attentiveness, through our consistent discipline, and through our loving relationship!

The next morning Eli called for Samuel. Although Samuel was afraid to tell Eli what the Lord had said, Eli exhorted Samuel to tell him everything. Samuel proceeded to do so.

The Bible says that "the Lord was with Samuel as he grew up, and he let none of his words fall to the ground" (1 Sam. 3:19). Samuel grew in his relationship with the Lord! He learned to listen to the Lord. He walked and talked with the Lord. The Lord "revealed himself to Samuel through his word" (1 Sam. 3:21). "And Samuel's word came to all Israel" (1 Sam. 4:1). In effect, Samuel's word became one with God's Word.

Samuel learned to listen to the voice of the Lord. As God spoke, Samuel heard God's Word; and because he learned to recognize the voice of the Lord, he became a great prophet to the people of Israel!

And young person, you can learn to recognize the voice of the Lord as well. As alluded to earlier, Jesus declared, "My sheep listen to my voice; I know them, and they follow me" (John 10:27). As a child of God, you are a sheep of Jesus the Good Shepherd. And you can learn to hear and proclaim the voice of the Good Shepherd. God's Word can be revealed to you as well!

1 Samuel 2:26 summarizes Samuel's childhood character: "And the boy Samuel continued to grow in stature and in favor with the Lord and with men." This statement is very similar to what is said about Jesus at the age of twelve: "And Jesus grew in wisdom and stature, and in favor with God and men" (Luke 2:52). Also similar to Samuel's character was Jesus' listening posture: "After three days they found him [Jesus] in the temple courts, sitting among the teachers, listening to them and asking them questions" (Luke 2:46). This is how to be a great student, young people: be a listener who asks good questions!

Both Jesus and Samuel were characterized by listening, which is necessary both for obedience and for learning. Young person, it's very important to your future that you learn to obey and respect your parents, teachers, pastors, the governing authorities, and any other authorities your parents place in your lives. Many problems in our world would be alleviated if youth learned to submit to authority through the consistent and loving discipline of their parents. It's very important for you to learn to say cheerfully, "Yes, Mom," and "Yes, Dad," and then follow through with obedience!

Young person, learn to listen! Obey your parents and teachers with a good attitude—it's good for your future! In the process, you will learn to hear the voice of the Lord!

Memory Verse

John 10:27 "My sheep listen to my voice; I know them, and they follow me."

DAVID

Make the Lord Your Confidence

The Lord designed his people—the nation of Israel—to be a theocracy, a kingdom ruled by God, who is a just, loving, and righteous King. However, over the course of time, the people of Israel clamored for a human king. The Bible says that their desire for a king was symptomatic of their rejection of the Lord as King. After the boy Samuel grew up, he became a national prophet to Israel; in effect he became Israel's leader. God told Samuel to warn the people of the consequences of having a human king. However, 1 Samuel 8:19-20 says, "But the people refused to listen to Samuel. 'No!' they said. 'We want a king over us. Then we will be like all the other nations, with a king to lead us and to go out before us and fight our battles.'"

Therefore, the Lord directed Samuel to give the people a king. Israel's first king was King Saul. When Saul became king, he stood out because of his appearance. The Bible says that he was "an impressive young man without equal among the Israelites—a head taller than any of the others" (1 Sam. 9:2). However, King Saul became disobedient—even rebellious against the Lord's clear instructions and authority. As he disobeyed God, the Spirit of the Lord left him. Israel's first king showed that his heart was not right with God. Because of his rebellion, the prophet Samuel mourned over him.

In 1 Samuel 16:1, Samuel received the Lord's instructions: "How long will you mourn for Saul, since I have rejected him as king over Israel? Fill your horn with oil and be on your way; I am sending you to Jesse of Bethlehem. I have chosen one of his sons to be king." When Samuel expressed his fear that King Saul might hear of his purpose and kill him, the Lord gave Samuel instructions to make a sacrifice in Bethlehem so that Saul would not know his intent.

When Samuel came to Jesse's town and invited his family to the sacrifice, Jesse's sons came out. When Samuel saw the eldest Eliab, he thought, "Surely the Lord's anointed stands here before the Lord" (1 Sam. 16:6). However, God gave Samuel this guidance: "Do not consider his appearance or his height, for I have rejected him. The Lord does not look at the things man looks at. Man looks at the outward appearance, but the Lord looks at the heart" (1 Sam. 16:7). Seven sons of Jesse passed before Samuel, but Samuel said that the Lord had not chosen any of them. Finally, Samuel asked Jesse if these were all of his sons. Jesse replied, "There is still the youngest, but he is tending the sheep" (1 Sam. 16:11). When

Jesse's youngest son David came, the Lord told Samuel, "Rise and anoint him; he is the one" (1 Sam. 16:12). 1 Samuel 16:13 says that Samuel anointed David with oil and "from that day on the Spirit of the Lord came upon David in power."

Young person, please understand that it's people who look on the outward appearance, but it is God who looks on the heart. We can see this principle operating in David's life both as he was anointed to become king and later on as he answered Goliath's challenge. The Lord is able to see our inner motivations and our character. He's able to see whether we have a heart for God.

How do we gain a heart for God? Matthew 11:28-30 says, "Come to me, all you who are weary and burdened, and I will give you rest. Take my yoke upon you and learn from me, for I am gentle and humble in heart, and you will find rest for your souls. For my yoke is easy and my burden is light." As we come to Christ and take his yoke, we learn from him; we learn from his heart.

As a shepherd, David had gained a heart for God through spending time with him. In fact, it was David who wrote Psalm 23, which shows how David as a shepherd boy looked to the Lord as his Shepherd:

> The Lord is my shepherd, I shall not be in want. He makes me lie down in green pastures, he leads me beside quiet waters, he restores my soul. He guides me in paths of righteousness for his name's sake. Even though I walk through the valley of the shadow of death, I will fear no evil, for you are with me; your rod and your staff, they comfort me. You prepare a table before me in the presence of my enemies. You anoint my head with oil; my cup overflows. Surely goodness and love will follow me all the days of my life, and I will dwell in the house of the Lord forever.

We can see from this Psalm that David made the Lord his confidence. He had learned to trust God as the Good Shepherd to provide for him, to lead him, to protect him against evil, to be with him amid challenges, to comfort him, to feed him, to anoint him, and to love him.

Similarly, we know from David's Psalms that he was a worshiper of the Lord. He loved to worship God and extol him for who he is. Likewise, we gain a heart for God by learning from his heart—through worshiping him, walking with him, and reading his Word.

When David was called, he was "tending the sheep." David had the heart of a shepherd to take care of the sheep. This training as a shepherd prepared him to care for the people as their king. Psalm 78:70-72 says, "[The Lord] chose David his servant and took him from the sheep pens; from tending the sheep he brought him to be the shepherd of his people Jacob, of Israel his inheritance. And David shepherded them with integrity of heart; with skillful hands he led them."

David had both a heart for God and skill in working with people, two important skills for a godly leader.

As the Spirit of God came upon David, the Holy Spirit left Saul. In fact, Saul became tormented by an evil spirit. David had gained a reputation of being skillful with the harp. Because of his skill, David was called upon to use his musical ability to soothe Saul's mind from being tormented. The Bible says that the Lord was with David and that David gained Saul's favor.

Young person, it's very important that you let the Holy Spirit to be fully operating in your life. If you allow yourself to have disobedient, rebellious attitudes toward your parents and teachers, then the Holy Spirit will not be preeminent in your life. While the Holy Spirit left King Saul, the Holy Spirit was inspiring David. You want the Holy Spirit to be leading and guiding you! Keep your relationship with the Lord strong, stay in close relationship with your parents, and you will allow the Holy Spirit to inspire you to the life of a champion!

Well, the Philistines organized their military forces against the Israelites, who in turn gathered their forces to meet the Philistines in battle. The Philistines and the Israelites lined up for battle on opposite hills with a valley between them. Then the huge Goliath, standing over nine feet tall, came forward and shouted defiance against the Israelites: "Why do you come out and line up for battle? Am I not a Philistine, and are you not the servants of Saul? Choose a man and have him come down to me. If he is able to fight and kill me, we will become your subjects; but if I overcome him and kill him, you will become our subjects and serve us. This day I defy the ranks of Israel! Give me a man and let us fight each other" (1 Sam. 17:8-10). After hearing his taunts, none of the Israelites took Goliath's challenge. Lacking trust in God, King Saul and the Israelites were terrified.

Of course, King Saul, a very large man himself, was supposed to be Israel's champion. When he became king, people were impressed by his outward appearance; 1 Samuel 9:2 tells us that Saul was "an impressive young man without equal among the Israelites—a head taller than any of the others." However, as we have learned, man looks on the outward appearance, but God looks on the heart. The Israelites had replaced God with a human king. Instead of trusting the King of kings, they had put their trust in a human king; and now King Saul was found lacking. Having failed to trust God, the Israelites were now in trouble. They were not able to meet Goliath's challenge. The Bible says that each day for forty days Goliath would take his stand and ridicule the Israelites.

Meanwhile, David had been going back and forth from Saul's royal court to his home to care for his father's sheep. David was sent by his father to bring food to his three oldest brothers, who were soldiers in the Israelite army. Visiting his brothers, David heard Goliath's usual defiant taunts and saw the Israelites' fear firsthand.

David recognized that God's Kingdom through God's people was hanging in the balance. He spoke up for the cause of God! He said, "What will be done for the man who kills this Philistine and removes this disgrace from Israel? Who is this uncircumcised Philistine that he should defy the armies of the living God?" (1 Sam. 17:26). David was righteously indignant! His perspective was that we are God's people serving the living God. Who is this guy that is coming against God and his people?! David was on overcomer. As long as we are on the Lord's side, David knew that we can do all things through Christ who strengthens us!

David was angrily criticized for his comments by his oldest brother. When people overheard the ensuing conversations, word got back to King Saul. He heard of David's courageous and righteous words against Goliath. When David was brought before King Saul, David said, "Let no one lose heart on account of this Philistine; your servant will go and fight him" (1 Sam. 17:32). Because he knew that God was with him and that he was on the Lord's side, David was confident that his God would give the victory!

Saul was not so sure: "You are not able to go out against this Philistine and fight him; you are only a boy, and he has been a fighting man from his youth" (1 Sam. 17:33). Looking at David's outward appearance, Saul made a judgment. He was not taking into account David's trustful relationship with the Lord.

However, David shared with Saul about his experiences as a shepherd. He shared his resumé:

> Your servant has been keeping his father's sheep. When a lion or a bear came and carried off a sheep from the flock, I went after it, struck it and rescued the sheep from its mouth. When it turned on me, I seized it by its hair, struck it and killed it. Your servant has killed both the lion and the bear; this uncircumcised Philistine will be like one of them, because he has defied the armies of the living God. The Lord who delivered me from the paw of the lion and the paw of the bear will deliver me from the hand of this Philistine. (1 Sam. 17:34-37).

David's experiences overcoming the lion and the bear as a shepherd boy had prepared him for the giant Goliath! David knew that the Lord would win the battle for him!

After David convinced Saul of his confidence in the Lord, Saul said, "Go, and the Lord be with you" (1 Sam. 17:37). Whereas Saul had lost his faith in God, David showed his trust in the Lord. David's confidence came from his relationship with God!

The contrasts between Saul and David are very real. King Saul was the big man of Israel whereas David was just a boy. Saul gave David his armor to fight against Goliath; however, when David put on Saul's armor, it was too cumbersome for him to wear. Instead of all the typical battle armor, David simply took his staff and his sling, and gathered five smooth stones. While Saul had given up trusting the Lord, David expressed confidence in his God! With his staff, David was going as God's shepherd to defend the sheep of Israel!

We know that the Benjamites, one of Israel's tribes, were known for their skill with the sling. Judges 20:16 tells us, "Among all these soldiers there were seven hundred chosen men who were left-handed, each of whom could sling a stone at a hair and not miss." Through practice, David had achieved this same kind of skill with the sling. However, even though David had this skill, he still had to trust that the Lord was with him! David said about the Lord, "I saw the Lord always before me. Because he is at my right hand, I will not be shaken" (Acts 2:25). As David faced Goliath, he focused on the Lord's presence. That conscious awareness of God's presence gave David the strength that he needed! It gave him the needful courage to face the giant Goliath and not be shaken!

Young person, the example of David provides you with the answer to fear: to see the Lord always before you. I encourage you to develop a conscious awareness of the Lord's presence in your life. In fact, practice Christ's presence! It will help you to deal with any fear in your life. As you walk to school, as you go to your classes, as you try out for the sports team, as you approach any life challenge, develop the discipline of practicing the Lord's presence. See him walk with you, attend your classes with you, and train with you. Focus on the Lord; be aware of his presence always with you. Living this way will help you to become a courageous champion for the Lord and not be deterred by fear, nervousness, or anxiety!

When Goliath saw that the Israelites were sending a boy to fight him, he taunted David: "Am I a dog, that you come at me with sticks? . . . Come here, and I'll give your flesh to the birds of the air and the beasts of the field!" (1 Sam. 17:43-44).

David was not dismayed by Goliath's condemnations. He responded to Goliath with steely determination and declared his dependence on God Almighty:

> You come against me with sword and spear and javelin, but I come against you in the name of the Lord Almighty, the God of the armies of Israel, whom you have defied. This day the Lord will hand you over to me, and I'll strike you down and cut off your head. . . . and the whole world will know that there is a God in Israel. All those gathered here will know that it is not by sword or spear that the Lord saves; for the battle is the Lord's, and he will give all of you into our hands. (1 Sam. 17:45-47)

David was confident in his God! He is an example to all of us today of the kind of faith-filled relationship we're to have with Christ. Indeed, the Bible says, "I can do all things through him who gives me strength" (Phil. 4:13). God calls us to be an overcomer—a victor, not a victim! "The battle is the Lord's" (1 Sam. 17:47). Our trust is in the Lord!

Young person, I encourage you to be in *the Lord's* battle! Be on *his side*—in *his army*—and you will possess the confidence of Messiah. Don't get involved in petty fleshy battles with people. Fight the fight of faith in the Lord Jesus. Be confident in him to help you walk in victory over sin, over fighting with your siblings, and in having a true relationship with the Lord! As you walk this way, you will grow in confidence!

As David faced Goliath, he did not waver or hesitate. He ran quickly to the battle and got in position—into striking range. "As the Philistine moved closer to attack him, David ran quickly toward the battle line to meet him" (1 Sam. 17:48). David took out a stone and slung it at Goliath, killing him. David triumphed over the unrighteous Goliath!

Today Goliath is representative of those huge things in our life that may cause us fear. Proverbs 29:25 counsels us, "Fear of man will prove to be a snare, but whoever trusts in the Lord is kept safe." As David did, I encourage you to trust in the Lord. Make the Lord your confidence! No matter what you are facing, the Lord can help you to stand for righteousness, to be an overcomer, and to give him glory!

Memory Verse

> 1 Samuel 17:47 "All those gathered here will know that it is not by sword or spear that the Lord saves; for the battle is the Lord's, and he will give all of you into our hands."

JONATHAN to DAVID

Be a Self-sacrificing Friend for Others

Through David's interactions with King Saul and as a result of his courage in battle, David won the loyal friendship of Jonathan, King Saul's son. In John 15:13, Jesus said, "Greater love has no one than this, that he lay down his life for his friends." A great example of this "greater love" is the person of Jonathan. As you know, David achieved outstanding exploits, including killing Israel's enemy, the giant Philistine Goliath. At the same time, Jonathan was an ambitious young man himself. In addition to being part of the royal family and likely to become king one day, Jonathan was a courageous warrior in his own right.

One day as the Israelites battled against the Philistines, Jonathan and his armor bearer climbed up between two cliffs to kill about twenty Philistines. As Jonathan gave direction to his comrade, we can see his strong faith in God: "Come, let's go over to the outpost of those uncircumcised fellows. Perhaps the Lord will act in our behalf. Nothing can hinder the Lord from saving, whether by many or by few" (1 Sam. 14:6). The Bible says that the two of them climbed up a cliff and "killed some twenty men in an area of about half an acre" (1 Sam. 14:14). Jonathan was a brave warrior who trusted the Lord!

After David killed Goliath and met with Jonathan's father King Saul, David won Jonathan's heart. The Bible says, "After David had finished talking with Saul, Jonathan became one in spirit with David, and he loved him as himself" (1 Sam. 18:1). Jonathan did not get jealous of David's success and did not get possessive of his right to the throne; instead he reached out to David to make a covenant with him "because he loved him as himself" (1 Sam. 18:3). Jonathan made a symbolic humble gesture that communicated his love and preference for David over himself. He took off his robe, sword, and belt; and he gave them to David.

However, Jonathan's father King Saul reacted differently to David's success. As the people gave David more and more accolades, praising him more than King Saul, the king became jealous of David. In fact, Jonathan tried to appeal to his father in an attempt to bridge the developing gap between his father and David. As he did so, Saul reassured Jonathan that he wouldn't harm David. But after David had won another great victory over the Philistines, King Saul tried to kill David with a spear. David barely escaped with his life!

After that, David and Jonathan had an emotional conversation. David questioned Jonathan repeatedly regarding why his father was trying to kill him. David asked Jonathan, "What have I done? What is my crime? How have I wronged your father, that he is trying to take my life?" (1 Sam. 20:1). After David convinced Jonathan of his father's intentions to kill him, Jonathan decided to support David against even his own father: "Whatever you want me to do, I'll do for you" (1 Sam. 20:4). Out of friendship, Jonathan decided to sacrifice his own interests for those of David.

Young person, people need these kinds of friendships. Instead of being selfish and looking out for your own interests, I encourage you to be a friend that is willing to sacrifice for the sake of others. As brothers and sisters in Christ, God calls us to be these kinds of excellent friends for one another.

David made a plan with Jonathan to see if his father was resolved to harm him. David said of Saul: "If he loses his temper, you can be sure that he is determined to harm me" (1 Sam. 20:7). Then Jonathan shared with David how he would communicate with him if he saw his father's hatred toward David. During this conversation, Jonathan recognized that David would eventually become king; he willingly sacrificed his future out of loving friendship for David: "May the Lord be with you as he has been with my father" (1 Sam. 20:13). This statement indicated that Jonathan knew that *David* would become king just as *his father* had become king. To ensure David's safety, Jonathan promised David that he would communicate his father's intentions.

In return, Jonathan asked David to show kindness to his family: "But show me unfailing kindness like that of the Lord as long as I live, so that I may not be killed, and do not ever cut off your kindness from my family" (1 Sam. 20:14-15). Jonathan asked David to show kindness "like that of the Lord" to him and his family.

Jonathan covenanted with David the following: "May the Lord call David's enemies to account" (1 Sam. 20:16). As he made this declaration, Jonathan knew that David's enemies included his very own father. "And Jonathan had David reaffirm his oath out of love for him, because he loved him as he loved himself" (1 Sam. 20:17).

Jonathan told David how he would communicate his father's intentions toward David. He would shoot three arrows in a certain field where David would be hiding behind a big rock called Ezel. He would then tell the boy attending him to get the arrows. If he yelled to the boy that the arrows were on *this* side of him, then that would mean that David was safe; however, if he yelled to the boy that the arrows were *beyond* him, then that would mean that David was in danger and must flee.

After they made the plan, when Saul saw that David did not come to the king's table for a second day in a row, he asked Jonathan why David hadn't come to dinner. After Jonathan answered his father, Saul became enraged and ordered Jonathan to bring David to him so he could be put to death! When Jonathan questioned why David should die, his father threw his spear at Jonathan. At that point, Jonathan knew that his father meant to kill David.

According to their plan, Jonathan went to the field to shoot the arrows and to communicate with David. He shot the arrows and then called out after the boy: "Isn't the arrow beyond you?" (1 Sam. 20:37). Then he yelled to the boy a hidden message that was really for David: "Hurry! Go quickly! Don't stop!" (1 Sam. 20:38).

After the boy had left with Jonathan's weapons, David came out from hiding. Jonathan met with David for a tearful departure. David "bowed down before Jonathan three times, with his face to the ground. Then they kissed each other and wept together—but David wept the most" (1 Sam. 20:41). Jonathan and David expressed their great love for each other before David left to flee from King Saul.

Even though his father hated David and wanted to kill him, Jonathan loved David. Jonathan sacrificed his future for David.

As David fled, King Saul pursued David with his men to try to kill him. At one point, Jonathan found David and encouraged him. Jonathan "helped him find strength in God" (1 Sam. 23:16).

Young person, that's what godly friends do. When you find friends in need, help them to find strength in the Lord. Point them to God. If they're going in the wrong direction, don't encourage them in their wrongdoing; instead, help them to find the narrow path that leads to life, not the wide path that leads to destruction (Matt. 7:13-14). As you help them to follow God, you will be a true friend. Encourage them and stand with them in the Lord.

Jonathan clearly communicated that David would be made king and that he would be subordinate to David: "Don't be afraid. . . . My father Saul will not lay a hand on you. You will be king over Israel, and I will be second to you. Even my father Saul knows this" (1 Sam. 23:17). Again, as he was encouraging David, Jonathan was also sacrificing his own future—that of becoming king—for David.

Young person, the Lord will use you as a friend to communicate strength to others in their times of need. God gives courage to people when faced with difficult trials; at the same time, he often uses people like you to do it. Be a friend God can use to help and encourage others.

Jonathan clearly subordinated himself to David. He practiced what the Apostle Paul exhorted the Philippians to do: "Do nothing out of selfish ambition or vain conceit, but in humility consider others better than yourselves. Each of you should look not only to your own interests, but also to the interests of others" (Phil. 2:3-4). Jonathan sacrificed his own future for David. This is the kind of Christlike sacrificial love that pleases God.

Israel's war with the Philistines continued to rage. In a particularly fierce battle, David's beloved friend Jonathan and two of his brothers were killed. After being wounded, King Saul also died. When David heard of their deaths, he mourned for both Saul and his loyal friend Jonathan. David said, "Saul and Jonathan—in life they were loved and gracious, and in death they were not parted. They were swifter than eagles, they were stronger than lions" (2 Sam. 1:23).

Even though King Saul had tried to kill him, David was gracious and kind in his words toward him: "O daughters of Israel, weep for Saul, who clothed you in scarlet and finery, who adorned your garments with ornaments of gold" (2 Sam. 1:24). Of his great friend Jonathan, David expressed his heart: "I grieve for you, Jonathan my brother; you were very dear to me. Your love for me was wonderful, more wonderful than that of women" (2 Sam. 1:26).

Jonathan, David's friend, was now dead. But do you remember the covenant that Jonathan made with David? Well, David fulfilled his covenant with Jonathan by showing kindness to his son. After becoming king and defeating the Philistines, David asked his advisers, "Is there anyone still left of the house of Saul to whom I can show kindness for Jonathan's sake?" (2 Sam. 9:1). He found out about a man named Mephibosheth, Jonathan's son, who was crippled.

Now it was customary for a succeeding king to kill off all the family members of a previous king. However, King David did not pursue that course of action. Instead, he fulfilled his covenant to Jonathan. When David had Mephibosheth come before him, David told him not to be afraid. He said, "I will surely show you kindness for the sake of your father Jonathan. I will restore to you all the land that belonged to your grandfather Saul, and you will always eat at my table" (2 Sam. 9:7). By helping the crippled Mephibosheth and his family, David fulfilled his covenant toward his friend Jonathan.

Young person, we learn much from the life and example of Jonathan in his friendship toward David. We learn how to be a true friend. We learn to sacrifice our own interests for others. We learn to encourage and to stand with a friend even when it means that we are giving up our own ambitions. As Jesus said in John 15:13, "Greater love has no one than this, that he lay down his life for his friends." I encourage you to be this kind of friend to others.

Memory Verse

John 15:13 "Greater love has no one than this, that he lay down his life for his friends."

ABIGAIL

Be Wise in Your Dealings; Don't Be Foolish

While David was fleeing King Saul, many men gathered around David as their leader. 1 Samuel 22:2 says, "All those who were in distress or in debt or discontented gathered around him, and he became their leader. About four hundred men were with him."

As David was leading these men, he came into contact with a very mean man named Nabal, who was married to a woman named Abigail. In life, you will sometimes come across people who are difficult. You will even encounter people who are mean. How does God call us to deal with difficult people?

We can learn from Nabal's wife Abigail, who got caught in the middle of a serious conflict between her husband and David. Abigail showed much wisdom, godly character, and tact.

In 1 Samuel 25, we are introduced to this Nabal, whose name means "fool." Nabal was a Calebite. One meaning of Caleb is that of a dog. Nabal was surly and mean as some dogs can be. Like a dog, Nabal growled at people.

In contrast, Nabal's wife Abigail was a wise person. 1 Samuel 25:3 tells us that Abigail "was an intelligent and beautiful woman."

On the run from King Saul, David moved with his men to the Desert of Maon. Nabal, who was very rich, lived there with *his* men. Instructing his men to greet Nabal with good will, David hoped to receive favor from Nabal since David's men had previously protected Nabal's men and flocks at Carmel. David requested food from Nabal for his men. Showing respect, David told his men to greet Nabal with the following: "Long life to you! Good health to you and your household! And good health to all that is yours! (1 Sam. 25:6). In his message to Nabal, David even referred to himself as "your son David" (1 Sam. 25:8).

How did Nabal respond to David's respectful greeting and good will?

Nabal answered David's servants in a mean-spirited way: "Who is this David? Who is this son of Jesse? Many servants are breaking away from their masters these days. Why should I take my bread and water, and the meat I have slaughtered for my shearers, and give it to men coming from who knows where?" (1 Sam. 25:10-11).

When David's men reported Nabal's message, David angrily reacted with an order for his men: "Put on your swords!" (1 Sam. 25:13). David and about four hundred of his men prepared to go to battle against Nabal!

Meanwhile, one of Nabal's servants told Abigail how her husband had treated David's men. He told Abigail that Nabal is "such a wicked man that no one can talk to him" (1 Sam. 25:17).

Have you ever encountered a person like that? A person so difficult that it seems that no one can talk to him? We can learn from God's character in Abigail about how to deal with difficult people.

At this point in time, Abigail was caught in the middle—between David and her husband Nabal. Have you ever felt caught between people who are being difficult?

Abigail was in a very difficult spot. Nabal's—*and Abigail's*—whole household was about to be destroyed. How did she handle this terrible circumstance? Abigail took wise and speedy action!

Abigail quickly prepared an enormous amount of food for David's men—exactly what David wanted for his men in the first place. There is a saying: "The way to a man's heart is through his stomach." Well, Abigail was a very wise woman: she prepared a gift of abundant food for David and his men. Proverbs 18:16 affirms her wisdom: "A gift opens the way for the giver."

As Abigail rode on a donkey toward David, David was riding furiously to battle against Nabal. David was fuming, beside himself over Nabal's meanness. David was so angry he did something we should never do: he cursed himself if he didn't achieve his goal of destroying all of Nabal's men by the next morning.

When Abigail reached David, she showed great humility. "When Abigail saw David, she quickly got off her donkey and bowed down before David with her face to the ground" (1 Sam. 25:23). This action showed humble respect for David. Young person, when dealing with conflict, it's very wise to take on a humble posture. The Bible teaches that God gives grace to the humble.

Next, Abigail took responsibility for her husband's poor behavior. Then she asked to be heard. She said to David: "Pay no attention to that wicked man Nabal" (1 Sam. 25:25).

Young person, God calls us not to get upset over foolish people. We're not to give them undue attention. In fact, Titus 3:10-11 commands leaders: "Warn a divisive person once, and then warn him a second time. After that, have nothing to do with him. You may be sure that such a man is warped and sinful; he is self-condemned."

As we have shared, David was very angry, so much so that he was determined to kill all of Nabal's men. Abigail was attempting to turn that wrath around. She practiced a principle expressed in Proverbs 15:1: "A gentle answer turns away wrath, but a harsh word stirs up anger." Abigail used soft communication. When dealing with difficult situations, we're to speak with gentleness and self-control.

In addition to taking responsibility for Nabal's wrongdoing, Abigail appealed to David to avoid doing something which would impugn his integrity. She said, "Please forgive your servant's offense, for the Lord will certainly make a lasting dynasty for my master, because he fights the Lord's battles. Let no wrongdoing be found in you as long as you live" (1 Sam. 25:28). Abigail was advising David to abstain from doing something he would later regret.

She encouraged David, "Even though someone [which was King Saul] is pursuing you to take your life, the life of my master will be bound securely in the bundle of the living by the Lord your God" (1 Sam. 25:29). She was telling David that your life is secure. She was reminding David that the Lord's life-giving favor was with him!

Young person, as a Christian, as God's disciple, you are bought by his blood; you are also in the "bundle of the living"! No matter what conflict you may have to endure, remember that you have security in the Lord Jesus.

In addition, Abigail declared that David's enemies would be hurled away like stones in "the pocket of a sling" (1 Sam. 25:29). In other words, God would take care of David's enemies. She appealed to David to remember that God had a purpose for him and to avoid doing something that would become a burden on his conscience: "When the Lord has done for my master every good thing he promised concerning him and has appointed him leader over Israel, my master will not have on his conscience the staggering burden of needless bloodshed or of having avenged himself" (1 Sam. 25:30-31).

Abigail gave David very wise advice. Sometimes we can make rash decisions as David did when he angrily commanded his comrades: "Put on your swords!" (1 Sam. 25:13). In other words, "Let's fight!" But Abigail appealed to David that it was not right to pursue vengeance.

Romans 12:17-21 hammers home the point:

> Do not repay anyone evil for evil. Be careful to do what is right in the eyes of everybody. If it is possible, as far as it depends on you, live at peace with everyone. Do not take revenge, my friends, but leave room for God's wrath, for it is written: "It is mine to avenge; I will repay," says the Lord. On the contrary: "If your enemy is hungry, feed him; if he is thirsty, give him something to drink. In doing this, you will heap burning coals on his head." Do not be overcome by evil, but overcome evil with good.

Remember, young people, vengeance—revenge—is God's job, not yours. Abigail in her wisdom was overcoming evil with good.

Abigail convinced David to stop his vengeful rage. To his credit, David listened and was won over. It's important for us to listen to others and be willing to change our attitude, to be willing to change our perspective. Matthew 18:15 instructs us, "If your brother sins against you, go and show him his fault, *just between the two of you*. If he listens to you, you have won your brother over" (italics added).

In addition, David recognized that God had sent Abigail. Young person, perhaps God will send *you* to talk with your boss or with a teacher, and to do it in a way that maintains respect and favor for that authority.

David recognized Abigail's good judgment and sensed that he had been rescued by Abigail from doing something he would later regret. He commended Abigail: "May you be blessed for your good judgment and for keeping me from bloodshed this day and from avenging myself with my own hands" (1 Sam. 25:33). David was grateful to Abigail for her wisdom and for her courage to confront him in the right way!

David changed and granted Abigail's request. David adjusted his attitude. For all of us, we need to be willing to change our perspective. I have learned in my role as a principal that when two students have a conflict, one student seems right until I listen to the other student. Often my perspective changes. Proverbs 18:17 gives us wisdom: "The first to present his case seems right, till another comes forward and questions him."

A very wise woman, Abigail looked for the right time to speak to mean Nabal. When she did, Nabal became "like a stone," (1 Sam. 25:37) probably having a stroke. (Recall Abigail's previous prophetic reference to David's enemies becoming like stones in a sling.) Now Nabal's "heart failed him and he became like a stone" (1 Sam. 25:37). We're told that ten days later Nabal was struck by the Lord and died. Again, vengeance is God's job, not ours.

David recognized that he had escaped from doing something foolish. In addition, he saw that Nabal's wrongdoing had been brought "down on his own head" (1 Sam. 25:39).

Young person, do you see someone behaving badly? Don't worry if it appears that he's getting away with it. The weight of sin has its own consequences. In fact, instead of hoping for the worse for your enemies, pray that God's grace will cause that person to repent and turn to God.

Abigail was rewarded for her wisdom and godly character. She became David's wife. Abigail's attitude was one of servanthood, an attitude so contrary to that of this world. In fact, the Apostle Paul calls us to have a radically different attitude from what we see in this world: "Your attitude should be the same as that of Christ Jesus: Who, being in very nature God, did not consider equality with God something to be grasped, but made himself nothing, taking the very nature of a servant, being made in human likeness. And being found in appearance as a man, he humbled himself and became obedient to death—even death on a cross!" (Phil. 2:5-8). The passage goes on to emphasize that since Jesus had an attitude of humble service, "God exalted him to the highest place" (Phil. 2:9).

Attitude—Attitude—Attitude! *An Attitude of Servanthood!* That's what distinguished wise Abigail. In fact, we all sometimes need a person like Abigail when our anger might cause us to do something we would later regret.

God provided Abigail for David. She provided David with courageous wisdom to protect his integrity and his future. I encourage you to learn from the wisdom and courage that God placed in Abigail.

Memory Verse

1 Sam. 25:32-33 "David said to Abigail, 'Praise be to the Lord, the God of Israel, who has sent you today to meet me. May you be blessed for your good judgment and for keeping me from bloodshed this day and from avenging myself with my own hands.'"

ELIJAH

Obey the Word of the Lord and Speak It

Elijah was a great champion of the Lord. Time and again, he obeyed the word of the Lord and spoke it. Elijah had to stand alone. However, through all of the battles, there was one person standing with him—the Lord himself!

God used Elijah in a cosmic battle between good and evil—a battle that played out between a righteous godly prophet and an evil pagan king. God used Elijah to speak against King Ahab, his wife Jezebel, and the prophets of Baal and Asherah.

King Ahab, who was king of Israel, was very evil. 1 Kings 16:33 tells us the following: "Ahab also made an Asherah pole and did more to provoke the Lord, the God of Israel, to anger than did all the kings of Israel before him."

In 1 Kings 17, Elijah spoke the word of the Lord directly to King Ahab. He told him that a drought was coming. This meant that there would be a lack of water and food, resulting in hunger. God was punishing the people for their worship of the pagan gods Baal and Asherah.

Baal and Asherah were nature gods supposedly responsible over the elements, including rain. Now Elijah was saying that there wasn't going to be any rain! This decree directly contradicted what these pagan gods supposedly could provide.

God's people had involved themselves in worshiping these false gods. Now Elijah was declaring that God—not these pagan deities—is supreme and that a drought was coming. Elijah, whose name means "The Lord is my God," was being used by God to oppose the worship of Baal. God raised up Elijah to confront this ungodly national sin of pagan worship.

God directed Elijah to go by himself to the Kerith Ravine. This canyon would provide him with water amid the drought. He said that ravens would provide him with food. Imagine being provided by ravens in a ravine!

Elijah obeyed God's Word. He went to the Kerith Ravine. All alone by a brook, Elijah was prepared by God for the coming battle.

God provided Elijah with food and water while Israel was starving because of the drought. The ravens provided Elijah with plenty of bread and meat, both in the morning and in the evening.

This miracle also had clear symbolism: God used ravens—a symbol of death—to bring food and life to Elijah. Ahab and Israel were depending on Baal while Elijah was depending on God's word.

After a while, when the brook dried up because of the drought, God continued to provide for Elijah. God told him to "go at once to Zarephath of Sidon" (1 Kings 17:9). Zarephath was the center of the Baal worship; it also was the hometown of Ahab's evil wife Jezebel. (Jezebel was even more evil than King Ahab.) God told Elijah that he would be provided for by a widow in Zarephath. Of course, often a widow is someone that *others* need to provide for, especially in tough times. Now, Elijah was being told that a widow would provide for *him*.

However, Elijah didn't question the Lord. Again, he obeyed the word of the Lord, relying on God for his provision. When he saw the widow, "He called to her and asked, 'Would you bring me a little water in a jar so I may have a drink?' As she was going to get it, he called, "And bring me, please, a piece of bread'" (1 Kings 17:10-11).

One can sense some exasperation in the widow's voice as she responded to Elijah's second request: "*As surely as the Lord your God lives*, I don't have any bread—only a handful of flour in a jar and a little oil in a jug. I am gathering a few sticks to take home and make a meal for myself and my son, that we may eat it—and die" (1 Kings 17:12, italics added).

Although her response would not inspire very much confidence, Elijah encouraged her to do what he had said—to obey God's word and trust that God would provide for her. In effect, Elijah was challenging the widow to give her all—to trust God completely!

In obeying Elijah, the widow was obeying God. A desperate widow chose to trust and obey God's word. Amid all Israel starving, God provided for Elijah through a widow.

However, later on the widow's son became ill, grew increasingly worse, and eventually died. Of course, the widow was distraught. She questioned what Elijah had against her.

Amid the widow's distress, Elijah took her son from her arms and cried out to the Lord. He took the boy to his room, stretched out his body three times on him, and asked God for his life to be returned to him. And God listened and restored the boy's life!

"Then the woman said to Elijah, 'Now I know that you are a man of God and that the word of the Lord from your mouth is the truth'" (I Kings 17:24).

A long while later, God told Elijah to show himself to Ahab to tell him that God—not the Baal—would send rain. Elijah responded in characteristic fashion: he obeyed God. He is an example to all of us: our courageous challenge is to obey the Word of the Lord and speak it, just like Elijah did!

The terrible famine continued to drag on. Then, in her rage, Ahab's wife Jezebel started killing off God's prophets. Meanwhile, a godly man named Obadiah, who was in charge of Ahab's palace, tried to protect some of God's prophets. Obadiah hid one hundred of God's prophets in two caves.

As the effects of the drought became more and more problematic, King Ahab tried to solve the problem on his own. He divided the nation's land between him and Obadiah to find grass to feed the animals so they would not die. Instead of repenting as a result of the famine, King Ahab tried to do what so many political leaders do: try to come up with a man-made solution to the spiritual problem of idol worship.

Sometimes we do the same thing. When we have a problem, we often try to come up with our own man-made solutions to our problems. Instead, what we really need to do is turn back to the Lord and give our lives to him. Then we can commit our problems to the Lord and let *him* lead us.

While Obadiah was traversing the land at Ahab's direction, he met Elijah. Obadiah bowed down and asked Elijah, "Is it really you, my lord Elijah?" (1 Kings 18:7).

Elijah told Obadiah to tell King Ahab, "Elijah is here" (1 Kings 18:8). However, at this juncture Obadiah was fearful for his life. He was afraid that Ahab would kill him if he told Ahab that Elijah was here but couldn't produce him. Elijah assured Obadiah that he would present himself to Ahab that same day.

When Ahab and Elijah finally met, Ahab said, "Is that you, you troubler of Israel?" (1 Kings 18:17).

Elijah responded to Ahab's taunt by correctly identifying the sin issue: "I have not made trouble for Israel. But you and your father's family have. You have abandoned the Lord's commands and have followed the Baals" (1 Kings 18:18).

Then Elijah challenged Ahab to call the people of Israel as well as the four hundred and fifty prophets of Baal and the four hundred prophets of Asherah to meet him at Mount Carmel for a confrontation. Elijah was going to match the one true God against these two pagan gods.

When they all had convened on Mount Carmel, "Elijah went before the people and said, 'How long will you waver between two opinions? If the Lord is God, follow him; but if Baal is God, follow him.' But the people said nothing" (1 Kings 18:21).

Elijah issued a challenge that remains to this day: You can't waver between following God and following the idols of this world. You have to be "all in" by trusting, worshiping, and serving God wholeheartedly; you can't waver between two different ways. Elijah was saying to the people that you have to decide; you can't worship both. Make a decision to follow the one true God wholeheartedly!

Another champion named Joshua issued the same challenge to the people of God:

> Now fear the Lord and serve him with all faithfulness. Throw away the gods your forefathers worshiped beyond the River and in Egypt, and serve the Lord. But if serving the Lord seems undesirable to you, then choose for

yourselves this day whom you will serve, whether the gods your forefathers served beyond the river, or the gods of the Amorites, in whose land you are living. But as for me and my household, we will serve the Lord. (Joshua 24:14-15)

As we lead our families today, God issues the same challenge to us!

Jesus shared a similar challenge in Matthew 6:24: "No one can serve two masters. Either he will hate the one and love the other, or he will be devoted to the one and despise the other. You cannot serve both God and Money." Whether you are a parent or a young person, the call remains the same today: Obey, serve, and honor the one true God—not a false god, whether it be a Baal, money, or the things of this world. Be devoted to the one true God!

And so we have the dramatic story of Elijah's victory over Ahab and the prophets of Baal. Elijah, the only one of the Lord's prophets left, went up against the 450 prophets of Baal. He called for a test. He said let's get two bulls. He told the prophets of Baal to call on the name of their god while Elijah would call on the name of the Lord. Elijah declared, "The god who answers by fire—he is God" (1 Kings 18:24). The people agreed to this test.

The prophets of Baal went first. They called on the name of Baal all morning, but Baal did not respond. They started dancing, but still no response. "At noon Elijah began to taunt them. 'Shout louder!' he said. 'Surely he is a god! Perhaps he is deep in thought, or busy, or traveling. Maybe he is sleeping and must be awakened'" (I Kings 18:27).

Desperately, as was their custom, the evil prophets started cutting themselves with spears and swords until their blood flowed. In regard to this evil custom, I want to share something very important for young people. I would encourage you to contrast this pagan action to that of the Biblical injunction to treat our body as the temple of the Holy Spirit. Leviticus 19:28 tells us, "Do not cut your bodies for the dead or put tattoo marks on yourselves. I am the Lord." While in Christ there is no condemnation if some have previously gotten a tattoo, my encouragement to young people is not to treat their body as a god to be worshiped with tattoos and all kinds of body piercings.

While at the beach, many young people like to go to a tattoo parlor and get a tattoo. In addition, we see professional athletes, instead of glorifying the Lord with their play, seeking glory for themselves and tattooing their body with all kinds of images that glorify man and the creation as opposed to the Creator. Instead of worshiping and magnifying our bodies, I encourage young people to view their bodies as created by God to be the temple of the Holy Spirit—literally as a home for God himself!

Of course, no one, least of all an idol, responded to the cries, dances, and body slashings of the Baal prophets. When it was Elijah's turn to test his God, he went to a different extreme: he had the altar absolutely drenched with water. If fire was sent, all the people would have to acknowledge that this was done by none other than the Lord—a miracle wrought by the one true God!

Elijah prayed a direct prayer to God to vindicate his command to Elijah. Praying redemptively, Elijah wanted the hearts of the people to turn back to God: "Answer me, O Lord, answer me, so these people will know that you, O Lord, are God, and that you are turning their hearts back again" (I Kings 18:37).

The Lord gave a spectacular answer to Elijah's prayer! Everything on the altar, including the water, was licked up by fire sent by the Lord! God heard Elijah! God honored Elijah's faith because he obeyed him—because Elijah did exactly what God said!

The people responded by falling down and crying, "The Lord—he is God! The Lord—he is God!" (1 Kings 18:39).

After Elijah carried out the just punishment against the evil prophets for their crimes, the Lord brought rain and ended the drought which had served as Israel's punishment. Elijah told Ahab that he heard the sound of rain. After Elijah told his servant to look at the sea a seventh time, his servant said he saw the following: "A cloud as small as a man's hand is rising from the sea" (I Kings 18:44). A cloud—even a very small cloud—means that rain is on the way; of course, that rain meant the end of the drought! Indeed, a very great storm came—not from the pagan gods—but from the one true God!

And then Elijah—probably the fastest runner of all time—ran past Ahab's chariot, showing once again the mighty power of the one true God over all other so-called gods!

Time and again this champion Elijah received instructions from the Lord. He followed them, and he spoke God's Word boldly. The challenge for us is to do the same: to obey the Word of the Lord and speak it!

Young person, I encourage you to obey God's Word and speak it with your friends. Parents, speak God's Word in your families—with your young people and with your small children. Obey and speak God's Word when you're experiencing opposition and when you don't "feel" like it. Speak God's Word in faith and with conviction. God will honor his Word!

Memory Verse

1 Kings 17:24 "Then the woman said to Elijah, 'Now I know that you are a man of God and that the word of the Lord from your mouth is the truth.'"

ELISHA

Follow and Learn from a Father in the Faith

It's important to find Christ-like examples for us to emulate. Jesus counsels us, "A student is not above his teacher, but everyone who is fully trained will be like his teacher" (Luke 6:40). We become like the person who is teaching and leading us. The challenge for us is to find, follow, and learn from Christian leaders, or fathers in the faith. We become a servant leader for Messiah by following a servant leader. One such example is that of Elisha who followed Elijah.

In 1 Kings 19, Elisha was hard at work when he was called by Elijah. Elisha "was plowing with twelve yoke of oxen, and he himself was driving the twelfth pair. Elijah went up to him and threw his cloak around him" (1 Kings 19:19). In this introduction to Elisha, we find that he was a man diligent in his daily work. My parents have often taught this principle for ministry: "First comes the natural; then comes the spiritual." In other words, a person first demonstrates work ethic, godly character, and servant leadership in the natural world; and then that experience prepares the person to exercise servant leadership in the Kingdom of God. Promotion is from the Lord, the one person who sees all. Elisha was a diligent worker with a strong work ethic—and God promoted him. The Lord saw this quality in Elisha in the natural world, and then he called Elisha to be a servant leader in his spiritual Kingdom.

When Elijah threw his cloak on Elisha, he was symbolically transferring his mantle of spiritual authority to Elisha. However, ultimately one's call is from the Lord. After Elisha asked Elijah to say goodbye to his parents, Elijah said, "Go back. What have I done to you?" (1 Kings 19:20). Elijah was saying that it's not I who am calling you, but the Lord himself; your call is from the Lord.

Elisha proceeded to sell everything to follow the Lord. "He took his yoke of oxen and slaughtered them. He burned the plowing equipment to cook the meat and gave it to the people, and they ate. Then he set out to follow Elijah and became his attendant" (1 Kings 19:21).

I recall when I was called to become a pastor. I had been immersed in my first calling—to disciple, teach, and encourage young people in their walk with the Lord. Having been a teacher and a principal for many years, I had enjoyed that ministry tremendously. I remember thinking, "Am I really giving this up?" Ultimately, in God's sovereign plan, as I obeyed the Lord's call to become a pastor, the Lord restored my calling to children as well, and we started a school as a ministry of the church.

Well, Elisha was from a rich family. He had a good job. He had the riches of this world. He was prospering in his occupation. But Elisha decided to sell it all—he gave it all up to follow the Lord!

Elisha became Elijah's "attendant," the same term used for Joshua who followed Moses for many years. After Moses died, Joshua led God's people to take the promised land. For many years, Joshua was Moses' attendant just as Elisha was Elijah's attendant.

Young person, the question I have for you is this: Are you willing to become someone's attendant? Are you willing to serve someone else's vision? Are you willing to learn from a Christian leader? That is what the Lord is calling you to.

Later on as Elisha served Elijah, Elisha became aware that "the Lord was about to take Elijah up to heaven in a whirlwind" (2 Kings 2:1). When Elijah told Elisha to stay at Gilgal while Elijah went to Bethel, Elisha responded, "As surely as the Lord lives and as you live, I will not leave you" (2 Kings 2:2). Elisha totally committed himself to following Elijah. When the prophets told Elisha that the Lord was taking Elijah today, Elisha told them not to speak of it. Elisha refused to leave Elijah's side. He stayed attentive to following Elijah.

Elisha was focused on his commitment to serving Elijah. However, there was a two-fold attack on Elisha's focus. First, Elisha had to continually tell the other prophets not to speak of the Lord taking Elijah. Secondly, Elisha had to continually deny Elijah's requests for Elisha to leave him. Elisha showed tenacity in following Elijah; he would not be distracted from his goal of staying by Elijah's side until the Lord took him!

2 Kings 2:6 emphasizes their close relationship:

> Then Elijah said to him, "Stay here; the Lord has sent me to the Jordan."
>
> And he replied, "As surely as the Lord lives and you live, I will not leave you." So the two of them walked on.

The two of them walked on together—Elijah and Elisha in relationship! God often links one leader with another to advance his Kingdom. Young person, God may link you with a fellow servant to be champions working side by side for the Lord's cause—partnering together for his Kingdom!

This principle of learning from a Christ-like leader should be taking place in many ways. When a young person works with an experienced teacher at Vacation Bible School or in Kids Church, this principle is in operation. When a committed disciple serves as an assistant to a Home Group leader, this principle is in operation. When a developing worship leader serves under an experienced worship leader, this principle is in operation. When a young person learns under a teacher and then serves as a tutor or as a leader at a summer camp, this principle is in operation.

After Elijah used his cloak to miraculously divide the Jordan River and they both passed over it on dry land, Elijah asked what he could do for Elisha before the Lord would take him. Elisha responded, "Let me inherit a double portion of your spirit" (2 Kings 2:9). Elisha was not being greedy for possession; rather, he was invoking an inheritance principle of parents to the firstborn to express his desire to continue his spiritual father's ministry. When you latch on to a spiritual father, you receive that person's heart and spirit to continue on! Instead of inheriting worldly possessions, you inherit the spirit which energizes you to carry on your spiritual father's ministry. You stand on your spiritual father's shoulders and make further advances for God's Kingdom!

Elijah told Elisha, "You have asked a difficult thing, yet if you see me when I am taken from you, it will be yours—otherwise not" (2 Kings 2:10). We learn from watching our leaders; we learn from watching a servant leader for Messiah! As we walk with that person, we gain what that person has. At the same time, it's not that person calling you. While the Lord is using that person to disciple you, it's the Lord who calls you. God is still in control. You are not called by another human being; you are called by God. God uses human hands; but rest assured, it's the Lord's call!

When the Lord calls you, answer the call! The Bible says, "Many are called but few are chosen" (Matt. 22:14). When God calls you, he is looking for your heart response and for his character to be born up within you. When God calls you to be a servant leader for him, answer the call! Embrace God's destiny for your life. Tell him that you're willing to follow him where he leads you. Make yourself totally available to him. As you do so, he chooses you—chooses you to do great and mighty exploits for his Kingdom!

As Elisha continued to walk with and tenaciously attend to Elijah, he saw an incredible sight. All of a sudden, a chariot and horses of fire came and took Elijah away to heaven! Elisha's spontaneous reaction to this miraculous experience was to cry out, "My father! My father! The chariots and horsemen of Israel!" (2 Kings 2:12). Elisha had achieved his goal of seeing Elijah taken away by the Lord; at the same time, he was filled with grief at losing his spiritual father.

We need fathers in the faith! Young people need spiritual fathers and mothers—older ones that they can reach out to and that can help them to grow in their relationship with the Lord. Young people need to look to these mentors to help them to take on the mantle of servant leadership! This process of generational mentoring between those older and those younger alludes to our mission: to make disciples for Christ and to equip servant leaders for God's Kingdom!

Malachi 4:5-6 expresses this spiritual dynamic of Elijah as a father to the next generation:

> See, I will send you the prophet Elijah before that great and dreadful day of the Lord comes. He will turn the hearts of the fathers to their children, and the hearts of the children to their fathers; or else I will come and strike the land with a curse.

As Elijah came before and prepared Elisha, this prophecy speaks of how John the Baptist would come before and prepare the way for Jesus Christ. It emphasizes our utter need for fathers' hearts to be turned to the next generation, and for children's hearts to be turned to their fathers. Obviously, this fatherly connection with children is one of the fundamental needs of our world. Through the Lord's work, we can see that this turning of hearts is occurring—one family at a time. There is nothing more powerful than a child looking up to and seeing his dad worship God with all his heart. The impact of the father's example is powerful!

2 Kings 2:13 says that Elisha "picked up the cloak that had fallen from Elijah and went back and stood on the bank of the Jordan." Elisha taking up Elijah's cloak is symbolic of his taking up the mantle of servant leadership. There is the mantle given and the mantle taken. Sometimes the mantle is offered but not taken up. Elisha chose to take up Elijah's mantle. He chose to embrace God's call upon his life.

Young person, when you take up the mantle, you are deciding to be a participant in the Lord's ministry. It's *his* ministry. Jesus tells us, "Take my yoke upon you and learn from me, for I am gentle and humble in heart, and you will find rest for your souls. For my yoke is easy and my burden is light" (Matt. 11:29-30). God calls us to take up his yoke and his burden—the call to minister his life and to serve others. And the Lord says it will not be overly burdensome. In Christ's ministry, there is a sense of resting in him. Rest assured, the Lord will not give you more than you can handle; his grace is sufficient for you. However, we're called to take up God's yoke decisively! We hold it lightly, but hold it we do!

Elisha took up the mantle! "Then he took the cloak that had fallen from him and struck the water with it. . . . When he struck the water, it divided to the right and to the left, and he crossed over" (2 Kings 2:14). His mentor Elijah was known for incredible miracles, but Elisha ended up performing twice as many miracles as Elijah! He truly received a "double portion" of the Lord's Spirit! As the Lord was with Elijah, he was with Elisha mightily as well!

The other prophets said of Elisha: "The spirit of Elijah is resting on Elisha" (2 Kings 2:15). That was the spirit of Christ! And the Spirit of Messiah can rest on you as well! It's only by making Jesus your Savior and Lord! It's only by taking up your cross and following him daily! It's only by responding to the Lord's call for your life! Elisha counted the cost, desired to be used by God, asked to be used by God, and took up the mantle of ministry—the mantle of taking on God's will and purpose for his life! Elisha sold all for Christ!

Elisha embodied what Jesus expressed in Matthew 10:38-39: "Anyone who does not take his cross and follow me is not worthy of me. Whoever finds his life will lose it, and whoever loses his life for my sake will find it." Elisha lost his life for the sake of Christ. He was willing to sell all, take up his cross, and follow the Lord.

As he chose to sell all for the Lord, Elisha learned by following the champion Elijah. Likewise, we learn by selling all for Jesus and following fathers and mothers in the faith! It's all about servant leadership—if you are willing to serve the Lord by serving others, you have a role to play in God's adventurous ministry! I encourage you to find a spiritual father or mother—a mentor who is willing to disciple you. Ask that person to teach you, walk with you, and to disciple you in the things of God! This is how you grow into leadership—servant leadership after Jesus!

I encourage you to pray this prayer: "Lord, I thank you for the Holy Spirit! Help me to sell all for you! Help me to be willing to grow in you by walking with and serving a father or mother in the faith! Help me to become the servant leader you're calling me to be! Thank you for the great adventure of following your call! In Jesus' name, Amen!"

Memory Passage

2 Kings 2:9-10 "When they had crossed, Elijah said to Elisha, 'Tell me, what can I do for you before I am taken from you?'

'Let me inherit a double portion of your spirit,' Elisha replied.

'You have asked a difficult thing,' Elijah said, 'yet if you see me when I am taken from you, it will be yours—otherwise not.'"

JABEZ

Pray about Your Future!

God works through prayer! There are different prayers in the Bible, such as the Lord's Prayer in Matthew 6, that teach us how to pray. One example of a prayer is known as "The Prayer of Jabez." In the middle of many family histories called genealogies in 1 Chronicles, a man named Jabez stood out. He stood out because of his prayer. Jabez shows how someone can be distinctive in their family history by trusting the Lord.

Amid all of these genealogies, Jabez was prominent. Exactly why did he stand out? He stood out because of his faith-filled prayer about his future! 1 Chronicles 4:9-10 tells of Jabez and his prayer:

> Now Jabez was more honorable than his brothers, and his mother called his name Jabez, saying, "Because I bore him in pain." And Jabez called on the God of Israel saying, "Oh, that You would bless me indeed, and enlarge my territory, that Your hand would be with me, and that You would keep me from evil, that I may not cause pain!" So God granted him what he requested. (NKJV)

What did Jabez pray for? He prayed that the Lord would bless him, that God would enlarge his territory, that God's hand would be with him, and that God would keep him from evil.

First, Jabez prayed that God would bless him. Of course, everyone desires to be blessed. The beatitudes in Matthew 5:3-12 speak of being blessed. *Beatitudes* are *attitudes* of *being*—attitudes of being that bring blessing! When we walk according to Biblical attitudes, we will be blessed. For instance, one beatitude is the following: "Blessed are the peacemakers, for they will be called the sons of God" (Matt. 5:9). When we cultivate an attitude of making peace, we are imitating Christ, the Prince of Peace, and are called sons of God.

Second, Jabez prayed that God would enlarge his territory. In that rural community, Jabez was praying that the Lord would enlarge his land, his real estate. Today, when we pray that prayer, we're praying that the Lord would enlarge our sphere of influence—that we would righteously and positively influence our peers. We're asking that God would bless us not simply for our own sake but also for others. We're asking that we would bless others by our godly influence. Jabez had a desire to be great. We *should* have a desire to be great—but not so that we can show off our greatness. We should desire to walk in the greatness of serving God and serving others.

Third, Jabez prayed that God's hand would be with him. He was praying for God's presence! The presence of God in our lives is the secret of courage—the secret of facing into fear and being a champion for the Lord. David said, "I have set the Lord always before me. Because he is at my right hand, I will not be shaken" (Psalm 16:8). God commanded Joshua, "Be strong and courageous. Do not be terrified; do not be discouraged, for the Lord your God will be with you wherever you go" (Joshua 1:9). When the Lord commissioned his disciples to make disciples of all nations, he said, "And surely I am with you always, to the very end of the age" (Matt. 28:20). As with other champions of the Bible, Jabez was asking for the Lord to be with him! Indeed, focusing on the Lord's presence gives us the courage to embrace the challenging tasks God has for us!

Lastly, Jabez prayed that God would keep him from evil. Why did he pray that? Well, Jabez surely knew what his name meant. It means "he will cause pain." However, Jabez made a decision. He decided that his name would not define him. Instead, he prayed that he would live in such a way that he would not cause pain! Turning his name around, Jabez decided to shun evil and not cause pain in others' lives! What a great prayer!

When Jabez prayed about his future, he prayed in faith. What is faith? More importantly, what is faith in **God**? Faith is **confidence** that if we call out to God and seek him with all our heart, that we're going to connect with him, that God is hearing and will answer us, and that we will find him! Faith in God is an adventure—it's an adventure to see God work in our lives and to experience amazing breakthroughs!

In my adventure of faith, I've seen God work in powerful and exciting ways through prayer. In college, I was going through a trial of faith and needed help. I called out to God to "send someone or something" to help me! He sent an elderly man named K. B. Hoover, who just happened to be out walking on a cold wintry day. Meeting me on a covered bridge, he saw that I was distraught. With compassion, he talked with me and invited me to his home that evening. I went to his house many times that year, and he helped to nurture me at a critical time in my faith journey.

As I continued on my adventure of faith, the Lord helped me to gain the victory with being overly preoccupied with sin consciousness; as a young man, I would confess sin after sin after sin. A thought would pop into my mind and I would confess it as sin, not understanding the Biblical strategy to "take captive every thought to make it obedient to Christ" (2 Cor. 10:5). Instead of being focused on Christ, my mind was preoccupied with avoiding sin. I'll never forget what happened as I was driving home from college by myself one night. As I was driving down the highway and about to confess another sin, a huge eighteen-wheeler truck came right into my line of vision as it went over a bridge right in front of me. I looked up, and on that truck were the following huge letters: G-R-A-C-E. At that point, I knew that God was sending me a message! During the rest of my drive home, my mind wasn't on sin anymore; rather, I was praising God! I believe that the Lord sent me a message that day to learn what it means to walk by his GRACE!

Similarly, I recall struggling with suicidal thoughts as a young man. (I don't think I was actually suicidal; I believe the enemy was attacking my mind, which is the battlefield in our lives.) As I worked my mowing maintenance job, I was preoccupied with negative thoughts. One day as I was taking my lunch break and reading God's Word, the Lord gave me a passage of Scripture from 1 Peter 5:8-11 that has stayed with me to this day. Interestingly, the passage is addressed to young men. It says the following:

> Be self-controlled and alert. Your enemy the devil prowls around like a roaring lion looking for someone to devour. Resist him, standing firm in the faith, because you know that your brothers throughout the world are undergoing the same kind of sufferings.
>
> And the God of all grace, who called you to his eternal glory in Christ, after you have suffered a little while, will himself restore you and make you strong, firm and steadfast. To him be the power for ever and ever. Amen.

This passage was a word directly from the Lord to help me to overcome. It has become part of my testimony. It became a rallying cry for me as I went back out to work; whenever the negative thoughts returned, I confessed that Scripture passage with conviction. I could imagine my Christian brothers all over the world undergoing the same battle, and we were standing together in Christ! Now, whenever my thoughts seem to get out of control, I simply state that passage with conviction and I overcome! That Scripture has become part of my very being, just as much as my right arm!

After I graduated from college, I became an English teacher. One responsibility of an English teacher is to grade compositions. With that responsibility comes subjectivity: Is this grade a B+ or an A-? I got so caught up in the subjectivity of that task that Satan started accusing me of grading the compositions inaccurately; he even accused me of giving wrong grades purposely. Well, through that trial, I learned to walk in faith. The Bible says, "The righteous will live by faith" (Rom. 1:17). I learned to commit to the Lord the grading of the compositions and to trust him that he is guiding my decisions. And now, to this day, with all the decisions I have to make as a principal and as a pastor, I trust the Lord to guide me. I commit every day and every decision into the Lord's hands for his guidance. Praise the Lord—He has helped me to learn to walk in faith and to make confident decisions for the people with whom I work!

Next, I saw a very important answer to prayer regarding my future—the Lord's provision of my wife Silvia Cristina! As I prayed for my wife before meeting her, the Lord gave me a vision of what kind of lady she would be. I'm five years older than my wife; and when I was in college, she was in high school. In fact, in my wallet I have a beautiful picture of my wife when she was in seventh grade. That picture reminds me of how God protected Silvia through trying circumstances in her youth. Looking back, we see how God answered my prayer to protect her even though I didn't know her at the time. Eventually the Lord worked to bring Silvia from Honduras to Massachusetts to Maryland where we met. She became the Spanish teacher at the Christian school where I was the English teacher. I knew within a month that Silvia was the one that I had been praying for, the one in the vision. It was simply a matter of recognizing God's work. Today we work together in the pastoral ministry and in raising up champions for the Lord at our Christian school.

As a young couple, my wife and I underwent a trial of faith. We had to trust the Lord's continued provision and direction for his calling in our lives. The school at which I had been working closed near the end of one summer. What was I going to do? We lifted up our need to the Lord in prayer. I called a Christian school in another part of Maryland and told them that I was looking for a teaching job. The administrator on the other end of the line said that *they* needed an English and physical education teacher. I thought, "Did I say that or did you say that?" Being an English and PE teacher was exactly what I did! I went in for the interview and got the job. The Lord provided for my wife and me at a critical time as a young couple! I enjoyed three rewarding years of teaching and coaching young people at that school.

In fact, it was during that period of my life, that the Lord led my wife and me to start a Christian camp called Camp Courage, one with a mission of encouraging champions for the Lord. As I prayed about our future, I believe the Lord led me to start this camp. However, as we approached the first year, things weren't looking good. The financing of the camp didn't seem to be coming together. We were at a critical juncture. I almost felt like giving up. But I cried out to the Lord in prayer. He answered our prayer, and we were able to have a significant financial event. We then proceeded to enjoy a successful first summer of camp. Camp Courage has now been encouraging young champions for God for twenty-seven years.

A little while later, I experienced a health concern. I was eating my lunch one day, and all of a sudden I experienced my jaw locking. As I pursued medical help, my doctor told me that it was the dentist's responsibility to take care of it; and my dentist told me that it was the doctor's responsibility. What was I to do? I was at a standstill; the medical professionals in my life couldn't help me. At a Christian home group meeting, I asked for prayer for the healing of my jaw. As I received prayer, a warm sensation pervaded my jaw, and I was immediately healed. To this day, I have not had a problem with my jaw.

Early in our marriage, my wife and I were told that Silvia had a condition which hindered her ability to have children. Of course, this news was very hard for us—we had been *called* to work with children and now the doctor was saying that it might be difficult for my wife to bear a child! I recall lying prostrate on the floor, crying out to the Lord in prayer for a child. In addition, prayer intercessors gave me Biblical promises to pray over our marriage, my wife, and her womb. Sometimes I grew weary of praying those prayers, but we persevered in interceding for a baby. I'll always remember when my wife Silvia shared the news that she was pregnant; it was a great cause for rejoicing and giving thanks to the Lord for his answer to our prayers! When our baby Anna was born, we were so grateful to the Lord for his beautiful work. And now, Anna has three brothers: Caleb, Nehemiah, and Joshua. God answered our prayers!

As I grew in the Lord, I continued to pray about God's plans for our future. I was initially called to teach and disciple young people, helping them to grow in their walk with the Lord. After being an educator for almost twenty years, the Lord called me to the pastoral ministry. This was a major leap of faith for me. I had enjoyed working with children immensely, and I recall wondering, "Am I really giving this up?" I loved doing what I was doing. However, in faith, I decided to sell all for the cause of Christ. The Lord called me to pastor his people, leading them into the promised land God has for us. Through this process, I learned Jesus' principle of giving up one's life: "Whoever finds his life will lose it, and whoever loses his life for my sake will find it" (Matt. 10:39). As I embraced the pastoral calling, the Lord proceeded to redeem our first call; he called my wife and me to start a school as a ministry of the church—Living Grace Christian School, a school with a mission of raising up champions for the Lord. In addition to the pastoral call, the Lord redeemed his call to teach and disciple children. It had never really left. We just needed to trust God for our future. Following the Lord's direction, we had to trust and obey him.

In fact, as we grew as a church and as a school, we continued to pray about our future. Previously, we had the impression that it would be almost impossible to build an expanded facility on our church's property because of "the powers that be." However, we continued to pray about our future, and the Lord started opening doors within our community. We started to see God give our church more favor in our community—more GRACE! As we continued to pray for God's direction for our church, he opened the way; and now the Lord has given us a beautiful expanded facility. He has given us room to grow—all for his purposes!

As a Christian, you too can live an exciting adventure of faith! I encourage you to pray about your future. As you pray, you will see God work miracles big and small in your life, your marriage, and your family! Praying about your future is an amazing adventure as you learn to trust God!

Like Jabez, we are called to pray about our future—a future focused not on ourselves but on impacting others for the Lord. And like Jabez, we are called to pray in faith believing. The writer of the book of Hebrews emphasized the following about faith:

> Now faith is being sure of what we hope for and certain of what we do not see. This is what the ancients were commended for. . . . And without faith it is impossible to please God, because anyone who comes to him must believe that he exists and that he rewards those who earnestly seek him. (Heb. 11:1-2, 6)

How do we please God? We please him by walking in faith. Again, the Bible emphasizes, "The righteous will live by faith" (Rom. 1:17). When we pray in faith about our future, we please God.

Our faith is not just faith in faith. Our faith is faith in **God**, the creator of the universe! When we call out to God, he hears us. "Everyone who calls on the name of the Lord will be saved" (Joel 2:32). Jeremiah 29:11-14 declares the following: "'For I know the plans I have for you,' declares the Lord, 'plans to prosper you and not to harm you, plans to give you hope and a future. Then you will call upon me and come and pray to me, and I will listen to you. You will seek me and find me when you seek me with all your heart. I will be found by you.'"

Young person, I encourage you to pray about your future. The Lord knows your future. He knows the plans he has for you, and it's a good future! When you call upon God in prayer, he listens! When you seek God with all your heart, that's walking in faith. You're making God your trust! As you pray in faith, you will find God; and at the right time, he will reveal his plans for you!

You may be asking, "What exactly should I be praying about my future?" Three major areas are the following: pray to have a close relationship with the Lord Jesus Christ, pray to understand your life calling in serving the Lord, and pray for your life mate—the person with whom you will walk this great adventure of faith. I encourage you to pray about your future in the Lord!

As you pray in faith about your future, pray with persistence. When it seems as if nothing is happening, don't give up on your prayers. After Jesus taught his disciples how to pray in Luke chapter 11, he shared the need for persistence and boldness in prayer. He shared the parable of a man who went to his friend at midnight to get bread that he needed to feed a visitor. The friend inside the house didn't want to be bothered because he was in bed with all his children. (If he got up, he would wake up his little ones and cause a commotion.) Jesus said, "I tell you, though he will not get up and give him the bread because he is his friend, yet because of the man's boldness he will get up and give him as much as he needs" (Luke 11:8).

Jesus proceeded to emphasize the following about prayer: "Ask and it will be given to you; seek and you will find; knock and the door will be opened to you. For everyone who asks receives; he who seeks finds; and to him who knocks, the door will be opened" (Luke 11:9-10). He said, "Which of you fathers, if your son asks for a fish, will give him a snake instead? Or if he asks for an egg, will give him a scorpion? If you then, though you are evil, know how to give good gifts to your children, how much more will your Father in heaven give the Holy Spirit to those who ask him!" (Luke 11:11-13).

Young person, when you pray, realize that you're praying to your all-loving Heavenly Father who wants to bless you with good gifts, such as the gift of the Holy Spirit! Pray for God's gifts to bless others as opposed to earthly riches that will pass away. Pray for God's kingdom and will to come into your life, into your family's lives, and into your friends' lives. Pray in confidence because your God loves you as a loving Father! As Jabez did, pray in faith about God's plans for your future!

Memory Verse

1 Chronicles 4:10 "And Jabez called on the God of Israel saying, 'Oh, that You would bless me indeed, and enlarge my territory, that Your hand would be with me, and that You would keep me from evil, that I may not cause pain!' So God granted him what he requested" (NKJV).

DAVID

Take Responsibility for Your Actions

My dad taught my brothers and me the following truth: When you are caught in a fault, acknowledge the fault and the blame will stop. In other words, we can't be faultless—no one is perfect; but we can be blameless if we take responsibility for our actions. If we lie about what we've done, try to make excuses, or blame others, the blame will keep coming our way. But when we finally admit to the truth—to our sin—the blame will stop.

The best thing to do when you've done wrong is to go to the applicable authority—often your parents or teacher—and confess to what you've done before you're even confronted about it. However, when your parents or teachers do confront you for wrongdoing, acknowledge it immediately and fully. The Bible says, "All have sinned and fall short of the glory of God" (Romans 3:23). We've all sinned; none of us are without wrongdoing. When we are at fault, we need to take full responsibility for our actions before the Lord and before the proper authorities as needful.

In 1 Chronicles 21, we see that King David acknowledged his fault and took responsibility for his sin. 1 Chronicles 21:1 says, "Satan rose up against Israel and incited David to take a census of Israel." Perhaps to punish Israel for their sin, God in his sovereignty allowed the adversary Satan to tempt King David to do wrong by commanding his people to take a census. Now a census in itself is not sinful; however, this census, which was the counting of Israel's fighting men, was indicative of King David placing his confidence in manpower as opposed to God.

The Apostle Paul refers to Satan as the tempter: "I was afraid that in some way the tempter might have tempted you and our efforts might have been useless" (1 Thess. 3:5). One way that Satan tempts us is to place prideful confidence in our own strength as opposed to humbly trusting the Lord. Young person, the Lord calls you to place your full confidence in the Lord—he will build you up as you learn to trust him.

David's faithful assistant Joab expressed serious concern regarding David's command to count the fighting men of Israel. Three times Joab questioned David: "May the Lord multiply his troops a hundred times over. My lord the king, are they not all my lord's subjects? Why does my lord want to do this? Why should he bring guilt on Israel?" (1 Chron. 21:3). However, Joab's concerns went unheeded by David; the king's behest of a census was summarily carried out.

Still, Joab expressed his strong dislike of David's command. Because the order was odious to him, Joab didn't fully obey it. He didn't count the fighting men from all the tribes of Israel; he left out the tribes of Levi and Benjamin. More importantly than Joab's concern was God's disapproval of David's action: "This command was also evil in the sight of God; so he punished Israel" (1 Chron. 21:7).

After the census was taken, David came to the realization that he had sinned against God. He said to the Lord about his commanding a census: "I have sinned greatly by doing this. Now, I beg you, take away the guilt of your servant. I have done a very foolish thing" (1 Chron. 21:8). David confessed his sin and acknowledged his guilt. He recognized that he had done wrong by ordering the census of the fighting men.

In the prophet Samuel's parallel account of this episode, the Bible says that David was "conscience-stricken" (2 Sam. 24:10). This means that David's conscience—that part inside him that knew right from wrong—was telling him that he had greatly sinned. Young person, it's very important that you learn to listen to your conscience. When your conscience tells you that you've done wrong, you need to make it right. You do that by going to the applicable authority—normally your parents and your teachers—to confess what you've done and to seek forgiveness.

You restore to yourself a good conscience by confessing your sin to the Lord. 1 John 1:9 tells us, "If we confess our sins, he is faithful and just and will forgive us our sins and purify us from all unrighteousness." However, "If we claim to be without sin, we deceive ourselves and the truth is not in us" (1 John 1:8). If we don't listen to our conscience and continue to violate it by sinning, we may even start to deceive our own selves. At that point, the truth is not operational in our lives. Being in a state of self-deception is very serious. Sometimes we can violate our conscience so much so that our conscience doesn't bother us anymore. We think we've done nothing wrong; at that point, we're not only deceiving others but also deceiving ourselves.

However, "If we walk in the light, as he is in the light, we have fellowship with one another, and the blood of Jesus, his Son, purifies us from all sin" (1 John 1:7). You see, when we hide our sin, we have no fellowship—no relationship. When we hide sin from our parents, we have no true relationship with them. And when we hide our sin from God, we have no true relationship with him. That's why it's very important that we learn to take responsibility for our actions; by doing so we receive forgiveness and can have prosperous relationships not only with God but also with our parents.

In Psalm 51:3-4, David expressed that his sin was against God: "For I know my transgressions, and my sin is always before me. Against you, you only, have I sinned and done what is evil in your sight, so that you are proved right when you speak and justified when you judge." Ultimately, our sin is against God because it's God's standard that we are breaking. It's God who made the standard in the first place.

The Lord used David's friend Gad to help David repent of his sin. Sometimes the Lord uses a true godly friend to help us to turn from wrongdoing and to find the right path going forward. Through David's friend, God gave David three choices for his punishment: "Take your choice: three years of famine, three months of being swept away before your enemies, with their swords overtaking you, or three days of the sword of the Lord—days of plague in the land, with the angel of the Lord ravaging every part of Israel" (1 Chron. 21:11-12). From these choices, the Lord allowed David to decide his punishment.

David chose to put himself in the hands of the Lord. He reasoned that he would depend on the Lord's mercy; therefore, he chose the three days of the sword of the Lord.

David saw firsthand how his wrong actions affected others. A plague proceeded to kill seventy thousand men in his kingdom. Young person, our actions impact others. This realization should have a sobering effect on us, particularly as we grow older and become responsible for others. Our sinful actions can destroy our family. If we are in a leadership position, sinning can destroy whole organizations and ministries. It can cause heartache and life-altering consequences. Sin can shatter people's lives and relationships.

God calls us to be courageous leaders for the advancement of his kingdom through being responsibility takers. We need to realize that we are responsible not only for ourselves but also for others. As servant leaders, our actions affect others. This understanding should sober us and motivate us to depend on Christ every day of our lives—to live for Christ instead of living for our own selfish desires.

The Lord sent a destroying angel to the city of Jerusalem. He was about to devastate God's city! The Biblical account reveals that the Lord's destroying angel was about to kill a particular family—the family of Araunah. We see in this passage that sin hurts real people!

The destroying angel was standing at the threshing floor of Araunah, who was working with his four sons. Here a family was minding their own business and going about their work—people who through no fault of their own were about to be destroyed as a result of King David's wrongdoing. However, the Lord had compassion and mercy; he commanded the angel who was about to kill this innocent family with the following: "Enough! Withdraw your hand" (1 Chron. 21:15).

When David saw the destroying angel poised to attack Jerusalem and others' lives because of his sin, he cried out to God: "Was it not I who ordered the fighting men to be counted? I am the one who has sinned and done wrong. These are but sheep. What have they done? O Lord my God, let your hand fall upon me and my family, but do not let this plague remain on your people" (1 Chron. 21:17).

Young person, through David's experience, this is what we realize: our sin impacts real people. It hurts others' lives. This sobering understanding serves to motivate us to do nothing that will bring shame to the cause of Jesus Christ.

However, when we do sin in a way that hurts others, we need to be quick to take responsibility—to acknowledge our fault—as David did. David took responsibility for his sin.

I recall as a principal being in charge of students on a trip to an amusement park. There was a certain ride—an eight-track driving course—that was designated for an older age group. For our seventh and eighth grade class, I realized that according to the stated rules for the ride, some of the students were old enough to go on this ride and some weren't old enough. However, I relented to the younger students' pressure and allowed all of them to go on the ride. Sure enough, as the students started driving the little cars, an underage student had an accident which hurt others, including one of our teachers. In the process, I knew that I had done wrong. At the hospital, I took responsibility for my failure in allowing the underage students to drive the car on the track. I apologized to the teacher who was hurt. I took responsibility for my sin and my fault. I am so grateful to the Lord that that teacher forgave me. I am still working with her to this day.

After David appealed to the Lord that only he be punished for his wrongdoing and not others, the Lord's angel told Gad to tell David to build an altar on Araunah's threshing floor. You see, young person, in order for sin to be forgiven, there needs to be a sacrifice. In the Old Testament, a sacrifice of an animal was made for the forgiveness of sins.

Thank God, we now have the ultimate sacrifice of Jesus Christ for our sins. Because of Jesus' sacrificial death on the cross, in which he took the punishment for our sin, we can be forgiven. Romans 6:23 says, "For the wages of sin is death, but the gift of God is eternal life in Christ Jesus our Lord." You see, the punishment for sin is death; but thanks be to God, Jesus took our punishment upon himself! By dying for us, he became our substitutionary sacrifice. That's why we all need to come to Christ for salvation. Jesus saves us from our sin so that we don't need to spend eternal death in hell but instead can live eternally in heaven!

David obeyed the Lord's instructions to make an altar. When the Lord's destroying angel appeared to Araunah, his four sons hid from the angel. But at that moment, King David came to this family and Araunah bowed down to him. David asked Araunah to use his threshing floor for the altar: "Let me have the site of your threshing floor so I can build an altar to the Lord, that the plague on the people may be stopped. Sell it to me at the full price" (I Chron. 21:22).

In response to King David, Araunah said, "Take it! Let my lord the king do whatever pleases him. Look, I will give the oxen for the burnt offerings, the threshing sledges for the wood, and the wheat for the grain offering. I will give all this" (1 Chron. 21:23).

However, David insisted on paying the price for the sacrifice himself: "No, I insist on paying the full price. I will not take for the Lord what is yours, or sacrifice a burnt offering that costs me nothing" (1 Chron. 21:24). You see, young person, a sacrificial offering is part of our worship of almighty God. David had sinned against the Lord. It would have been wrong for him to bring an offering to the Lord that cost him nothing. He needed to bring a sacrifice to the Lord. There is a cost to truly following the Lord.

There is a cost to true discipleship. When we make a sacrifice, we feel that sacrifice. It could be a sacrifice of time, of money, or of our own desires. One way we make that sacrifice is by sacrificing our time to serve the Lord. Another way is by giving the tithe to the Lord—a tenth of our earnings, the first fruits of our income. Giving a sacrificial offering to the Lord is part of our worship.

David paid the full price for the sacrifice. He would not let the cost of his sin's sacrifice be passed on to someone else. He paid for both the land and the animals needed for the sacrifice. The parallel passage of 2 Samuel 24:24 tells us, "So David bought the threshing floor and the oxen."

After purchasing the site, David burnt both sacrificial offerings for his sin and fellowship offerings to demonstrate his rededication to the Lord. God dealt with David's sin, and fellowship was restored between God and David. 1 Chron. 21:26 shares of David's restoration: "He called on the Lord, and the Lord answered him with fire from heaven on the altar of burnt offering." You see, young person, when we bring a sacrificial offering to the Lord, we call upon Christ. We call on him for forgiveness, for cleansing, and for restoration of a pure heart so that we can serve him! Our relationship with the Lord is restored!

Well, the Lord received David's sacrifice! The Lord stopped the destroying angel: the angel "put his sword back into its sheath" (1 Chron. 21:27). In his parallel account, Samuel reports, "Then the Lord answered prayer in behalf of the land, and the plague on Israel was stopped" (2 Sam. 24:25).

The Lord worked redemption through David's sin. In addition to the site being used as a sacrifice for sin, God used it for a larger purpose. The Lord used it to build his temple, the house of the Lord, the place for his very presence! In this redemptive act, we see that God can use all things—even our sin and failures—to turn things around for his glory! Romans 8:28 reminds us of how God can use even our bad failures for his good purpose: "And we know that in all things God works for the good of those who love him, who have been called according to his purpose." David dedicated the property that he bought from Araunah to be used to build God's temple: "The house of the Lord God is to be here, and also the altar of burnt offering for Israel" (1 Chron. 22:1).

Young person, if we learn to take responsibility for our actions, God can use our failures to advance his kingdom. One purpose that God has for our sin is that he teaches us through our failures; this growth in learning enables us to help others. In Psalm 51:10-13, David expressed the following: "Create in me a pure heart, O God, and renew a steadfast spirit within me. Do not cast me from your presence or take your Holy Spirit from me. Restore to me the joy of your salvation and grant me a willing spirit, to sustain me. *Then I will teach transgressors your ways, and sinners will turn back to you*" (italics added). The goal is that we learn from our sin, be cleansed, be built back up, and then be used by the Lord to teach others.

In addition, the Lord desires to be praised as a result of our experience: "O Lord, open my lips, and my mouth will declare your praise" (Psalm 51:15). Ultimately, the Lord wants to restore us to his service through humble brokenness: "The sacrifices of God are a broken spirit; a broken and contrite heart, O God, you will not despise" (Ps. 51:17). When we have the sacrifice of a broken and contrite heart, the Lord is able to use us. Out of our humble state, the Lord makes us clean vessels to help others! I encourage you to learn to take responsibility for your actions quickly. As you grow in this character, the Lord will use you mightily to advance his kingdom!

Memory Passage

Psalm 51:10-13 "Create in me a pure heart, O God, and renew a steadfast spirit within me. Do not cast me from your presence or take your Holy Spirit from me. Restore to me the joy of your salvation and grant me a willing spirit, to sustain me. Then I will teach transgressors your ways, and sinners will turn back to you."

JOSIAH

Discover, Read, and Obey God's Word

Can you imagine becoming a king at the age of eight? That's what happened to a boy named Josiah. He reigned as king for thirty-one years, from 640 to 609 B.C. The Bible says, "Even a child is known by his actions, by whether his conduct is pure and right" (Prov. 20:11). As a young king, Josiah became known for his righteous actions, and he determined to follow God. Although his father Amon did evil and didn't follow the Lord, Josiah resolved to follow God and do what is right. The Bible says, "He did what was right in the eyes of the Lord" (2 Chron. 34:2). In fact, when he discovered God's Word, he read it and obeyed it! He proceeded to lead the people in following God's Word. The courage challenge for us all is to discover, read, and obey God's Word!

At age 16, still in his youth, Josiah began to earnestly seek God. At age 20, he started to get rid of all the idols in the land: "Under his direction the altars of the Baals were torn down; he cut to pieces the incense altars that were above them, and smashed the Asherah poles, the idols and the images" (2 Chron. 34:4).

Josiah got rid of all the idols! He demolished the idols along with their high places. He took clear action to purify the land.

What is an idol? In ancient days, an idol was an image made by man and then worshiped as if it was a god. It would take the place of God in the people's worship. Some people today still worship these idolatrous images.

For us today, anything becoming more important to us than God—anything becoming obsessive to us—can become an idol in our lives. For instance, one big area for young people is video gaming. We need to be careful that we don't become obsessed with video gaming—or anything else—with our time. Otherwise, that thing can become an idol in our lives.

Then, at age 26, King Josiah committed himself to purifying the land and repairing God's temple. While his men were restoring the temple, guess what happened: the Word of God was found! "While they were bringing out the money that had been taken into the temple of the Lord, Hilkiah the priest found the Book of the Law of the Lord that had been given through Moses" (2 Chron. 34:14). While they were restoring the temple, the priest Hilkiah found God's Word!

If the priest *found* God's Word, that means that they had *lost* God's Word! Can you imagine not having the Bible? We are so blessed that we have God's Word to lead and instruct us. However, what happens if we don't read it? If we don't read God's Word, our hearts will start drifting away from God like a ship without an anchor. *We need to discover, read, and obey God's Word.* If we have lost God's Word in our lives, we need to rediscover it and obey it!

In order for us to grow in our walk with the Lord, we need to feed on God's Word for our daily nourishment. Hebrews 5:14 tells us, "But solid food is for the mature, who by constant use have trained themselves to distinguish good from evil." God's Word is like food for our spiritual growth. We need to read it every day of our lives—and do what it says!

Well, King Josiah had his secretary—Shaphan—read this Book to him. When Josiah realized that their fathers had not been keeping the Word of the Lord, he tore his robes in humble repentance for his people. He then had his Priest Hilkiah, his Secretary Shaphan, and his attendants inquire of the Lord about this newly rediscovered Word.

Following King Josiah's order, they inquired of the prophetess Huldah. She prophesied of the people's coming destruction because of their idolatry. However, she commended Josiah because of his actions: "Because your heart was responsive and you humbled yourself before God when you heard what he spoke against this place and its people, and because you humbled yourself before me and tore your robes and wept in my presence, I have heard you, declares the Lord" (2 Chron. 34:27).

As a young king, Josiah distinguished himself as one who humbly repented and then led the people in doing what is right. Josiah took personal responsibility. He didn't just blame others for their sin; he took responsibility for the sin of the people by humbling himself and repenting on behalf of the people and their forefathers.

Young person, God always responds positively to us when we humble ourselves and turn to him in repentance. We all need God's grace for our lives. No one is without sin. When we take responsibility for our sin through confession, God lovingly forgives us and gives us a clean start. However, if we refuse to acknowledge our sin, we will only waste away in selfish pride. God gives mercy and grace to the humble.

One way that you will be a leader is by taking personal responsibility. I referenced in the last chapter an experience that I had as a young principal, one that bears repeating in this chapter. We had our students at a carnival. And I made a compromising decision to let some students drive eight-track race cars, even though they were not of the age allowing them to drive. In the process, an accident occurred involving one of those younger students. People had to go to the hospital for treatment, including one of our teachers. Thank God everyone eventually was ok with no serious injuries. However, I realized that I had to take personal responsibility and confess that it was my fault for allowing the underage students to race the course. Through that process and as time progressed, I saw that I had grown in respect with the teacher hurt by the accident. Now many years later, I am still working with that teacher, and we have a great sense of teamwork and esteem for one another.

When I was a young man, my dad gave me the following great advice: "When you're caught in a fault, acknowledge the fault, and the blame stops." As long as we deny what we've done, lie about it, or try to shift the blame to others, the blame keeps coming. But if we learn to repent and confess our fault, we are forgiven and the blame ceases. We may still receive our just punishment, but we can start anew with a clean slate. It's important to take responsibility for our sin.

What is sin? Sin is missing the mark; it's missing the bull's eye of God's righteousness. Psalm 19:12-13 explains five progressions of sin: "Who can discern his errors? Forgive my hidden faults. Keep your servant also from willful sins; may they not rule over me. Then will I be blameless, innocent of great transgression." First, we all have "errors"; we make mistakes. It's part of our human condition. Second, we have "hidden faults"; these are like blind spots for a driver. When a driver is driving down the highway, he has blind spots between what he can see with his rear-view mirror and what he can see with his side-view mirror. That's why the driver needs to make a quick glance back to see if there is an oncoming car when he makes a lane change. Likewise, in our character we all have blind spots—or "hidden faults"—that our loved ones may have to share with us to help us change.

Third, this passage speaks of "willful sins." Willful sins are sins that we still sometimes do although we know them to be wrong. Quite frankly, sometimes we want to deceive ourselves into thinking that a "willful sin" is just a "hidden fault." Part of our process of maturing as a Christian is to recognize that they are really "willful sins" and that we need to stop doing them! If we don't address the "willful sins" in our lives, they can become sins that "rule over me," or ruling sins. These are sins that become our master.

In fact, the Lord made this point to Cain when he said, "If you do what is right, will you not be accepted? But if you do not do what is right, sin is crouching at your door; it desires to have you, but you must master it" (Gen. 4:7). Instead of becoming mastered by sin—sin that becomes addictive or obsessive, we need to master it. If we don't, then the sin will control our lives and could destroy us and hurt those around us. Being mastered by sin leads to the last destructive progression—the "great transgression." Of course, we don't want to go there; we need to deal with sin early and decisively! We don't want sin to become our master. Thank God that he gives us loving boundaries in which we are free to live for his Kingdom: "By them is your servant warned; in keeping them there is great reward" (Ps. 19:11).

In the process of ridding the land of idolatry, King Josiah got rid of all perversions. For example, he got rid of a place used for sacrificing children. Moreover, he removed houses and burned chariots dedicated to the sun.

In addition, King Josiah "got rid of the mediums and spiritists" (2 Kings 23:24). Mediums and spiritists have to do with evil occultic activity, which is consulting with Satanic forces. Of course, we must not be deceived by seemingly innocuous games, such as fortune telling, tarot cards, crystal balls, astrology, Ouija boards, dungeons and dragons, and other evil games. In addition, many secular colleges today offer courses on subjects such as witchcraft and other evil supernatural forces. We must shun all evil activity and be alert to its effects on our fellow students.

Young King Josiah distinguished himself: "Neither before nor after Josiah was there a king like him who turned to the Lord as he did—with all his heart and with all his soul and with all his strength, in accordance with the Law of Moses" (2 Kings 23:25). King Josiah followed the Sh'ma as given in Deuteronomy 6:5: "Love the Lord your God with all your heart and with all your soul and with all your strength." As we focus on loving God with all our being, we will stay clear from being drawn toward evil activities. A heart that loves God wholeheartedly is one that can be steered by God toward right living!

King Josiah proceeded to gather all the people together at the Lord's temple. He read God's rediscovered Word to the people. Next, he renewed the covenant in God's presence for the people to follow the Lord and obey his commands wholeheartedly. King Josiah dramatically led the people: "The king stood by his pillar and renewed the covenant in the presence of the Lord—to follow the Lord and keep his commands, regulations and decrees with all his heart and all his soul, and to obey the words of the covenant written in this book" (2 Chron. 34:31). Then he led the people in making a pledge to follow the Word of God!

Wow! Even though he was young, King Josiah was an outstanding leader! He took personal responsibility for the sin of the people, and he gathered the people together to turn from their sin. He then renewed their covenant to follow God and his Word and led the people in pledging to do so. This verse summarizes his actions as a leader: "Josiah removed all the detestable idols from all the territory belonging to the Israelites, and he had all who were present in Israel serve the Lord their God. As long as he lived, they did not fail to follow the Lord, the God of their fathers" (2 Chron. 34:33).

Finally, Josiah restored the people's observance of Passover. Passover is a remembrance of what God did when the angel of death "passed over" the Israelite homes. The angel passed over their homes because they had placed lamb's blood on their doorframes in preparation for the last plague on Egypt before Pharaoh finally let God's people escape bondage. Because of their obedience, the angel of death did not slay the firstborn child; the angel passed over their homes.

Passover points to Messiah as the perfect Passover Lamb for the sins of the world; as we apply the blood of Christ to our hearts in repentance and faith, God "passes over" our sin and does not count our sin against us. As Romans 6:23 says, "For the wages of sin is death, but the gift of God is eternal life in Christ

Jesus our Lord." When we observe the Lord's Table, we remember Jesus' sacrificial death on the cross as he took the penalty for our sin as the once-for-all, perfect Passover Lamb!

Commending King Josiah, the prophet Jeremiah declared the following: "'He did what was right and just, so all went well with him. He defended the cause of the poor and needy, and so all went well. Is that not what it means to know me?' declares the Lord" (Jer. 22:15-16).

Young person, I encourage you to be like young King Josiah. Discover, read, and obey God's Word. As you learn from God's Word, do the right thing! Don't just *hear* the Word; *do* the Word. And then lead your peers in following God's Word, as King Josiah did. Discover the truths of God's Word and stand for the Lord!

Memory Verse

Psalm 119:11 "I have hidden your word in my heart that I might not sin against you."

EZRA

Study God's Word, Teach God's Word, and Lead God's People in Following God's Word

Part of Jesus' Great Commission to his disciples was to teach God's Word to others. Jesus commissioned all of his disciples with the following: "Go and make disciples of all nations, . . . teaching them to obey everything I have commanded you" (Matt. 28:19-20). As a disciple, God calls you to be involved in teaching others God's Word. Although you may not be called to be a *school* teacher, God still commissions you to *teach* others in one way or another. For instance, you may teach a group Bible study, counsel others one-on-one, or become an evangelist. There are many different ways that God can use you to teach others his Word.

One such individual who studied and learned how to teach God's Word was a man named Ezra.

Ezra was a contemporary of Nehemiah, whom God used to lead his people in rebuilding the walls of Jerusalem. In fact, when the wall was dedicated, Ezra led the ceremonial procession. However, when Ezra was returning from Babylonian exile to Jerusalem before the wall's rebuilding, God's people had not been following his Word. God used both Nehemiah and Ezra to restore his covenant community. The Lord used Ezra to bring his people back together and to call the people to be committed to his Word. Ezra studied God's Word, taught God's Word, and led God's people in following God's Word!

Ezra was from the ancestral priestly line of Aaron. He was a "teacher well versed" in the Word of God, meaning he was very skilled in using the Scriptures (Ezra 7:6). As a scribe, he had studied, copied, and taught the Word of God.

In addition, the Bible is clear that the Lord was with Ezra: "The hand of the Lord his God was on him" (Ezra 7:6). Because the Lord was with Ezra, he courageously called the people to return to God's Word!

Ezra was all about God's Word! In fact, because of his devotion to God's Word, he became a leader of leaders! When he returned from Babylonian exile to Jerusalem, other Jewish leaders came with Ezra. In Ezra's life we see the dynamic that when you follow God's direction, God will give you the power and the strength to fulfill his call! Ezra 7:9 emphasizes this point about him: "For the gracious hand of his God was on him."

The Lord had led Ezra to become an outstanding student of the Word of God. Ezra had devoted himself to studying and teaching God's Word. In 2 Timothy 2:15

we see that the Apostle Paul exhorted the young Timothy to "study to show thyself approved unto God, a workman that needeth not to be ashamed, rightly dividing the word of truth" (KJV). Ezra certainly was a workman who rightly divided God's Word. He was a diligent student of God's Word.

Young person, we see here that the foundation of teaching God's Word is studying God's Word. In order to master any subject, you have to study it diligently. In order to be able to teach the Word of God, you have to study it. Because Ezra was a wholehearted student of God's Word, he became skilled at teaching it!

Ezra 7:10 reinforces this principle: "For Ezra had devoted himself to the study and observance of the Law of the Lord, and to teaching its decrees and laws in Israel." We see here a three-fold progression: study of the Word, observance of the Word, and teaching the Word. First, Ezra was a devoted student of the Word of God; he studied in order to learn God's Word. Because of his study, he gained great understanding of Biblical truth.

Secondly, Ezra observed God's Word. He put into practice what he studied. Jesus emphasized the importance of walking out his Word at the end of his Sermon on the Mount: "Therefore everyone who hears these words of mine and puts them into practice is like a wise man who built his house on the rock. The rain came down, the streams rose, and the winds blew and beat against that house; yet it did not fall, because it had its foundation on the rock" (Matt. 7:24-25). When we put God's Word into practice—not just hearing the Word but doing the Word—we build our lives on the rock; when the inevitable storms of life come, our house and our family will endure the storm because we have a sure foundation!

Finally, Ezra devoted himself to teaching the Word of God. His knowledge of God's Word enabled him to share it effectively. In the process, he became a respected leader among the people.

As Ezra prepared to go to Jerusalem, the Persian king, King Artaxerxes, gave him a letter. This letter permitted others to go with Ezra to Jerusalem. King Artaxerxes also gave Ezra gold and silver in order for him to buy animals to sacrifice to God. The king permitted Ezra to get anything he needed for the temple from the king's royal treasury. He ordered his treasurers to do the following: "Now I, King Artaxerxes, order all the treasurers of Trans-Euphrates to provide with diligence whatever Ezra the priest, a teacher of the Law of the God of heaven, may ask of you" (Ezra 7:21). In addition, the letter gave Ezra authority to appoint judges and officials to administer justice. The king's letter gave Ezra exceeding authority.

The Lord gave Ezra favor from King Artaxerxes, a pagan king. God used a pagan in Ezra's life to promote God's kingdom. Young person, as you grow in the

Lord, God will work favor in your life in such a way that he may even use unbelievers to help you advance his Kingdom!

Ezra gave all praise to the Lord! He praised God for favor with this pagan king who chose to honor God's house. Because God's hand was with Ezra, he took courage and became a leader of God's people! Ezra led these people as they returned to God's city of Jerusalem from their exile in Babylon. Ezra said, "Because the hand of the Lord my God was on me, *I took courage* and gathered leading men from Israel to go up with me" (Ezra 7:28, italics added).

As Ezra called the people to return to God and follow his Word, he led them in important ways. For example, when Ezra learned that God's people had defiled themselves by intermarrying with pagan peoples with their detestable practices, he led the people in repentance and confession of their sin.

You see, the nation of Israel was called to be a holy nation unto the Lord, a people set apart to him. The Lord had commanded them to do the following when they entered the promised land: "Do not intermarry with them [pagan peoples]. Do not give your daughters to their sons or take their daughters for your sons, for they will turn your sons away from following me to serve other gods, and the Lord's anger will burn against you and will quickly destroy you" (Deut. 7:3-4).

Israel was called to be a light to the nations, a people belonging to God, a people called out to be separate from pagan nations, which worshiped idols. Likewise, the Apostle Peter declared the following about the church: "But you are a chosen people, a royal priesthood, a holy nation, a people belonging to God, that you may declare the praises of him who called you out of darkness into his wonderful light" (1 Peter 2:9).

The New Covenant application of this principle for marriage is that we are not to be unequally yoked with unbelievers as husband and wife. To illustrate this point, my wife Silvia and I are of different physical nationalities but we are of *one spiritual holy nation*. The Biblical application now is that we should get married to a committed believer in the Lord as opposed to getting married to an unbeliever. Young people, when you get married, it's very important that you marry a devoted disciple of the Lord. For the lifetime covenant of marriage, it's important that you be "equally yoked" with a committed believer.

The Apostle Paul made this truth plain in 2 Corinthians 6:14-7:1:

> Do not be yoked together with unbelievers. For what do righteousness and wickedness have in common? Or what fellowship can light have with darkness? What harmony is there between Christ and Belial? What does a believer have in common with an unbeliever? What agreement is there between the temple of God and idols? For we are the temple of the living God. As God has said: "I will live with them and walk among them, and I will be their God, and they will be my people."

> "Therefore come out from them and be separate, says the Lord. Touch no unclean thing, and I will receive you."
>
> "I will be a Father to you, and you will be my sons and daughters, says the Lord Almighty."
>
> Since we have these promises, dear friends, let us purify ourselves from everything that contaminates body and spirit, perfecting holiness out of reverence for God.

The reason for not being unequally yoked in marriage is that of idolatry. Again, 2 Corinthians 6:16 asks, "What agreement is there between the temple of God and idols? For we are the temple of the living God." Since our body is the temple of the Holy Spirit, God calls us to marry a person whose God is the Lord, not idols. We are not to marry those who are walking in idolatry. Rather we should marry one who sees his or her body as the temple of the Holy Spirit.

As a leader, Ezra took personal responsibility for the sin of the people. Instead of judging others, Ezra joined in repentance, confession, and in crying out to God. He prayed the following:

> But now, O our God, what can we say after this? For we have disregarded the commands you gave through your servants the prophets when you said: "The land you are entering to possess is a land polluted by the corruption of its peoples. By their detestable practices they have filled it with their impurity from one end to the other. Therefore, do not give your daughters in marriage to their sons or take their daughters for your sons. Do not seek a treaty of friendship with them at any time, that you may be strong and eat the good things of the land and leave it to your children as an everlasting inheritance." (Ezra 9:10-12)

Notice that in Ezra's prayer of repentance, he used the pronoun *we*; instead of judging others, he included himself and took responsibility as a leader for the sins of the people.

In Ezra 10:1, a large group of people gathered around Ezra: "While Ezra was praying and confessing, weeping and throwing himself down before the house of God, a large crowd of Israelites—men, women, and children—gathered around him. They too wept bitterly." After Ezra's prayer, he waited for the people to respond. A man named Shecaniah came forward and confessed to their unfaithfulness to God and said that they should make a covenant to correct their sin. He then encouraged Ezra to take courage and to lead the people in doing what is right: "Rise up; this matter is in your hands. We will support you, so *take courage* and do it" (Ezra 10:4, italics added). Ezra proceeded to courageously lead the people in correcting their wrongdoing.

Ezra's legacy is that of a courageous champion who led the people in returning to God's Word. He was a student of the Word, a teacher of the Word, and a leader in calling God's people to follow God's Word!

Young person, Ezra led the people in taking responsibility for their sin, correcting their wrong, and doing what God had called them to be—the set-apart people belonging to God. Because Ezra had studied God's Word and practiced it, he had the courage of conviction to lead the people in bringing about repentance—the needed change—to follow God's Word. I encourage you to do the same: be a student of God's Word, put into practice God's Word, and when the opportunities of life come, lead your peers with all courage to follow God's Word! The Lord is with you!

Memory Passage

2 Timothy 3:16-17 "All Scripture is God-breathed and is useful for teaching, rebuking, correcting and training in righteousness, so that the man of God may be thoroughly equipped for every good work."

NEHEMIAH

Take Responsibility for Leading the Team to Achieve the Goal

In 446 B.C., a man named Nehemiah was the cupbearer to the king of Persia, King Artaxerxes. Nehemiah was a contemporary of Ezra. (We saw in the last chapter that the Lord used Ezra to restore his Word to his people.) Nehemiah served as cupbearer to the king, a very high position that put him in close proximity to the king. However, Nehemiah showed that he wasn't concerned with protecting his position and his wealth; instead he chose to be concerned for his people. Nehemiah was willing to give up position, riches, and even his life if necessary for God's cause. Nehemiah is an outstanding example of a leader who saw a very important need and took responsibility for leading his people to achieve a worthy goal.

In Nehemiah chapter one, Nehemiah's brother Hanani and others gave Nehemiah the following report: "Those who survived the exile and are back in the province are in great trouble and disgrace. The wall of Jerusalem is broken down, and its gates have been burned with fire" (Neh. 1:3). When Nehemiah heard of this terrible situation, he responded with great sorrow and weeping. He started fasting and praying before the Lord.

You see, Jerusalem was God's city. Because its walls were broken down, the city had both a security issue and a symbolic issue. Not only did it mean that the people were vulnerable to attack; it also meant that God's people were in disgrace. The lack of secure walls around Jerusalem served as an invitation to neighboring peoples to attack them. People would mock God and his people because of this state of affairs.

The first thing that Nehemiah did was to take responsibility before God. A man of prayer, Nehemiah had a relationship with God that enabled him to call upon God at any moment. He confessed the sins of his people, including his family's sins and his own sins. He took responsibility for failing to follow God's Word. And he also reminded the Lord that if his people repented, then God would gather them back "to the place I have chosen as a dwelling for my Name" (Neh. 1:9). Then Nehemiah asked God for favor as he began to take action to rectify this problem: "O Lord, let your ear be attentive to the prayer of this your servant and to the prayer of your servants who delight in revering your name. Give your servant success today by granting him favor in the presence of this man" (Neh. 1:11).

That man was the king he served as cupbearer—King Artaxerxes. Nehemiah asked God for favor when he would go before the king. While Nehemiah was performing his duty as cupbearer, the king noticed that Nehemiah was sad and asked him why. Although Nehemiah was very fearful to bring his request before the king, Nehemiah explained to him that "the city where my fathers are buried lies in ruins, and its gates have been destroyed by fire" (Neh. 2:3). When the king asked him what he wanted, Nehemiah breathed a quick prayer to the Lord before humbly asking the following: "If it pleases the king and if your servant has found favor in his sight, let him send me to the city in Judah where my fathers are buried so that I can rebuild it" (Neh. 2:5). The king granted Nehemiah's request and made him governor of Judah, the province wherein lies the city of Jerusalem.

Nehemiah proceeded to request letters for safe travel and for timber. "And because the gracious hand of my God was upon me, the king granted my requests" (Neh. 2:8). God's favor upon Nehemiah was making the way for him!

After Nehemiah traveled to Jerusalem, he assessed the problem. Going out secretly at night, he evaluated the broken walls and gates. He kept the matter to himself before going public.

After Nehemiah evaluated the matter, he took responsibility by gathering the people together and inspiring them to rebuild the walls of Jerusalem. He clearly showed them the problem—that it was an exceedingly serious one needing to be rectified: "You see the trouble we are in: Jerusalem lies in ruins, and its gates have been burned with fire" (Neh. 2:17). Then Nehemiah communicated the vision: "Come, let us rebuild the wall of Jerusalem, and we will no longer be in disgrace" (Neh. 2:17). After declaring the goal, Nehemiah made it clear that God was with him and was inspiring him to action: "I also told them about the gracious hand of my God upon me and what the king had said to me" (Neh. 2:18). Nehemiah was letting them know that our God is a living and active God who will help us. We only need to step out in faith!

The people responded enthusiastically to Nehemiah's leadership: "Let us start rebuilding" (Neh. 2:18). Thus this great building project was begun!

As they started the work, Nehemiah had to confront enemies that tried to snuff out the work before it even got off the ground. He had to confront pagan rulers commanding the larger province. Sanballat, Tobiah, and Geshem ridiculed Nehemiah and his people: "What is this you are doing? Are you rebelling against the king?" (Neh. 2:19).

Young person, as a leader you should expect that you will encounter opposition. If you are leading important work—work involving change—you can expect to receive pushback. Don't get discouraged. Keep your eyes on the Lord and on the work he has given you to do.

Nehemiah spoke forthrightly to the mockers: “The God of heaven will give us success. We his servants will start rebuilding, but as for you, you have no share in Jerusalem or any claim or historic right to it” (Neh. 2:20).

Well, the people went to work rebuilding the walls. Led by the example of the priests, they gave themselves wholeheartedly to the task: “Eliashib the high priest and his fellow priests went to work and rebuilt the Sheep Gate” (Neh. 3:1). Nehemiah organized the people into teams that had responsibility to complete a certain part of the wall. Often he had them work on sections close to their homes and neighborhoods.

Most of the people worked wholeheartedly, but some didn’t. Nehemiah 3:5 tells us that some “nobles would not put their shoulders to the work under their supervisors.” Young person, what does it mean to put your shoulders to the work? What does it mean to listen to your supervisors? For some reason, these particular nobles were unwilling to listen and to follow cheerfully. Perhaps they thought that the work was beneath them.

When we’re part of a team, we need to work willingly and wholeheartedly in whatever the Lord has given us to do. In fact, whether you’re working as a student, on your house chores, as a volunteer, on a job, or in the church, learn to give yourself wholeheartedly to the work. As you do so faithfully, you will experience promotion from the Lord.

As the building moved forward, we see that Nehemiah had to work with all kinds of different people. Most of the people worked wholeheartedly. Different groups contributed to rebuilding the wall. Often they worked together as families. For instance, Nehemiah 3:12 says that Shallum, who was the son of a district ruler in Jerusalem, “repaired the next section with the help of his daughters.” Here we see that children also participated in rebuilding the wall of Jerusalem.

As the work advanced, Nehemiah had to continue to deal with opposition. He encouraged the people through these distractions. Sanballat and Tobiah resumed their ridicule. Tobiah mocked them: “What they are building—if even a fox climbed up on it, he would break down their wall of stones!” (Neh. 4:3).

Nehemiah responded by praying: “Hear us, O our God, for we are despised. Turn their insults back on their own heads . . .” (Neh. 4:4). Instead of attacking Sanballat and Tobiah, Nehemiah appealed to God. Because Nehemiah would not let the people get distracted by the mockers, the people were able to continue to work: “So we rebuilt the wall till all of it reached half its height, for the people worked with all their heart” (Neh. 4:6).

When their enemies heard that Nehemiah and the people were making headway, they got extremely angry: “They all plotted together to come and fight against Jerusalem and stir up trouble against it” (Neh. 4:8). However, Nehemiah led the people by taking both spiritual action and practical action. Nehemiah 4:9 summarizes Nehemiah’s leadership philosophy: “But we prayed to our God and posted a guard day and night to meet this threat." Spiritually, Nehemiah led the people in prayer; practically, he posted a round-the-clock guard to watch out for any attacks.

Nehemiah took responsibility by refusing to be distracted from the goal. He refused to be intimidated by deceptive threats. He was committed to completely rebuilding the wall of Jerusalem! He kept his eyes on this God-ordained objective.

As they continued to work, Nehemiah had to encourage the people through weariness and discouragement. Internally, he had to deal with negative comments from his own people: "The strength of the laborers is giving out, and there is so much rubble that we cannot rebuild the wall" (Neh. 4:10). Externally, he had to deal with increasing threats from their enemies: "Before they know it or see us, we will be right there among them and will kill them and put an end to the work" (Neh. 4:11). After that threat, fellow Jews living near their enemies repeatedly made this discouraging comment: "Wherever you turn, they will attack us" (Neh. 4:12).

Young person, be courageous when you are faced with threats and opposition. Stand firm in the purpose the Lord has given you. In addition, sometimes it will seem that you are being attacked with bad news from all directions. Through the onslaught of attacks, I encourage you to stay steady.

Instead of getting discouraged by all these negative comments, Nehemiah took action to meet the threat: "Therefore I stationed some of the people behind the lowest points of the wall at the exposed places, posting them by families, with their swords, spears and bows" (Neh. 4:13). In other words, Nehemiah posted guards behind the workers so that they would be able to focus on their work without having to look over their shoulders to see if they were being attacked.

After Nehemiah made sure that his plan was in order, he stood before all the people and gave an inspiring speech: "Don't be afraid of them. Remember the Lord, who is great and awesome, and fight for your brothers, your sons and your daughters, your wives and your homes" (Neh. 4:14). By reminding the people to "remember the Lord," Nehemiah was telling them that the Lord was with them and would help them to overcome. He also encouraged them by challenging them to fight courageously for their families. This was a rallying cry! He encouraged them to fight for their family's freedom—to fight for this righteous cause! If you know you're in the right, that gives you courage!

Nehemiah dealt with the threatening crisis with faith-filled action and words! "When our enemies heard that we were aware of their plot and that God had frustrated it, we all returned to the wall, each to his own work" (Neh. 4:15).

Nehemiah continued to take clear leadership steps. He had half of the men work on the wall while the other half carried weapons in case of attack. He posted officers to stand guard behind those working on the wall. As workers carried materials, they carried the items in one hand and their weapon in the other hand. "Each of the builders wore his sword at his side as he worked" (Neh. 4:18).

In addition, Nehemiah continued to rally the people with practical and encouraging communication: "The work is extensive and spread out, and we are widely separated from each other along the wall. Wherever you hear the sound of the trumpet, join us there. Our God will fight for us!" (Neh. 4:19-20). The sound of the trumpet would be a signal for the people to gather together to fend off any attack. Strategically, Nehemiah knew that if they were attacked, it would be imperative that they stand together tightly to deter the enemy. Constantly encouraging the people with his words, Nehemiah knew the importance of unified teamwork.

The steps Nehemiah took as a leader enabled the people to keep their focus on rebuilding the wall. They worked from dawn until dark. In addition, Nehemiah was not afraid to call the people to some difficult requirements that he knew were needed for success. He communicated what was needed to the people: "Have every man and his helper stay inside Jerusalem at night, so they can serve us as guards by night and workmen by day" (Neh. 4:22). He required the workers to stay inside the city during the night to serve as guards.

At the same time, Nehemiah didn't ask the people to do what he was unwilling to do himself. He led by example: "Neither I nor my brothers nor my men nor the guards with me took off our clothes; each had his weapon, even when he went for water" (Neh. 4:23). Nehemiah provided both spiritual and practical leadership; he encouraged the people by word and by example. According to the historian Josephus in his work *Antiquities*, Nehemiah "himself made the rounds of the city by night, never tiring either through work or lack of food and sleep, neither of which he took for pleasure but as a necessity" (*Antiquities*, 11.5.8).

Because of Nehemiah's strong leadership, the project moved forward. Nehemiah continued to lead the people, including dealing with conflicts among his own people. When he was promoted, Nehemiah didn't take privilege to himself. Instead, he continued to lead by example. Nehemiah simply prayed the following: "Remember me with favor, O my God, for all I have done for these people" (Neh. 5:19).

In Nehemiah chapter six, we see that Nehemiah had to deal with purposeful scheming by his enemies. His enemies increasingly sought to sabotage the project. As the opposition saw the progress being made, they tried to deceive and distract him: "Sanballat and Geshem sent me this message: 'Come, let us meet together in one of the villages on the plain of Ono'" (Neh. 6:2). However, Nehemiah could see through their manipulations and kept his focus. He sent them this message: "I am carrying on a great project and cannot do down. Why should the work stop while I leave it and go down to you?" (Neh. 6:3).

Their scheming was relentless. Four times they sent the message, and four times Nehemiah persistently refused. As a leader, you can't give in to ungodly pressure and manipulation. Continue to take your cue from the Lord. You must stand firm and strong.

On their fifth message, Nehemiah's enemies made the false accusation that he was preparing a revolt and that he intended to have prophets proclaim him to be king. This was a very serious accusation because the Persian kings of that time would take severe action if they thought someone was seeking to usurp their power. In fact, Nehemiah's enemies sent the message in an "unsealed letter," meaning that their accusations could be broadcast to others (Neh. 6:5).

Young person, don't be intimidated when someone falsely accuses you publicly. This has happened to me when a person falsely accused me with an "unsealed letter." This person sent an email to me; but instead of just sending it to me, the person also sent it to many others as well. I could have been very disconcerted by this personal attack; but I entrusted myself to the Lord, and he looked out for my reputation. When this kind of manipulation occurs, don't be fearful. Just stay steady and know that the Lord will be your defense. Psalm 37:5-6 says, "Commit your way to the Lord; trust in him and he will do this: He will make your righteousness shine like the dawn, the justice of your cause like the noonday sun."

Well, even though Nehemiah was being falsely and publicly accused, he refused to be intimidated. He responded to Sanballat and Geshem with the following: "Nothing like what you are saying is happening; you are just making it up out of your head" (Neh. 6:8). Nehemiah called them out. He refused to be distracted from the work.

Young person, don't let people influenced by the enemy intimidate you! Keep your focus on the Lord and his work!

Nehemiah would not let the people get weak out of fear. "They were all trying to frighten us, thinking, 'Their hands will get too weak for the work, and it will not be completed'" (Neh. 6:9). You see, when the enemy attacks you with fear, you can become physically weak—your hands feel weak. However, if you focus on God's presence with you, he will give you the strength you need. Nehemiah prayed, "Now strengthen my hands" (Neh. 6:9). The Lord is our strength!

Still, the attacks didn't stop. Nehemiah's enemies made a last-ditch effort to stop the project. Sanballat hired a false prophet to try to deceive Nehemiah. This false prophet told Nehemiah, "Let us meet in the house of God, inside the temple, and let us close the temple doors, because men are coming to kill you—by night they are coming to kill you" (Neh. 6:10). This false prophecy was another manipulation to try to get Nehemiah to hide himself and to protect himself out of fear. In fact, the prophet was trying to get Nehemiah to hide himself inside God's temple. But what would that do? That would take Nehemiah away from the very people he was seeking to lead.

Nehemiah was a leader with a great cause. He needed to stay with the people and to continue leading them. If he went into hiding and was absent from them, the people would get discouraged. With God's help, Nehemiah kept his focus on the task. He said, "Should a man like me run away? Or should one like me go into the temple to save his life? I will not go!" (Neh. 6:11). Nehemiah again discerned that his enemies Tobiah and Sanballat had hired this prophet to get Nehemiah to do something wrong in an effort to protect himself, for it was against the law for a layman to go into the sanctuary. And Nehemiah was a layman, not a priest. Nehemiah would not hide in the temple even to save his life. Nehemiah knew that if he did such a thing, "then they would give me a bad name to discredit me" (Neh. 6:13).

When you are leading with conviction for a righteous cause, there will be people who will try to come up with ways to discredit you and to shame you. When this occurs, you have to deal righteously with those doing wrong. In the process, you most likely will come under attack. Although conflict is never pleasant, learn to recognize that this is part of being a leader. Instead of getting discouraged, keep your focus on the Lord and living according to his Word. He will be your defense!

Nehemiah courageously continued to lead the people and did not give into the temptation to protect himself out of fear. Therefore, the people's morale remained strong. Nehemiah encouraged them to stay with the task. That's what godly leaders do!

Nehemiah led his team by example. And he is an example for us today as well! I encourage you to learn from his life. Amid the opposition of his enemies, he again turned to the Lord in prayer: "Remember Tobiah and Sanballat, O my God, because of what they have done; remember also the prophetess Noadiah and the rest of the prophets who have been trying to intimidate me" (Neh. 6:14).

Young person, as you grow into leadership, I encourage you to be alert to people falsely seeking to intimidate you from the cause the Lord has given you. In order to keep moving in the right direction, keep your focus on the Lord and on his Word. When God gives you a purpose, stay focused on achieving that mission!

Nehemiah tells us of the completion of this great project: "So the wall was completed on the twenty-fifth of Elul, in fifty-two days. When all our enemies heard about this, all the surrounding nations were afraid and lost their self-confidence, because they realized that this work had been done with the help of our God" (Neh. 6:15-16). With the Lord's help, Nehemiah led the people to rebuild the walls of God's city in fifty-two days!

Young person, God needs builders for his kingdom—servants of the Lord who are willing to give of themselves to advance his cause! I encourage you to be a wholehearted servant leader who follows God's call. He is calling you to greatness! Let's learn from Nehemiah who had a close relationship with the Lord—one that inspired him to accomplish an important work for his kingdom!

Memory Verses

Nehemiah 4:9 "But we prayed to our God and posted a guard day and night to meet this threat."

Nehemiah 4:14 "Don't be afraid of them. Remember the Lord, who is great and awesome, and fight for your brothers, your sons and your daughters, your wives and your homes."

ESTHER AND MORDECAI

God Created You for a Reason

The Lord said in Jeremiah 29:11: "For I know the plans I have for you, plans to prosper you and not to harm you, plans to give you hope and a future." My mother often confessed that Scripture over my life, and it gave me a real sense of destiny that God had a special plan for my life. In the Bible, we see that God had a special purpose for a young lady who came to a very influential position. Indeed, God has always used those willing to follow him for his purposes. Let me tell you the inspiring story of Esther and her older cousin Mordecai.

In the capital of Susa, King Xerxes, the king of the Persian Empire, held a seven-day banquet. He and his guests had been indulging in too much wine, and the king used bad judgment. He commanded that his queen—Queen Vashti—come before them and parade herself before them, for she was beautiful to behold. Well, Vashti refused the king's request; and the king, out of anger for this slight, deposed her.

As a result of this action, King Xerxes consulted his advisors. Now that he had deposed his queen, what should he do? He decided to look for a new queen. In effect, he conducted a beauty contest! In all of his realm, a search for beautiful young maidens was made. The ladies chosen would undergo twelve months of beauty treatments before they would present themselves before the king, after which he would choose his new queen.

The Bible tells us that Mordecai, a Jew living in the city of Susa, was the older cousin of a beautiful young Jewish lady named Esther: "Mordecai had a cousin named Hadassah, whom he had brought up because she had neither father or mother. This girl, who was also known as Esther, was lovely in form and features, and Mordecai had taken her as his own daughter when her father and mother died" (Esther 2:7). In effect, Mordecai was like a father to Esther.

Esther, of Jewish nationality, was chosen to be part of the king's contest. After undergoing her twelve months of beauty treatments, she went before King Xerxes. Lo and behold, Esther was chosen by King Xerxes to be his new queen! However, following the instructions of Mordecai, Esther kept her family background and nationality a secret.

While Mordecai was keeping track of Esther at the king's gate, he overheard a plot to assassinate King Xerxes. He told Queen Esther who reported it to Xerxes;

she also gave credit to Mordecai for uncovering the plot to kill him. Mordecai's action of saving the king was recorded in the king's official record book.

Some time later, King Xerxes decided to honor a certain official in his royal court. This man's name was Haman. Because the king had bestowed honor on Haman, the royal officials would bow down to him at the king's gate; however, Mordecai would neither bow down to Haman nor honor him. The royal officials questioned Mordecai, "Why do you disobey the king's command?" (Esther 3:3). When they saw that Mordecai continued to refuse to obey the king's command, "they told Haman about it to see whether Mordecai's behavior would be tolerated for he had told them he was a Jew" (Esther 3:4).

When Haman found out that Mordecai was not honoring him and that he was a Jew, he was furious. However, in his rage, Haman resolved not only to kill Mordecai but also to exterminate all the Jewish people—all of God's people—from all over Xerxes' realm.

Once Haman had decided to take this extreme step, he used a game of chance to determine the date to obliterate the Jewish people. Haman oversaw the casting of the pur (the lot) to choose the date for this diabolical act. After this despicable decision, Haman secured King Xerxes' permission to destroy "a certain people" (Esther 3:8). (Of course, this "certain people" was God's chosen people, the Jews.) He then secured an edict written in the name of King Xerxes and sealed it with the king's signet ring: "Dispatches were sent by couriers to all the king's provinces with the order to destroy, kill and annihilate all the Jews—young and old, women and little children—on a single day, the thirteenth day of the twelfth month, the month of Adar, and to plunder their goods" (Esther 3:13). That was the day on which the pur—the lot of chance—had fallen.

Of course, this act was a blatant form of prejudice. In fact, it was prejudice against God's people. *Any* prejudice against a certain people is wrong. We should never prejudge a person based on their nationality. All people, no matter what their background, are created in God's image and have intrinsic value.

Well, Mordecai and the Jews wept bitterly over this decree. Out of his hatred, Haman was following through on a hideous plot to kill off an entire people. When Esther heard of Mordecai's distress, she found out the reason. Mordecai told Esther of Haman's evil plot to kill all the Jewish people in the empire.

Although Esther was understandably hesitant at first because of the serious risk involved, Mordecai convinced her to intervene and approach the king. It was a very dangerous step to come before the king without being called to do so. If the king did not bestow his golden scepter to the individual, that person would be summarily put to death.

However, Mordecai influenced her with convictional persuasion: "Do not think that because you are in the king's house you alone of all the Jews will escape. For if you remain silent at this time, relief and deliverance for the Jews will arise from another place, but you and your father's family will perish. And who knows but that you have come to royal position for such a time as this?" (Esther 4:13-14). Acting as Esther's father, Mordecai provided her with a convictional basis to stand with God's people and to be a courageous leader for a righteous cause, even as he knew that Esther would be risking her life by doing so. Also, through Mordecai's words, we can see that even though God is not mentioned, Mordecai is speaking of God's promise to keep and propagate his people.

Young person, Mordecai's message to Esther is important for all of us. First, Mordecai gave her convictional courage to stand for the Lord and his people. Second, he pointed out that if Esther missed this opportunity, deliverance would come through some other means.

Young person, if you miss God's opportunity for you, he will use someone else to achieve his plans. I encourage you to *desire* to be used by God! Remember that God created you for a reason! The distinguished American writer Mark Twain declared the importance of understanding one's purpose: "The two most important days in a person's life are the day he was born and the day he finds out why." There is a lot of truth to these words. For all of us, when the Lord sparks a fire within us regarding his plan, we need to recognize that plan and wholeheartedly pursue his purpose for our lives!

In addition, as a champion for the Lord, you need to speak up with convictional courage when you see wrong being done. We should not be silent when we have the opportunity to stand for what is right. With your peers, if others are bullying one of your classmates, you need to speak up and say, "That's not right!" You need to defend those being attacked.

Again, Mordecai challenged Esther that she may have ". . . come to royal position for such a time as this" (Esther 4:14). He helped her to see that this attack against her people (and God's people) may be the very reason for her becoming queen. In other words, it wasn't just circumstance that she had become queen; God wanted to use Esther in his sovereign purpose—to save his people!

Well, Esther responded courageously: "Go, gather together all the Jews who are in Susa, and fast for me. Do not eat or drink for three days, night or day. I and my maids will fast as you do. When this is done, I will go to the king, even though it is against the law. And if I perish, I perish" (Esther 4:16). In effect, Esther was willing to sacrifice her life—to risk everything—to be used by God to save her people. Of course, along with the fasting, the Jews would be praying for God's deliverance!

When the time came, Esther approached King Xerxes. She took her life into her own hands. She could have been killed for approaching the king without being summoned. However, King Xerxes showed Esther favor and extended his golden scepter, thus giving her an audience with the king.

Esther asked the king to come with Haman to a banquet she had prepared for him. At the banquet, King Xerxes asked Esther, "Now what is your petition? It will be given you. And what is your request? Even up to half the kingdom, it will be granted" (Esther 5:6). Esther then asked the king along with Haman to come to a second banquet the next day. Perhaps she was trusting the Lord for the right moment to share what was on her heart.

Young person, there will be times when something very important is on your heart. Perhaps you need to share something needful with a person in authority. However, it's very important that you commit that matter into the Lord's hands and trust him to provide you with the right opportunity to talk with that person. Proverbs 3:5-6 gives good counsel: "Trust in the Lord with all your heart and lean not on your own understanding; in all your ways acknowledge him, and he will make your paths straight." Commit the matter into the Lord's hands and trust him for the right timing. He will lead you by the Holy Spirit.

Well, the evil Haman went out from Esther's banquet feeling "happy and in high spirits" that he was the only one along with the king who was invited to the queen's banquet (Esther 5:9). However, "when he saw Mordecai at the king's gate and observed that he neither rose nor showed fear in his presence, he was filled with rage against Mordecai" (Esther 5:9).

When Haman complained bitterly to his friends and his wife about Mordecai, they advised him to have Mordecai hanged on a gallows. He took their advice and had the gallows built for the purpose of killing Mordecai.

Well, that night King Xerxes couldn't sleep. He had the king's official record book, which chronicled all the important actions of his reign, to be read to him. When he heard of how Mordecai had uncovered the plot to assassinate him, he realized that he should reward Mordecai for saving his life. Of course, through all of these developments, we can see God working behind the scenes to orchestrate events and to give Mordecai favor.

The next morning King Xerxes asked his advisor, the evil Haman, what he should do for the man he wishes to honor. Thinking that the king wanted to honor him, Haman told the king that he should give him a royal robe and "lead him on the horse through the city streets, proclaiming before him, 'This is what is done for the man the king delights to honor!'" (Esther 6:9).

Then the king gave Haman devastating news. He told Haman to honor the man Haman so utterly hated—Mordecai! What a turn of events for Haman! Of course, he was crestfallen! Even his wife and friends saw that he was doomed.

At the banquet the next day with Haman, the king asked Queen Esther what her petition was. Esther responded, "If I have found favor with you, O king, and if it pleases your majesty, grant me my life—this is my petition. And spare my people—this is my request. For I and my people have been sold for destruction and slaughter and annihilation. If we had merely been sold as male and female slaves, I would have kept quiet, because no such distress would justify disturbing the king" (Esther 7:3-4).

When King Xerxes asked Esther who was causing her people such terrible trouble, she answered, "The adversary and enemy is this vile Haman" (Esther 7:6).

This turn of events is a perfect example of what is called "poetic justice." Here Haman had lied to the king in order to bring about the extermination of the Jews. Now he would pay the price. The raging Haman had tried to hang Mordecai, who had previously uncovered a plot to kill the king; but through Esther's wisdom, the tables were turned *against* Haman and *toward* Mordecai, Esther, and the Jews. Haman was hanged on the very gallows that he had prepared for Mordecai.

The signet ring that the king had given to Haman now was given to Mordecai. After Esther appealed to King Xerxes once again about the terrible order to destroy her people, King Xerxes gave her and Mordecai permission to write another decree, sealed with the king's signet ring, to counterattack Haman's earlier order to kill the Jews.

Mordecai proceeded to write an order in the king's name that the Jews could protect themselves, defend themselves, and attack any army that intended to come against them. In every city and province the Jews celebrated! The Jews were victorious! The Jews became so influential that even people from other nationalities converted to Judaism!

Esther 9:3-4 tells us that Mordecai's influence spread far and wide on behalf of God's people: "And all the nobles of the provinces, the satraps, the governors and the king's administrators helped the Jews, because fear of Mordecai had seized them. Mordecai was prominent in the palace; his reputation spread throughout the provinces, and he became more and more powerful." And so to this day the Jewish people celebrate their victory with the festival of Purim on the fourteenth and fifteenth days of the month of Adar "as the time when the Jews got relief from their enemies, and as the month when their sorrow was turned into joy and their mourning into a day of celebration. [Mordecai] wrote them to observe the days as days of feasting and joy and giving presents of food to one another and gifts to the poor" (Esther 9:22). These two days are called Purim from the word *pur* for casting the lot, which Haman had used to choose the day of the Jews' destruction. However, Haman's plot was turned "back onto his own head" (Esther 9:25).

God blessed Mordecai's leadership: "Mordecai the Jew was second in rank to King Xerxes, preeminent among the Jews, and held in high esteem by his many fellow Jews, because he worked for the good of his people and spoke up for the welfare of all the Jews" (Esther 10:3). Mordecai served God's people well!

As we can see, God sovereignly protected, defended, and preserved his people. Far from being subject to Haman's game of chance, the Jews were in God's hands—God was (and is) always in control. The Lord used Mordecai and Esther to save his people. He created and prepared Esther for a distinct purpose; he created her for a reason—to save his people! God was watching over all these affairs to preserve his people, through whom would eventually come the Savior of the world, Jesus Christ!

And young person, God created you for a distinct purpose and reason as well! You are a work of art—God's creation! Ephesians 2:10 tells us, "For we are God's workmanship, created in Christ Jesus to do good works, which God prepared in advance for us to do." You may not know your future, but God does. He knows your future, and he has a definite plan for your life. You can be absolutely confident of that. To help you find out why you were created, I encourage you to seek God with all your heart as well as to listen to your parents just as Esther listened to Mordecai.

Remember: God is working behind the scenes. He is watching over you and has your best interests in mind. Trust him. Just as God used Mordecai and Esther for his sovereign purpose, he will use you for his purpose as well!

Memory Verse

Ephesians 2:10 "For we are God's workmanship, created in Christ Jesus to do good works, which God prepared in advance for us to do."

JOB

Trust God Even through Tragedy

The Bible speaks of a man named Job who was upright in all of his life. Although he was not sinless, Job was marked by integrity and righteousness. God blessed him with seven sons, three daughters, and large herds of many different kinds of livestock. Job 1:3 says, "He was the greatest man among all the people of the East."

However, Job was struck with tragedy. God broached with Satan the consideration of Job and his character: "Have you considered my servant Job? There is no one on earth like him; he is blameless and upright, a man who fears God and shuns evil" (Job 1:8).

Satan, whose name means "accuser," proceeded to challenge God regarding Job's character: "Does Job fear God for nothing? Have you not put a hedge around him and his household and everything he has? You have blessed the work of his hands, so that his flocks and herds are spread throughout the land. But stretch out your hand and strike everything he has, and he will surely curse you to your face" (Job 1:9-11). By this argument, Satan asserted that Job only followed God and was righteous because of God's protection and blessing on his life. Satan claimed that if God's blessing was taken away, Job would no longer seek to please him. To put the issue to the test, God gave Satan permission to do whatever he wanted to Job's possessions; however, he could not strike Job's physical body.

Have you ever felt as if bad news comes in droves? Well, that's what happened to Job. Job was bombarded with bad news from four different messengers. The first messenger shared that all of his oxen and donkeys had been stolen and the servants caring for them were killed. The second messenger reported that all of his sheep and his sheep servants were consumed by fire. The third messenger revealed that all of Job's camels were stolen and those servants were killed. Finally, the fourth messenger divulged the devastating news that in a "mighty wind" like a tornado, all of his sons and daughters were killed (Job 1:19).

Through all of this bad news, Job did not speak—until he heard that his children were killed. He then mourned. When he heard of his children's demise, "Job got up and tore his robe and shaved his head" in mourning (Job 1:20). Then Job responded by worshiping the Lord: "Then he fell to the ground in worship and said: 'Naked I came from my mother's womb, and naked I will depart. The Lord gave and the Lord has taken away; may the name of the Lord be praised'" (Job 1:20-21). Amid this heartbreaking tragedy, Job continued to worship God. He saw the work of God in his sovereignty.

Young person, we learn from Job a valuable lesson when faced with heartbreak. When going through tragedy, we may not know the reasons for it. Our natural response when bad things happen might be to lash out at God, but Job did not do so. Job passed the test! Job 1:22 says, "In all this, Job did not sin by charging God with wrongdoing." Job didn't sin by blaming God; rather, he continued to worship God.

Well, the test continued. In Job 2:3, God again asked Satan, "Have you considered my servant Job? There is no one on earth like him; he is blameless and upright, a man who fears God and shuns evil. And he still maintains his integrity, though you incited me against him to ruin him without any reason."

Satan again challenged God: "Skin for skin! A man will give all he has for his own life. But stretch out your hand and strike his flesh and bones, and he will surely curse you to your face" (Job 2:4-5). Satan was saying that if Job had to undergo severe physical pain, then he would curse God. God then made the decision to allow Satan to cause Job physical malady.

Satan proceeded to bring destruction on Job's health. He "afflicted Job with painful sores from the soles of his feet to the top of his head" (Job 2:7). As Job was trying to get some relief by scraping his sores with a broken piece of pottery, his wife scolded him: "Are you still holding on to your integrity? Curse God and die!" (Job 2:9). Even Job's wife berated him and told him to curse God.

Job admonished his wife: "You are talking like a foolish woman. Shall we accept good from God, and not trouble?" (Job 2:10). The Bible tells us that Job continued to honor the Lord: "In all this, Job did not sin in what he said" (Job 2:10).

Job's response to his wife teaches us that experiencing difficult tragedies doesn't necessarily mean that we are being disciplined for sin. The trials that we are undergoing may be for our growth and refinement in the Lord. They may be a test. In fact, we may never know why we are experiencing a certain trial until we get to heaven.

However, we do know that the enemy is silenced. After this point in Job's story, the accuser Satan no longer appears; we no longer hear from him for the rest of the book. Satan is silenced. In fact, Revelation 12:10-11 declares, "Now have come the salvation and the power and the kingdom of our God, and the authority of his Christ. For the accuser of our brothers, who accuses them before our God day and night, has been hurled down. They overcame him by the blood of the Lamb and by the word of their testimony; they did not love their lives so much as to shrink from death." Satan, the accuser and the father of lies, has been "hurled down." He has been silenced!

Satan is the ultimate "trash talker." Unfortunately, too often in professional sporting events, we see trash talkers—athletes who like to get in their opponents' heads and spew all kinds of negativity to get them off their game. Well, Satan is the ultimate trash talker. He is like a bully who tries to intimidate other students in school. However, we need to remember that Satan is on a leash. He can talk "trash," but he cannot hurt us if we remember our overcoming position in Messiah.

In order to overcome the attacks of the enemy, we need to remember God's strategy in Revelation 12:11: that of claiming the blood of Messiah and confessing the word of our testimony. We need to remember our testimony—how God has worked in our life. We need to use the sword of the Spirit, the Word of God, to take captive the lies and accusations of the enemy. And we know that we don't have to shrink from death because our eternity is secure with God in heaven! As Christians covered by the blood of Christ, the accuser Satan is silenced; his threats are null and void!

Well, Job's friends saw that his grief was great. In fact, it was so great that for the first seven days and nights, they just sat with him in silence. They should have kept silent! Often, the best thing you can do for someone enduring terrible tragedy is to be with that person and just offer a sympathetic heart without too many words.

Eventually Job's "friends" began to speak. One friend said that Job was experiencing this suffering because of his *sin*. Another friend told Job that he should *repent* of his sin. His third friend *pleaded* with Job to repent of his sin. In other words, all three friends assumed that Job was enduring his terrible suffering because of some sin that he had committed.

In Job 13:13-18 Job defended himself before his friends:

> Keep silent and let me speak; then let come to me what may. Why do I put myself in jeopardy and take my life in my hands? Though he slay me, yet will I hope in him; I will surely defend my ways to his face. Indeed, this will turn out for my deliverance, for no godless man would dare come before him! Listen carefully to my words; let your ears take in what I say. Now that I have prepared my case, I know I will be vindicated.

Job knew that God would ultimately vindicate him. Job would speak face to face with the Lord. Job would not curse God, and he would not run from God. Instead, he would confront God directly. He said that even if God would kill him, he would still place his hope in the Lord. What faith!

We see in this passage that Job would "surely defend my ways to his face" (Job 13:15). Job defended his ways directly to God. Instead of turning away from God and running from him, Job faced God.

We learn from Job that when faced with difficult tragedies, we can have questions and even complain, but we need to talk directly to God. If we are complaining, complain to God; if we are questioning, question God. But don't run from him! Don't turn away from God. Even if you're angry and upset, stay engaged with God. Deal directly with God!

Sometimes when I am going through a trial, I'll go on a run to a wooded area along a creek that is very secluded. At a certain point when I know that no one else is around, I might yell out, "God!!!" I cry out to God. I pour out my heart to him. It's been my experience that the Lord answers the cry of my heart. He helps me at my point of need. Sometimes we just need to cry out to God.

In addition, we learn from Job that "though he slay me, yet will I hope in him" (Job 13:15). Job was saying that even if God kills me, I will still trust in him. Job is an example of one who trusted the Lord no matter what happened to him.

Job's friends continued to crush Job with their ill-informed words. Unfortunately, they did not understand God's ways. Their misguided theology was very hurtful to Job. They were not helpful to him. Young person, remember that the best thing you can do for a person struck by tragedy is to listen, to comfort, and to pray.

Through all of his friends' erroneous talk, Job continued to defend his righteousness. In Job 19:25-27 Job expressed that through his physical suffering and eventual death he would see God: "I know that my Redeemer lives, and that in the end he will stand upon the earth. And after my skin has been destroyed, yet in my flesh I will see God; I myself will see him with my own eyes—I, and not another. How my heart yearns within me!"

I recall when my wife's mother contracted cancer. At the time, she didn't know the Lord. However, through that terrible experience my wife was able to share the Lord with her, and her mother became born again. Now we have the hope that we will see her again in heaven.

Amid any tragedy, heaven is our ultimate hope! We may not know why we are experiencing tragedy until we are with God in heaven. This hope is not only for us but also for our loved ones. I encourage you to share the Lord with your family and friends so that they can see God with you in heaven as well!

As Job continued to question God, we're told that "the Lord answered Job out of the storm" (Job 38:1). Indeed, when we're going through unending trials, it feels as if we're going through a mighty storm. The Bible says that the rain falls on the righteous and the unrighteous (Matt. 5:45). We all deal with the rain and storms of life. Rain can bring good things such as water for crops, but it can also bring bad things such as flooding and destruction. Everyone experiences the storms of life.

Out of the storm, the Lord said the following to Job: "Who is this that darkens my counsel with words without knowledge?" (Job 38:2). God was telling Job that his complaints against him were resulting from unclear knowledge. Then the Lord told Job, "Brace yourself like a man; I will question you, and you shall answer me" (Job 38:3).

The Lord proceeded to share how he had set boundaries for our good. He asked Job many questions: "Where were you when I laid the earth's foundation? . . . Who marked off its dimensions? . . . Who stretched a measuring line across it? On what were its footings set, or who laid its cornerstone?" (Job 38:4-6). Of course, the implication of these questions is that Job had not observed the Lord setting these needful boundaries. God had done all these things and more. Man hadn't.

Job was now gaining more understanding that God is just and his ways are higher than our ways. Who are we to question God and his ways? We don't know why tragedy sometimes happens. No matter what we're going through, we can trust that the Lord is righteous in all his ways.

In Job 40:2, the Lord said to Job, "Will the one who contends with the Almighty correct him? Let him who accuses God answer him!"

Job replied sheepishly, "I am unworthy—how can I reply to you? I put my hand over my mouth. I spoke once, but I have no answer—twice, but I will say no more" (Job 40:4-5). Job knew not to defend himself anymore.

The Lord confronted Job in his thinking. Again, the Lord told Job to brace himself as he questioned him. Job had to stand up and face God! Young person, if you want to become a champion for God, there is no place for self-pity. You have to refuse feeling sorry for yourself. Although I encourage you to cry out to God, don't fall into the trap of self-pity. God may call you to stand up and to be questioned—to face him and to endure his pressure. As you face into the Lord, he will ultimately give you the perspective you need to move forward. Allow the Lord to use the tragedy to help you grow closer to him.

The Lord challenged Job with the following:

> Would you discredit my justice? Would you condemn me to justify yourself? Do you have an arm like God's, and can your voice thunder like his? Then adorn yourself with glory and splendor, and clothe yourself in honor and majesty. Unleash the fury of your wrath, look at every proud man and bring him low, look at every proud man and humble him, crush the wicked where they stand. Bury them all in the dust together; shroud their faces in the grave. Then I myself will admit to you that your own right hand can save you. (Job 40:8-14)

Young person, ultimately our life, including our vindication, is in God's hands. We can't save ourselves. We are not God; only God is God. The Lord alone is our Savior.

To show God's power over all of creation, the Lord then gave Job examples of mighty creatures such as the behemoth (perhaps the hippopotamus) and the leviathan (possibly the crocodile) whom God created in addition to humanity. God is the Creator of all things. He created us and the entire world—all creatures. To remember God as Creator puts in perspective the trials that we may endure. God knows all things and has a perspective that goes far beyond our earthly concerns—a perspective that includes all of eternity.

As he listened to the Lord, Job came to increased *understanding* of God's ways toward him, and he repented for his presumptuous *misunderstanding*: "I know that you can do all things; no plan of yours can be thwarted. You asked, 'Who is this that obscures my counsel without knowledge?' Surely I spoke of things I did not understand, things too wonderful for me to know" (Job 42:2-3). As he dealt directly with the Lord, Job repented. He recognized that God's ways were higher than his.

Job continued to share how he had changed: "You said, 'Listen now, and I will speak; I will question you, and you shall answer me.' My ears had heard of you but now my eyes have seen you. Therefore I despise myself and repent in dust and ashes" (Job 42:4-6). How had Job changed? Before Job had only "heard" of God; now Job "sees" God. Early on in his suffering, Job said, "What I feared has come upon me; what I dreaded has happened to me" (Job 3:25). In other words, at the beginning of his suffering, Job shared that he had previously *feared* that bad things could happen to him—and bad things did happen to him. However, as he continued in his suffering and dealt directly with the Lord, Job's mindset changed. Whereas Job previously *feared* what might happen to him, now Job is not fearful. He says, "My ears had heard of you but now my eyes have seen you" (Job 42:5). Having endured terrible suffering, he is now able to *see* God. Job now sees God with the eyes of faith and knows him more intimately.

Having fully surrendered himself to God, Job is not fearful anymore about his future. Now Job has more knowledge of God—he sees God for who he is. As Job communicated directly with God, including sharing his questions, his appeals, and his frustrations, he never cursed God. Satan's prediction did not come true. Throughout his suffering, Job honored God.

God proceeded to rebuke Job's three friends. In Job 42:7, he said the following to Eliphaz: "I am angry with you and your two friends, because you have not spoken of me what is right, as my servant Job has." God said, "My servant Job will pray for you, and I will accept his prayer and not deal with you according to your folly" (Job 42:8). Job was vindicated by the Lord! The Lord called out Job's friends for their misguided and foolish counsel.

God told Job to pray for those who had hurt him in his suffering. When people in their misguided ways hurt us in our tragic disappointments, we're called to pray for them. Praying for them will enable us to resist being resentful toward them. Prayer helps us to love those who hurt us.

Psalm 26:1 says, "Vindicate me, O Lord, for I have led a blameless life; I have trusted in the Lord without wavering." Well, the Lord certainly vindicated Job! After he had stood the tests, the Lord blessed Job double-fold. Job became two times as wealthy as he had been. In addition, he had ten more children, lived to the age of 140, and saw his grandchildren and his great grandchildren.

Young person, we see that Job grew in his understanding of God through his experience of suffering. Even in his anger, Job dealt truthfully with God. Unlike his friends who were puffed up in theological pride, Job talked directly with God. Sometimes friends may have a lot of correct-sounding theology but not have a right understanding of God. Sometimes well-meaning friends hurt us. But we can still love them by praying for them.

We learn from Job's experience that we don't always understand why we go through trials. We don't understand God's ways—his ways are higher than our ways! James 1:2-5 says, "Consider it pure joy, my brothers, whenever you face trials of many kinds, because you know that the testing of your faith develops perseverance. Perseverance must finish its work so that you may be mature and complete, not lacking anything. If any of you lacks wisdom, he should ask God, who gives generously to all without finding fault, and it will be given to him." When we are suffering trials, we may not know the reasons for those experiences. But we can ask God for wisdom. When you are going through suffering, ask God for wisdom to learn from it. God does have a purpose for our suffering. He uses our suffering for our good. My encouragement to you is the following: don't waste your suffering; use it to grow to be the champion he's calling you to be!

Romans 5:2-5 gives us the Lord's perspective: "And we rejoice in the hope of the glory of God. Not only so, but we also rejoice in our sufferings, because we know that suffering produces perseverance; perseverance, character; and character, hope. And hope does not disappoint us, because God has poured out his love into our hearts by the Holy Spirit, whom he has given us." This is our hope amid any tragedy! Through the suffering, we can allow God to work in us perseverance, character, and ultimately hope. This hope doesn't disappoint us because Jesus, who is the hope of glory, lives in us! Through any tragedy, we have this assurance: the Lord is with us, and we will one day see him in heaven!

Memory Passage

Job 19:25-27 "I know that my Redeemer lives, and that in the end he will stand upon the earth. And after my skin has been destroyed, yet in my flesh I will see God; I myself will see him with my own eyes—I, and not another. How my heart yearns within me!"

ISAIAH

Be the Lord's Champion by Making Yourself Available

In Isaiah chapter 6, we observe the Lord's calling of Isaiah. Isaiah was commissioned to hold God's people accountable because of their disobedience. They had mocked God with their words: "Let God hurry, let him hasten his work so we may see it. Let it approach, let the plan of the Holy One of Israel come, so we may know it" (Isa. 5:19). They had rebelled against God by calling "evil good and good evil" and placing "darkness for light and light for darkness" (Isa. 5:20). Indeed, in our society today we see this rebellion against God in which wrong is called right and right is called wrong. In our "politically correct" society, those things that God calls sin are often labeled as right; however, we need to live our lives according to the eternal principles of God's Word, not according to the changing norms of culture.

In 740 B.C. Isaiah "saw the Lord seated on a throne, high and exalted" (Isa. 6:1). He saw a glorious vision that included angels. Angels called seraphs were surrounding the Lord and worshiping him; because of the glory of the Lord's presence, these seraphs covered their faces and feet with their wings. However, Isaiah's focus was on the Lord; his eyes were fastened on the Lord who was seated on the throne as the King of kings. As Hebrews 12:2 exhorts us, "Let us fix our eyes on Jesus, the author and perfecter of our faith."

As Isaiah saw the vision of God's glory, he noticed that the seraphs continually called out to each other the following chorus: "Holy, holy, holy is the Lord Almighty; the whole earth is full of his glory" (Isa. 6:3). They sang this refrain over and over again, emphasizing God's unending holiness! Holiness is one of the main attributes of God. It means that the Lord is perfectly moral, pure, and sinless with total integrity. Along with Isaiah, these angels saw the Lord in his holiness; they experienced him in all his glory! Their eyes were fastened on the Lord, praising him with all of their being!

In order for you, young person, to see God's vision for your life, you need to learn to praise him—with all of your heart and with abandon! When I was a young college student entering my sophomore year, I had just had a terrible summer of trials and severe personal weakness. Working as a security guard often on the graveyard shift (the night-time shift), I was very unstable. I was a "security" guard who wasn't secure. Instead, I was marked by insecurity. I was very weak and had hardly any confidence. I really was just surviving day to day.

To illustrate this point, one night around midnight I went to work but couldn't figure out what building I was supposed to work in that night. I drove around to different places. Finally I drove to the headquarters to find my night's assignment. Flustered and disconcerted because I was late for work, I ran into the headquarters. When I ran back out of the building to my car, I found that my car was gone! I turned around and found that my car had drifted across the parking lot and was leaning up against a curb! (In my rush, I had forgotten to put up the emergency brake.) Thank God it was late at night; because the parking lot was empty, my drifting car hadn't hit any other cars. But that incident illustrated my mental state. I was in bad shape.

After barely making it to the end of the summer, I went to a Christian camp. The night before camp started, in my brokenness and weakness, I totally surrendered to the Lord. I got before the Lord and prayed in effect, "Lord, you see me for who I am. I am very weak; I don't have much to offer you. You see my life. If you can do anything with me, here I am." That week while praising and glorifying the Lord in total abandon and surrender, the Lord called me to my life purpose. The Lord shared with me how I could serve him. He gave me vision for my life. This calling motivates me to this day, one that I am still doing thirty-five years later.

As I praised the Lord with all my heart amid my personal weakness and desperation, God made something out of my life. Psalm 72:19 declares, "Praise be to his glorious name forever; may the whole earth be filled with his glory." Psalm 85:9 assures us, "Surely his salvation is near those who fear him, that his glory may dwell in our land." In a sense, my salvation was praising the Lord—praising him as if my life depended on it! As I praised the Lord, he gave me an identity. He called me and commissioned me to my life's work! God's call has made the difference in my life!

Just as I had come to the end of myself, we see that Isaiah came to the end of himself. In Isaiah 6:5, he cried out to God, "Woe to me! I am ruined! For I am a man of unclean lips, and I live among a people of unclean lips, and my eyes have seen the King, the Lord Almighty." Isaiah said that he was ruined. He saw himself for who he was—a man of unclean lips, a sinful man.

Isaiah said that his lips were unclean. Think of it: our lips—our mouth with our words—are used to do very sinful things. Jesus said the following about a person's mouth: "What goes into a man's mouth does not make him 'unclean,' but what comes out of his mouth, that is what makes him 'unclean'" (Matt. 15:11). When his disciple Peter asked Jesus to explain what he meant, Jesus replied, "Don't you see that whatever enters the mouth goes into the stomach and then out of the body? But the things that come out of the mouth come from the heart, and these make a man 'unclean.' For out of the heart come evil thoughts, murder, adultery, sexual immorality, theft, false testimony, slander. These are what make a man 'unclean'; but eating with unwashed hands does not make him 'unclean'" (Matt. 15:17-20). Jesus was saying that being clean is an issue of our hearts, not our hands. It's through our mouth that we understand the state of our heart.

Young people, I encourage you with the exhortation of Proverbs 4:23: "Above all else, guard your heart, for it is the wellspring of life." We need to guard our heart with all diligence for out of it come the issues of life. It's a matter of our heart. If you store up good things in your heart, then good things will come out of your mouth. If you store up bad things in your heart, then bad things will come out of your mouth. For out of the heart the mouth speaks (Matt. 12:34-35). We need to focus on allowing God to clean our heart.

It's our lips that are used to sin. Often it's our words that sin against others and cause them harm. Jesus rebuked the self-righteous Pharisees with the following:

> Make a tree good and its fruit will be good, or make a tree bad and its fruit will be bad, for a tree is recognized by its fruit. You brood of vipers, how can you who are evil say anything good? For out of the overflow of the heart the mouth speaks. The good man brings good things out of the good stored up in him, and the evil man brings evil things out of the evil stored up in him. But I tell you that men will have to give account on the day of judgment for every careless word they have spoken. For by your words you will be acquitted, and by your words you will be condemned. (Matt. 12:33-37)

Isaiah realized that his lips were unclean. It's our mouth—our words—that show our sinfulness.

James reinforced this understanding: "With the tongue we praise our Lord and Father, and with it we curse men, who have been made in God's likeness. Out of the same mouth come praise and cursing. My brothers, this should not be. Can both fresh water and salt water flow from the same spring? My brothers, can a fig tree bear olives, or a grapevine bear figs? Neither can a salt spring produce fresh water" (James 3:9-12).

Before a holy God, Isaiah realized his terrible sinfulness. Because he had seen God, Isaiah expected that he would die. "Then one of the seraphs flew to me with a live coal in his hand, which he had taken with tongs from the altar" (Isa. 6:6). This hot coal was taken from the altar, the place of getting right with God. God was dealing with Isaiah's sin and purifying him. God forgave Isaiah, and he was cleansed.

As with Isaiah, it's the same with us. We need the fire of God to come into our lives to purify us! We need God's fire to make us fit for his service. We need to be cleansed so that we can serve the living God! In fact, Isaiah 1:25 stresses this point: "I will turn my hand against you; I will thoroughly purge away your dross and remove all your impurities." This purging away the dross in our lives refers to the Lord's purifying fire!

Thank God for his cleansing power! And thank him that his mercies are new every morning! With the hot coal, the seraph touched Isaiah's lips and declared, "See, this has touched your lips; your guilt is taken away and your sin atoned for" (Isa. 6:7). When God through the angel touched Isaiah's lips with the hot coal, he was forgiven. He was no longer guilty.

After Isaiah had been cleansed and forgiven, the Lord asked him two questions that would lead into his life purpose: "Whom shall I send? And who will go for us?" (Isa. 6:8). God asked Isaiah these questions, giving him a chance to make a clear commitment. The issue was whether Isaiah was willing to serve the Lord. Grateful to be forgiven, Isaiah responded with the heart of a servant: "Here am I. Send me!" (Isa. 6:8).

Isaiah said, "Here am I"! This expression is the Hebrew *hineni*; other great champions of the Bible have used it as well. When called to be the Lord's servant, they responded with "hineni," declaring their willingness to serve. This expression of "Here am I" declares an availability, a willingness to serve God!

Young person, when you serve God, you are making yourself *available* to him; you are *volunteering* to serve him. You're not forced to serve him; you're willing. You're expressing a willingness to do whatever God asks of you. God asks you, "Are you willing to serve me?" If you want to know God's *will*, let him know that you are *willing*!

Isaiah responded to the Lord's call with a clear declaration: "Send me!" He would take God's message to the people, no matter the outcome.

When God has forgiven us, cleansed us, and changed us—raised us up out of the dirtiness of sin—what else can be our response but to be a willing servant? When God has changed us through his love, what else can be our response but to make ourselves totally available for his use!

In Isaiah 6:9, the Lord gave Isaiah his assignment as his commissioned servant: "Go and tell this people: 'Be ever hearing, but never understanding; be ever seeing, but never perceiving.'" Isaiah would tell the people that they are constantly hearing the message but not understanding it; that they are constantly seeing, but not perceiving what is being said. In other words, the people were not heeding the message and not changing their evil ways.

Young person, the Lord calls us to have hearts of good soil into which the seed of God's Word can be planted. When we receive God's Word with hearts of good soil, God brings a good crop into our lives. He calls us not simply to be hearers of the Word, but to be doers of the Word. Our Christian life is one of constant change. As we apply God's Word to our lives, we're continually being changed to become more like Jesus.

Isaiah received a commissioning to preach the Word to a people who would not listen to his message. Isaiah's ministry would seem to be a failure without much fruit. The vast majority of the people would not respond to his message. In Isaiah 6:11, Isaiah asked the Lord "how long" would the people stay in a state of having hard hearts that would not receive his message and change. The Lord responded with this answer: "Until the cities lie ruined and without inhabitant, until the houses are left deserted and the fields ruined and ravaged, until the Lord has sent everyone far away and the land is utterly forsaken" (Isa. 6:11-12). In other words, total devastation would have to occur before the people would respond to the message and return to the Lord.

Even the remnant of God's faithful people would experience this devastation: "And though a tenth remains in the land, it will again be laid waste" (Isa. 6:13).

However, God's Word does not return void. The Lord gave Isaiah this word of encouragement: "But as the terebinth and oak leave stumps when they are cut down, so the holy seed will be the stump in the land" (Isa. 6:13). Old tree stumps, seemingly cut off and dead, can have tiny green shoots that will sprout from the wood. Although many would refuse to listen to Isaiah's message, a minority—a remnant—would heed. That remnant would be the stump of holy seed in the land. Life would eventually spring forth again!

What does the message of Isaiah's commissioning mean for us? As servants of the Lord, we can't get discouraged in the commission that the Lord has given us. We need to continue in the Lord's ministry even if there seems to be no fruit. Just as God called Isaiah to stay faithful, he calls us to stay faithful. God's Word will not return void!

We learn from the commissioning of Isaiah an important life lesson regarding following God. Young person, when you make yourself totally available to God—no matter your state, he will use you. He will love you, purify you, build you, equip you, and make you his servant. He will make you a champion for his Kingdom purpose! No matter your present condition, I encourage you to make yourself totally available to God. Be a champion for the Lord!

Memory Verse

Isaiah 6:8 "Then I heard the voice of the Lord saying, 'Whom shall I send? And who will go for us?' And I said, 'Here am I. Send me!'"

JEREMIAH

The Lord Created You for a Purpose

When God called Jeremiah, he was only a youth, probably around 16-18 years old. He was a shy, sensitive boy who lacked confidence. When Jeremiah was called, he initially tried to dissuade the Lord: "Ah, Sovereign Lord, I do not know how to speak; I am only a child" (Jer. 1:6). However, the Lord both admonished and encouraged Jeremiah: "Do not say, 'I am only a child.' You must go to everyone I send you to and say whatever I command you. Do not be afraid of them, for I am with you and will rescue you" (Jer. 1:7-8). Jeremiah would need to remember that encouragement over and over throughout his life.

As God called Jeremiah, he emphasized that he had created him: "Before I formed you in the womb I knew you, before you were born I set you apart; I appointed you as a prophet to the nations" (Jer. 1:5). It is clear that God, the all-knowing one, knew Jeremiah even before he was in the womb.

The Psalmist confirms the truth that God created us in our mother's womb in Psalm 139:13-16:

> For you created my inmost being; you knit me together in my mother's womb. I praise you because I am fearfully and wonderfully made; your works are wonderful, I know that full well. My frame was not hidden from you when I was made in the secret place. When I was woven together in the depths of the earth, your eyes saw my unformed body. All the days ordained for me were written in your book before one of them came to be.

Young person, when the Lord says that all your days were ordained for you "before one of them came to be," it is clear that he is saying that he created you for a purpose! He not only created you; he also has a God-ordained purpose for you! You are not an evolutionary animal with no value, meaning, and purpose. Rather you have been created in the image of God—with great value and meaning! As one created in God's image, you are intrinsically linked to God! God is your Creator; evolution didn't create you! And you have been created as a work of art: "For we are God's workmanship, created in Christ Jesus to do good works, which God prepared in advance for us to do" (Eph. 2:10). Never forget—you are God's beautiful creation!

The book of Jeremiah is a strong advocate for God as Creator. Speaking of man-made idols, Jeremiah announced, "Tell them this: 'These gods, who did not make the heavens and the earth, will perish from the earth and from under the heavens'" (Jer. 10:11). Idols didn't create the earth, and the earth didn't just happen by accident. Creator God made the earth! Jeremiah emphasized this truth: "But God made the earth by his power; he founded the world by his wisdom and stretched out the heavens by his understanding" (Jer. 10:12).

Jeremiah preached the obvious uselessness of making and following man-made idols: "Everyone is senseless and without knowledge; every goldsmith is shamed by his idols. His images are a fraud; they have no breath in them" (Jer. 10:14). Of course, we should not elevate man-made things—idols—above God. When we use our rational minds, we are able to understand the truth that this earth and all we see was not made by happenstance but on purpose by a loving God.

Related to our understanding of God as Creator is the truth of his creating babies in the womb. Young person, never fall prey to the ungodly argument that the fetus in the womb is not a person. Never fall prey to the thinking that the fetus is just a piece of tissue or a part of the mother's body. No, be assured that that fetus is a real developing baby. It is never right to kill a baby. Let's be clear: abortion is wrong. And as God had a purpose for Jeremiah's life, God has a purpose for you and for all people, including babies in the womb. Always remember: God created you for a purpose!

And God can do whatever is needed to equip you for your life purpose. When he calls someone, he also provides what is necessary to fulfill that call. God appointed Jeremiah to be a prophet to the nations, and God equipped him for that call.

I can personally identify with Jeremiah's contesting the Lord's call in his life by his saying, "I do not know how to speak" (Jer. 1:6). As a tenth grader I gave a speech in English class. At the end of my speech, a girl sitting *right in front of me* made the following pronouncement to the teacher before the whole class: "I couldn't understand a word he said." Of course, I was completely humiliated. Like Jeremiah, I was a very shy person who lacked confidence. However, the Lord called me to be a teacher and a pastor; and in the Lord's timing, he has equipped me to preach and teach his Word—to use my words to communicate God's truth. Young person, just as God equipped Jeremiah to his appointment as a prophet to the nations, be assured that the Lord will equip you with everything you need to fulfill *his* appointment for *your* life!

As we have seen, God did not concede Jeremiah's excuse of being slow of speech. In fact, he gave Jeremiah courage and promised him that he would be with him: "Do not be afraid of them, for I am with you and will rescue you" (Jer. 1:8). In addition, the Lord supernaturally touched Jeremiah's mouth with his hand. He encouraged Jeremiah with these words: "Now, I have put my words in your mouth" (Jer. 1:9). Young person, as you pursue God's call, he will put *his* Word in your heart to be expressed with your mouth. God will give you the power to accomplish the call he gives you. The Holy Spirit inside you will inspire you with his Word!

In fact, this shy sensitive boy became a strong preacher of God's Word. Jeremiah 23:29 is an apt description of Jeremiah's preaching: "'Is not my word like fire,' declares the Lord, 'and like a hammer that breaks a rock in pieces?'" Jeremiah preached like fire and like a hammer!

Jeremiah was given a hard call; it would not be easy for him. In Jeremiah 1:10 the Lord described his commission: "See, today I appoint you over nations and kingdoms to uproot and tear down, to destroy and overthrow, to build and to plant." Jeremiah was called primarily to prophesy destruction because of the sin of the people of Judah, but there would be hope beyond God's discipline—the Lord would eventually rebuild and plant his people.

Jeremiah had to stand for the truth no matter the consequences. Because the people of Judah had turned away from God, Jeremiah had to confront much wrongdoing. As he confronted their sin, he encountered extreme conflict. His life focused on sharing the consequences of people's rebellion against God. Therefore, he was very much hated by the rebels.

However, God gave Jeremiah the strength he needed with a clear call to action: "Get yourself ready! Stand up and say to them whatever I command you. Do not be terrified by them, or I will terrify you before them" (Jer. 1:17). God called Jeremiah to stand and proclaim God's Word courageously: "Stand at the gate of the Lord's house and there proclaim this message" (Jer. 7:2). Throughout his life, God fortified Jeremiah to stand and deliver his message!

God described the kind of strength Jeremiah needed to fulfill his call: "Today I have made you a fortified city, an iron pillar and a bronze wall to stand against the whole land—against the kings of Judah, its officials, its priests and the people of the land" (Jer. 1:18). God was preparing Jeremiah to stand against everyone: rulers, priests, officials, and indeed all the people of the land if necessary! In order to do that, God made Jeremiah "a fortified city, an iron pillar and a bronze wall" (Jer. 1:18). God made Jeremiah strong in the Lord! God took this sensitive youth and made him a strong man of God! The entire nation would rebel—they would come against Jeremiah and his God—but Jeremiah would remain true to the Lord! Jeremiah became so courageous in God that he was able to stand against everyone!

As he proclaimed God's Word, God equipped Jeremiah to be a tester of the people. The Lord pronounced the following about Jeremiah: "I have made you a tester of metals and my people the ore, that you may observe and test their ways" (Jer. 6:27). As metal needs to be tested and refined to get out the impurities, Jeremiah would be the tester of the people of Judah.

Because of the people's evil, Jeremiah announced the destruction of the Kingdom of Judah.

Since he proclaimed an unpopular message, he was attacked from all sides. The people of Judah did not like his message: specifically, that because of their sin, God was bringing them judgment—the judgment of being overtaken by Babylonian rule. Jeremiah had to tell the people that they were not to fight against Babylonian rule but that they were required to submit to it. To those who wanted to fight against and throw off the Babylonian captivity, this was a very unpopular message.

In Jeremiah 1:19 God assured Jeremiah of his watching over him as he delivered the terrible message: "They will fight against you but will not overcome you, for I am with you and will rescue you." Even as he told Jeremiah that all these people would fight against him, he assured Jeremiah that he would help him overcome. Remember, young person, the Bible says, "If God is for us, who can be against us?" (Rom. 8:31). If you know that you are following the Lord's bidding and that he is with you, that is all you need.

Jeremiah endured intense opposition throughout his lifetime. He was exceedingly unpopular. For many young people, peer pressure is a very real thing. Well, Jeremiah encountered extreme pressure. When I was in high school, I chose not to go to ungodly parties with my peers. I wasn't popular and often walked alone. But what I experienced was nothing compared to Jeremiah. I still had a good number of friends in my church youth group. Not so with Jeremiah—he had very few friends.

In fact, God didn't even allow Jeremiah to have his own family. He was denied some of the basic comforts of life, such as having a wife and children. He served God alone without a family. Because the next generation would endure terrible destruction, the Lord told him not to get married and have children:

> "You must not marry and have sons or daughters in this place." For this is what the Lord says about the sons and daughters born in this land and about the women who are their mothers and the men who are their fathers: "They will die of deadly diseases. They will not be mourned or buried but will be like refuse lying on the ground. They will perish by sword and famine, and their dead bodies will become food for the birds of the air and the beasts of the earth." (Jer. 16:2-4)

Without the support of a wife and children, Jeremiah had to stand alone as he preached the coming destruction. Jeremiah was beaten, put in prison, and humiliated. He endured many putdowns. As Jeremiah 17:23 says, the people of Judah would not listen to him: "Yet they did not listen or pay attention; they were stiff-necked and would not listen or respond to discipline." However, the call of God and the presence of God empowered him to fulfill his purpose!

As Jeremiah disciplined the people, he also communicated hope. God's punishment for the people of Judah was that they would have to endure a seventy-year exile under Babylonian rule, a period which included Nebuchadnezzar's terrible destruction of God's city Jerusalem and of Solomon's temple in 586 B.C. However, Jeremiah communicated that after their punishment, rebirth and righteousness of the heart would come. As Jeremiah anticipated the fulfillment of God's judgment followed by hope, we receive one of the greatest passages in the Bible in Jeremiah chapter 29.

While verses from Jeremiah 29 are quoted by many Christians over and over, it is helpful to examine this passage in context. As alluded to earlier, Jeremiah was saying that the people of Judah would have to endure a seventy-year exile—in effect, a punishment lasting seventy years! However, there would be hope amid the discipline!

Jeremiah prophesied the following: "When seventy years are completed for Babylon, I will come to you and fulfill my gracious promise to bring you back to this place" (Jer. 29:10). God was saying that he would bring his people back to their homeland after their discipline! God communicated great hope for them through the discipline: "For I know the plans I have for you, plans to prosper you and not to harm you, plans to give you hope and a future" (Jer. 29:11). Not only for them but also for us who follow the Lord, we can be assured that God has good plans for us!

Jeremiah continued God's encouraging message: "Then you will call upon me and come and pray to me, and I will listen to you. You will seek me and find me when you seek me with all your heart" (Jer. 29:12-13). With these words, God is promising us that when we return to God and seek him with all our heart, we can be assured that we will find him. As we find him, God will also reveal his plans for us.

Finally, the Lord declared the following: "I will be found by you and will bring you back from captivity. I will gather you from all the nations and places where I have banished you and will bring you back to the place from which I carried you into exile" (Jer. 29:14). This word is such an encouragement to us whenever we are undergoing discipline, whether we're being disciplined by God or by our parents. There is hope amid the discipline!

When you are disciplined, embrace the discipline, learn from it, and change. You will then live in great hope! There is hope through the discipline! The discipline helps us to grow into the likeness of Christ. It helps us to become the champions God has created us to be!

It is evident from Jeremiah's life that as he dealt with the people's sin, that he still loved and prayed for them. In Jeremiah 31:31-34, Jeremiah shared of a great new kind of covenant that God would make with his followers:

> "The time is coming," declares the Lord, "when I will make a new covenant with the house of Israel and with the house of Judah. It will not be like the covenant I made with their forefathers when I took them by the hand to lead them out of Egypt, because they broke my covenant, though I

> was a husband to them," declares the Lord. "This is the covenant I will make with the house of Israel after that time," declares the Lord. "I will put my law in their minds and write it on their hearts. I will be their God, and they will be my people. No longer will a man teach his neighbor, or a man his brother, saying, 'Know the Lord,' because they will all know me, from the least of them to the greatest," declares the Lord. "For I will forgive their wickedness and will remember their sins no more."

This new covenant would be written upon the hearts of God's people! Instead of God's commands being written upon external stone tablets, his word would be written upon the internal hearts of men and women and boys and girls all over the world! It would be fulfilled in the born-again experience of Messiah as one yields to the Holy Spirit. This new covenant is a transformation of one's heart on the inside through a personal relationship with God himself.

Young person, we learn much from this champion Jeremiah who stood alone for God amid extreme opposition throughout his lifetime. We learn that God created you and that he created you for a purpose! God has great plans for your life. When you seek God with all your heart, he will eventually reveal those plans to you. When you yield to the Holy Spirit wholeheartedly, he can't help but share his plans with you. He will fulfill his will for your life. As you walk by faith, he will direct your steps to walk into his promised land. Remember that your life is for God's purpose! And what a great thing it is to live for *his* purpose!

Memory passage

> Jeremiah 29:11-13 "'For I know the plans I have for you,' declares the Lord, 'plans to prosper you and not to harm you, plans to give you hope and a future. Then you will call upon me and come and pray to me, and I will listen to you. You will seek me and find me when you seek me with all your heart.'"

EZEKIEL

Eat the Word and Speak It Fearlessly

In the last chapter, we saw how God needed to give Jeremiah much strength to fulfill a very difficult call. God had to do a similar work in a prophet named Ezekiel. After Ezekiel fell facedown upon seeing an awesome vision of the Lord's glory, God challenged him: "Son of man, stand up on your feet and I will speak to you" (Ezek. 2:1). Ezekiel was on his face—seeking God in prayer—and the Lord challenged him to stand up and receive his assignment! God was calling Ezekiel to receive his courage challenge!

God was calling Ezekiel to proclaim his Word to his people. The thing is, those people were in rebellion! What does it mean to be in rebellion? Rebellion is coming against the rightful authority. Of course, God is the ultimate authority—he is the most high authority! When people come against God and his Word, they are in rebellion. The people of Israel had rebelled against God. In fact, God's people were being punished for their disobedience by having to live in exile—away from their home.

As God spoke to Ezekiel, the Holy Spirit proceeded to inspire him. God gave Ezekiel a challenging task: "Son of man, I am sending you to the Israelites, to a rebellious nation that has rebelled against me; they and their fathers have been in revolt against me to this very day. The people to whom I am sending you are obstinate and stubborn" (Ezek. 2:3-4). What an assignment! Ezekiel was being commissioned to go speak to a stubborn and rebellious people!

God proceeded to tell Ezekiel to not be afraid of these rebellious people: "And whether they listen or fail to listen—for they are a rebellious house—they will know that a prophet has been among them. And you, son of man, do not be afraid of them or their words. Do not be afraid, though briers and thorns are all around you and you live among scorpions. Do not be afraid of what they say or terrified by them, though they are a rebellious house" (Ezek. 2:5-6).

Have you ever walked through briers and thorns? Ever step on a scorpion? Maybe you haven't stepped on a scorpion, but virtually all of us have had the experience of being stuck by a thorn or a brier. When we walk through thorns and briers, it causes us to lack confidence to continue going that way. However, the Lord is calling us to be champions that are willing to take on difficult tasks!

Rebellious people are like briers and thorns to an individual who is seeking to follow the Lord. The Lord was preparing Ezekiel for the challenges he would face. Ezekiel would need to persevere through every obstacle to do God's work!

In Ezekiel 2:8, God commanded Ezekiel: "Listen to what I say to you. Do not rebel like that rebellious house; open your mouth and eat what I give you." God called Ezekiel to eat the words he was giving him. And young person, God calls you to eat his Word as well!

Then God showed Ezekiel a vision of a scroll, which had words of lament, mourning, and woe—not a very pleasant message. Because of their sin, Ezekiel was being commissioned to proclaim God's judgment to a rebellious people.

God told Ezekiel to eat the scroll, which had God's words on it. He said, "Eat this scroll I am giving you and fill your stomach with it" (Ezek. 3:3). Likewise, we are called to eat and to fill our stomach with God's Word.

How do we eat God's Word? Just like physical food, we're called to eat spiritual food from God's Word. We're called to feed on God's Word—to chew it, digest it, and make it part of our being. We do this by reading God's Word and reflecting on it. We do this by reading God's Word slowly and prayerfully. We're called to hide God's Word in our heart. We do this by memorizing key passages of Scripture that relate to important areas of our lives. Psalm 119:9-11 shares the power of God's Word to you as a young person: "How can a young man keep his way pure? By living according to your word. I seek you with all my heart; do not let me stray from your commands. I have hidden your word in my heart that I might not sin against you." When we hide God's Word in our hearts, it enables us to overcome those sin areas that can hamper our progress as the Lord's disciples.

I recall receiving a Word from the Lord at a critical time of my life. When I was a young man, the enemy Satan was buffeting me with suicidal thoughts. Although I don't think I was suicidal, I was struggling with controlling my thoughts. Working at my maintenance job, I wrestled with my thoughts over and over again. Well, at my lunch break one day, the Holy Spirit inspired me with the following Word from 1 Peter 5:8-11:

> Be self-controlled and alert. Your enemy the devil prowls around like a roaring lion looking for someone to devour. Resist him, standing firm in the faith, because you know that your brothers throughout the world are undergoing the same kind of sufferings. And the God of all grace, who called you to his eternal glory in Christ, after you have suffered a little while, will himself restore you and make you strong, firm and steadfast. To him be the power for ever and ever. Amen.

When the Holy Spirit gave me that message from the Word of God, I immediately memorized it; in fact, it became part of my very being. Going back out to work, I was now armed with the Sword of the Spirit, the Word of God (Eph. 6). When those terrible thoughts returned, I used the Sword of the Spirit! By proclaiming that Word, Satan and his bad thoughts were defeated. Even now, many years later, whenever I feel as if my thoughts are getting out of control, I confess that Scripture and godless thoughts are taken captive! Through God's Word, I gained the victory!

1 John 2:13 expresses this dynamic of the Word enabling us to overcome: "I write to you, young men, because you are strong, and the word of God lives in you, and you have overcome the evil one."

When you eat God's Word, God's Word becomes part of you. His message is planted deep within your heart, and you are able to share it with others!

At first when Ezekiel ate the scroll containing God's Word, it was sweet like honey. Psalm 19:7-11 speaks of the sweetness of the Word of God:

> The law of the Lord is perfect, reviving the soul. The statutes of the Lord are trustworthy, making wise the simple. The precepts of the Lord are right, giving joy to the heart. The commands of the Lord are radiant, giving light to the eyes. The fear of the Lord is pure, enduring forever. The ordinances of the Lord are sure and altogether righteous. They are more precious than gold, than much pure gold; they are sweeter than honey, than honey from the comb. By them is your servant warned; in keeping them there is great reward.

God's Word has a tremendous effect on our lives. It revives us, makes us wise, gives us joy, gives us light for our path, helps us to walk in purity, enables us to withstand the inevitable storms of life, and warns us from harming ourselves and others! It is our daily bread; it is our food. We need God's Word every day of our lives.

God warned Ezekiel: "But the house of Israel is not willing to listen to you because they are not willing to listen to me, for the whole house of Israel is hardened and obstinate" (Ezek. 3:7). A friend in our church often reminds our congregation: God calls us to be faithful, not necessarily successful. As we share God's Word with others, we may very well be rejected; there may not be any response whatsoever. However, whether or not people respond, we're still called to proclaim God's Word!

God encouraged Ezekiel: "I will make your forehead like the hardest stone, harder than flint. Do not be afraid of them or terrified by them, though they are a rebellious house" (Ezek. 3:9). Young person, God calls you to set your face like a flint in the purpose he has given you! The Lord will give you the strength and courage you need for the task he gives you!

We saw in the last chapter that God had to give Jeremiah similar strength:

> Get yourself ready! Stand up and say to them whatever I command you. Do not be terrified by them, or I will terrify you before them. Today I have made you a fortified city, an iron pillar and a bronze wall to stand against the whole land—against the kings of Judah, its officials, its priests and the people of the land. They will fight against you but will not overcome you, for I am with you and will rescue you. (Jer. 1:17-19)

Again, God told Jeremiah that he was a fortified city, an iron pillar, and a bronze wall! What an encouragement! In the face of opposition, do not fear! God will give you the strength you need each and every day!

God commanded Ezekiel to listen attentively to him: "Son of man, listen carefully and take to heart all the words I speak to you" (Ezek. 3:10). Listening is a very important quality. It's characteristic of obedience. Likewise, not having a listening posture is characteristic of rebellion. God calls us to listen to authority—listening to our parents, our teachers, our pastors, and of course to the Most High God.

We started out by explaining how rebellion is coming against the rightful authority. Those who do not listen to authority are walking in rebellion. But God called Ezekiel to speak his words to the rebellious, whether they would listen or not. Likewise, we are also called to be faithful to speak the word to others in our lives, whether they listen or not.

After Ezekiel received the vision of eating the scroll, he was overwhelmed. For seven days, he just sat there, awestruck! And he had a bitterness of spirit. At first, when eating the words of God, he tasted the sweetness of God's call, but now he experienced bitterness: "The Spirit then lifted me up and took me away, and I went in bitterness and in the anger of my spirit, with the strong hand of the Lord upon me" (Ezek. 3:14). Failure can be bitter. When people reject us and we don't see any fruit, that experience can be very bitter. When we serve people time after time and fail to see them respond, that process can be very bitter to our souls. But God calls us to still be faithful.

Young people, true discipleship comes with a cost—the cost of Christ, the cost of the cross. The cost of being a disciple of Messiah is that of suffering and rejection. It's the cost of truly communicating to God "not my will but your will." When you truly accept God's call, he may call you to a very difficult assignment. However, God gives you the grace for that calling. He says, "I will be with you!" Through the challenges, always remember that you possess the sweetness of God's Word to encourage you along the journey.

God continued to call Ezekiel to be a watchman for his people—a guard at his post—one whose duty was to warn the people of danger. God told Ezekiel that if you don't warn a wicked person of danger, then God would hold Ezekiel accountable for that person's death. However, if Ezekiel did warn a wicked person of the danger of continuing in sin, then that wicked person would die for his own sin but Ezekiel would be saved.

Likewise, God warned Ezekiel that if he didn't warn a *righteous person* when he turned to *wrongdoing*, then Ezekiel would be held accountable for his death. "But if you do warn the righteous man not to sin and he does not sin, he will surely live because he took warning, and you will have saved yourself" (Ezek. 3:21).

Young person, you are called to speak the truth to others. Share it out of a heart of lovingkindness for others. Ezekiel was held accountable by God for speaking the truth. As a watchman, he was called to sound the alarm. When a watchman sounds the alarm, he has done his duty—he has sounded the alarm so the people can escape danger! It's up to the people to respond to that alarm and get to a place of safety. Although Ezekiel couldn't control how people would respond to the alarm, he was still called to sound it.

It's the same for us in sharing about how the Lord can save us from the judgment of sin. We're called to care for people by sharing the truth of the wages of sin and the good news of the gift of eternal life through Christ (Rom. 6:23). We're called to speak the truth to others, whether they listen or not. When we share with an individual, perhaps that person may initially have a negative reaction but then later take the warning to heart. Remember, life and death is at stake. We have to care enough for others to share the truth.

God encouraged Ezekiel that he would give him the needed words at the proper time: "But when I speak to you, I will open your mouth and you shall say to them, 'This is what the Sovereign Lord says.' Whoever will listen let him listen, and whoever will refuse let him refuse; for they are a rebellious house" (Ezek. 3:27).

Young person, be encouraged that the Lord will give you the right words at the right time. Sometimes the task may seem to be too difficult, but go to the Lord—He will give you the grace you need! Only be faithful to what he calls you to, for he will give you the strength and the courage *and the words* to fulfill his call in your life!

I encourage you to pray this prayer right now: "Lord, I thank you for your Word! Help me to eat your Word daily; make it part of my very being. Help me to share your Word boldly and fearlessly with others. Help me to be motivated by your love to be faithful. Help me to live your Word and speak your Word. In Jesus' name, amen!"

Memory Verses

Matthew 4:4 "Jesus answered, 'It is written: "Man does not live on bread alone, but on every word that comes from the mouth of God."'"

Jeremiah 1:17-19 "Get yourself ready! Stand up and say to them whatever I command you. Do not be terrified by them, or I will terrify you before them. Today I have made you a fortified city, an iron pillar and a bronze wall to stand against the whole land—against the kings of Judah, its officials, its priests and the people of the land. They will fight against you but will not overcome you, for I am with you and will rescue you."

EZEKIEL

Swim in the Fresh Water of the Lord— Swim in the Holy Spirit

Water is so essential to life. Fresh water is important to our lives. It quenches our thirst. Without it we have no food. It also cleans us. It provides us with recreation—swimming refreshes us. In many different ways, water brings life!

Everyone needs water! In Ezekiel 47:1 the angel of the Lord guided Ezekiel to see "water coming out from under the threshold of the temple." Water was flowing from God's house!

First the angel led Ezekiel into water that was ankle deep, as one experiences when stepping into a lake of cold water. Then the angel led Ezekiel into knee-deep water and then waist-deep water.

In Ezekiel 47:6, the angel asked Ezekiel, "Son of man, do you see this?" Water was so deep that Ezekiel had to swim. I recall visiting a lake on vacation with my extended family. I was looking across to the other side of the lake and assessing its distance. In fact, my niece used her phone to find out its distance (about half a mile). After consulting with my wife Silvia and praying, I decided to swim across that lake. I started out swimming too fast and was breathing hard. I was tempted to panic and turn back, but the Lord encouraged me to keep going. Before I started the swim, the Lord had encouraged me to relax and enjoy the adventure. That focus helped me to take my time, breathe the life-giving encouragement of the Holy Spirit, and to keep going. Before long, I could see the other side of the lake getting closer. I was greatly encouraged when I reached the other side and waved to my family.

As champions of God, we are called to swim. We can't just step into the Kingdom of God ankle deep or knee deep or even waist deep. We must dive in and swim! We must be all in! We have to let go and yield ourselves to God. We must surrender and release ourselves totally to God. We are called to sell all for Christ—our reputation and our desires. We're called to stake our future—our very life—on the Lord Jesus!

When we swim in total abandonment to the Lord, our life is changed. When we walk by faith, we please God. As we swim, the water of the Holy Spirit cleanses us so we may serve the living God! As the Lord is holy, we become holy. We're changed—a new power in our life gives us the ability to love and serve others.

The angel led Ezekiel back to the river's bank. Ezekiel noticed that there were "a great number of trees on each side of the river" (Ezek. 47:7). I like to run alongside a flowing river. When you do so, you notice that there are many trees and much vegetation along the river's bank. There's abundant life because of the flowing water there!

This passage illustrates the flowing life of the river. There are trees, vegetation, and much fruit. Wherever the river flows, everything lives! In Ezekiel 47:8, the angel tells Ezekiel that "this water flows . . . into the Arabah, where it enters the Sea. When it empties into the Sea, the water there becomes fresh." The "Sea" refers to the Dead Sea, a lifeless body of water. The Arabah is a region without water between Jerusalem and the Dead Sea. The Dead Sea is the lowest sea in the world, and because it's the saltiest, it's also known as the Salt Sea. It's known for a lack of life. It's described by its name—the Dead Sea. But when this water from God's temple enters the Dead Sea, the water of the Dead Sea becomes fresh. The Hebrew indicates that it "becomes healed." The water becomes fresh and life-giving. An amazing miracle of God occurs!

Have you ever gone fishing? Have you ever gone fishing and not caught any fish? Conversely, have you ever gone fishing and caught a lot of fish? Well, the Bible says that this fresh water is teeming with marine life—many different fish for fishermen! Ezekiel 47:9 says, "Where the river flows everything will live."

God calls us to enjoy this life-giving water, its abundance, and its healing power in our lives. At the same time, we're called not to keep this life-giving water just for ourselves. We're called to share it with others! We're called to go back to the river and to lead others to swim! We're called to bring this abundant life to others. Jesus said, "'If anyone is thirsty, let him come to me and drink. Whoever believes in me, as the Scripture has said, streams of living water will flow from within him.' By this he meant the Spirit, whom those who believed in him were later to receive" (John 7:37-39).

What is this water that brings healing and abundant life? It's the Holy Spirit! If we have turned from sin and received Jesus as our Lord and Savior, we have the Holy Spirit within us. We're called to let the Holy Spirit to flow from within us to others! We're called to use our mouth—our words—to bring this river of LIFE to others!

This water is the life-giving Spirit within us. What are some of the things this water brings? It brings fruit and healing! It brings the freshness of spring water—cleansing. It brings many kinds of fish—food. It brings fruit trees of all kinds—the fruit of the Holy Spirit. It produces leaves that bring healing!

Ezekiel 47:12 says that the fruit trees bear fruit every month, not just seasonally, "because the water from the sanctuary flows to them." The water flows from the temple of the Holy Spirit within us. (As Christians, our bodies are the temple of the Holy Spirit.) In addition, the water flows from the temple of God's people as we worship the Lord together in the midst of the assembly.

This life-giving river brings healing to the nations, including different people groups. I encourage you to be ones who bring the life-giving power of the Holy Spirit to others.

The last verse of the book of Ezekiel shares its purpose: "And the name of the city from that time on will be: THE LORD IS THERE!" (Ezek. 48:35). God is there—Forever! And if you have the Holy Spirit within you, *the Lord is with you* as well!

I challenge you to be champions who bring the life-giving water of the Holy Spirit to others! That's what our world needs. Let's resolve to bring the Holy Spirit—his presence—to this world—a world so desperately needing Jesus' love!

Memory Passage

John 7:37-39 "'If anyone is thirsty, let him come to me and drink. Whoever believes in me, as the Scripture has said, streams of living water will flow from within him.' By this he meant the Spirit, whom those who believed in him were later to receive."

DANIEL

Honor the Lord in an Ungodly Society

I have a question for you. If you were tried in a court of law, would there be enough evidence against you to convict you of being a Christian? What evidence would exist to show that you were truly following Christ? How would witnesses testify against you that you were different—that you were living out God's Word? Well, an Israelite named Daniel was definitely convicted for being steadfast in following God. Daniel teaches us how to honor the Lord in an ungodly society.

Daniel was an Israelite of the people of Judah. Because of their disobedience, the people of Judah were living in captivity and were deported to Babylon under King Nebuchadnezzar. As a young man, Daniel was placed in King Nebuchadnezzar's school, one which sought to train the best administrators for his kingdom. For his school, the king pursued "young men without any physical defect, handsome, showing aptitude for every kind of learning, well informed, quick to understand, and qualified to serve in the king's palace" (Dan. 1:4). In this school, they would be taught Babylonian language and literature. They would undergo training for three years; and if qualified, they would become servants to the king.

Daniel, whose name means "God is my judge," was given a new name—Belteshazzar. Also, three of his companions' names were changed to Shadrach, Meshach, and Abednego. They were given pagan names to make clear that they were now under King Nebuchadnezzar's authority, a pagan king. However, even though they were in captivity to a pagan king, these four individuals determined to honor the one true God.

As part of their training, the Israelites had to eat the king's food, food which violated God's command to them as his people. Daniel, however, was committed to honoring the Lord. Daniel 1:8 says, "But Daniel resolved not to defile himself with the royal food and wine." Even though he was now captive in an ungodly society, Daniel was committed to staying faithful to God and his Word. Because of his conviction, Daniel "asked the chief official for permission not to defile himself this way" (Dan. 1:8). Daniel respectfully appealed to the one in charge of their training to be released from the food requirement.

Now the Bible tells us that Daniel had gained the chief official's favor; however, the chief official was understandably afraid. If he granted Daniel's request and then Daniel and his friends looked worse than the other trainees, then the king would have him killed. So Daniel proposed an experiment to the guard overseeing them: "Please test your servants for ten days: Give us nothing but vegetables to eat and water to drink. Then compare our appearance with that of the young men who eat the royal food, and treat your servants in accordance with what you see" (Dan. 1:12-13). The guard agreed to Daniel's proposal of a ten-day test.

Daniel showed wisdom in his request. Instead of directly rebelling against the king's requirements, he asked if he could try something different to see if it worked well. Sure enough, after the ten days, Daniel and his companions looked more healthy than those eating the king's food. Therefore, Daniel's request was granted.

Young person, Daniel teaches us how to walk as Christians when we find ourselves caught in an ungodly society. Daniel didn't compromise. At the same time, he maintained respect for the authority. He was considerate of the official's position—that the official could get into trouble with the king. Remember that non-Christians are not our enemies. As Ephesians 6:12 tells us, "Our struggle is not against flesh and blood." At school and at work, by being respectful with people in authority, we can often gain favor with them, whether or not they are Christians.

As they pursued their education, these four young men stood out in their training as excellent students. "To these four young men God gave knowledge and understanding of all kinds of literature and learning" (Dan. 1:17). Notice that the Bible says "God gave" these things. These abilities were gifts from God. And God gave Daniel a very special gift: that of understanding and interpreting dreams and visions.

At the end of their training, these four Israelites were tested by the king: "In every matter of wisdom and understanding about which the king questioned them, he found them ten times better than all the magicians and enchanters in his whole kingdom" (Dan. 1:20). The king was impressed with Daniel, Shadrach, Meshach, and Abednego.

The Lord used Daniel's special gift to interpret dreams in a powerful way. After King Nebuchadnezzar had a dream regarding future kingdoms, he wanted someone to tell him the dream's meaning. However, the king would not tell his advisors what the dream was. When no one could tell the king his dream, let alone interpret it, the king ordered that all of his wise men, including Daniel and his comrades, be killed.

Daniel again showed great wisdom in how he handled this matter. Daniel 2:14 says, "When Arioch, the commander of the king's guard, had gone out to put to death the wise men of Babylon, Daniel spoke to him with wisdom and tact." After asking why the king had issued such a terrible decree, Daniel himself "went in to the king and asked for time, so that he might interpret the dream for him" (Dan. 2:16). Daniel then asked his three friends to pray fervently to the Lord. Sure enough, that night God revealed both the dream and its interpretation to Daniel.

Daniel proceeded to share with King Nebuchadnezzar about future world kingdoms. After those kingdoms would come and go, God's Kingdom would be inaugurated. He then declared the following about God's kingdom: "In the time of those kings, the God of heaven will set up a kingdom that will never be destroyed, nor will it be left to another people. It will crush all those kingdoms and bring them to an end, but it will itself endure forever" (Dan. 2:44). Indeed, the Lord's kingdom does live forever in the hearts of men and women and boys and girls all over the world!

After Daniel told Nebuchadnezzar his dream as well as interpreted it, King Nebuchadnezzar honored Daniel's God: "Surely your God is the God of gods and the Lord of kings and a revealer of mysteries, for you were able to reveal this mystery" (Dan. 2:47). King Nebuchadnezzar proceeded to promote Daniel to be ruler over the Babylonian province. In addition, Daniel asked that Shadrach, Meshach, and Abednego be the administrators over that province; his request was granted.

As time went on, Daniel continued to serve powerful kings. He served through the reigns of Nebuchadnezzar and Belshazzar. After King Belshazzar was killed, Darius the Mede became king. Then King Darius made Daniel one of three administrators who oversaw his kingdom. Daniel 6:3 tells us that Daniel stood out as an administrator: "Now Daniel so distinguished himself among the administrators and the satraps by his exceptional qualities that the king planned to set him over the whole kingdom." Because of his character and gifting, the king planned to put Daniel in charge of the entire kingdom.

Young person, how do we distinguish ourselves? We do so over time by how we work through various situations and dilemmas. As others observe us, we show our character. We show integrity by being truthful with our supervisors. When we get various assignments, we show whether we are responsible. We use the gifts that God has given us to bless others. We stand out by working hard and making no excuses. In the process, others learn that they can trust us.

Well, when the other administrators saw that King Darius was going to promote Daniel, they tried to find a way to bring Daniel down. As they considered what charges to bring against Daniel, they realized that he was a man of integrity and that they could find nothing against him: "They could find no corruption in him, because he was trustworthy and neither corrupt nor negligent" (Dan. 6:4). Still, they schemed together to see what they could do to destroy Daniel's reputation in the eyes of the king.

However, because Daniel was a leader in righteousness—a man who walked uprightly in all his dealings, they couldn't find anything wrong with Daniel. At last they realized that they could find nothing against Daniel unless it had to do with God. They schemed the following against Daniel: "We will never find any basis for charges against this man Daniel unless it has something to do with the law of his God" (Dan. 6:5).

To come against Daniel, they decided to go together to the king to propose a law that appealed to the king's pride: "O King Darius, live forever! The royal administrators, prefects, satraps, advisers and governors have all agreed that the king should issue an edict and enforce the decree that anyone who prays to any god or man during the next thirty days, except to you, O king, shall be thrown into the lions' den" (Dan. 6:6-7). Falling prey to their flattery, the king agreed to their law and decreed it in writing. Their law was based on deception; they had deceived the king. They had not "all agreed" to this law. Daniel was the foremost administrator, and he hadn't agreed to it! So the whole foundation for the law was a lie.

When Daniel heard of the law, he didn't change his behavior. When he heard of this unrighteous law, he didn't compromise. Of course, Daniel prayed only to the one true God. As he had always done, Daniel went home and prayed with his window open to Jerusalem: "Three times a day he got down on his knees and prayed, giving thanks to his God, just as he had done before" (Dan. 6:10). Daniel put into practice an active prayer life. The source of Daniel's strength was his relationship with the Lord. He regularly communicated with God. As Psalm 55:17 says, "Evening, morning and noon I cry out in distress, and he hears my voice."

Daniel had nothing to hide! He was doing nothing wrong. This law was an unrighteous one, and at risk to his life, Daniel chose to follow God's Word as he had always done. Daniel showed courage of conviction, meaning that he was willing to die if necessary for his belief in following the Lord.

Young person, we learn from Daniel not to fear man. When faced with pressure to do things contrary to God's Word, we need to continue to fear God and obey his Word. We learn that even if everyone else is going the wrong way, we need to be willing to stand alone and do the right thing. We learn from Daniel to stand for God—even if it means standing alone! I encourage you to be a leader in righteousness.

After the other administrators spied on Daniel and witnessed him still praying to God as he had always done, they went as a group to report Daniel's violation of the law to King Darius: "Daniel, who is one of the exiles from Judah, pays no attention to you, O king, or to the decree you put in writing. He still prays three times a day" (Dan. 6:13). They reported to the king that Daniel was breaking the king's law! However, the king was not angry with Daniel; rather he was very upset that he had done something that could harm Daniel, for he respected Daniel very much. Very disturbed, King Darius did everything he could to save Daniel.

However, the group went to King Darius and held him accountable to the law: "Remember, O king, that according to the law of the Medes and Persians no decree or edict that the king issues can be changed" (Dan. 6:15). (Persian custom was that once the king made a decree, that it couldn't be changed.) Although Daniel had gained the king's favor and the king did everything he could to keep Daniel from having to be punished, the king's hands were tied. He reluctantly commanded Daniel to be thrown into the lions' den.

Young person, if you are falsely accused of something, I encourage you to simply continue to do what is right. Be humble, be faithful in your duties, and work diligently. Trust the Lord that he is looking out for you. Obey the laws of the land, but if a law is set up against God's law—against God's Word, you must obey God. Be respectful with the authorities and don't try to make issues; however, if you are faced with a choice between obeying man and obeying God, choose to obey God.

Often this kind of issue will play out in the work field. A coworker or even a supervisor may expect you to do something that you know to be wrong. You then have a choice regarding what you are going to do. Are you going to go along with the crowd and do wrong? Or are you going to choose to do what is right? It may be very uncomfortable for you to take a godly stand. You may be persecuted; you may be made to be an outcast. You may be laughed at and ridiculed.

Sometimes, even your supervisor may order you to do something wrong. At that point, you may have to pray about confronting your supervisor forthrightly. In the process, you might suffer negative consequences because of your stand. But always remember, the Lord is with you; he is looking out for you.

Now a lions' den was a pit of lions with a small hole at the top. It was impossible for anyone to escape the lions in this kind of pit. But Daniel's faith had impacted King Darius. When Daniel was thrown into the lions' den, the king shared his care for Daniel: "May your God, whom you serve continually, rescue you!" (Dan. 6:16).

Well, King Darius had a long night. He could not sleep. Early that next morning, the king ran to check on Daniel in the lions' den. He cried out to Daniel, "Daniel, servant of the living God, has your God, whom you serve continually, been able to rescue you from the lions?" (Dan. 6:20). It is clear that Daniel had influenced King Darius, who had come to recognize the one true God as protector and rescuer.

The king was greatly relieved to hear Daniel's response: "O king, live forever! My God sent his angel, and he shut the mouths of the lions. They have not hurt me, because I was found innocent in his sight. Nor have I ever done any wrong before you, O king" (Dan. 6:21-22). Referring to God as "my God," Daniel gave the Lord glory. Daniel was innocent of any wrongdoing. He had no wounds on his body. Why? Because he trusted God. Daniel's personal relationship with God saw him through the danger. 1 Corinthians 15:58 could be said of Daniel: "Therefore, my dear brothers, stand firm. Let nothing move you. Always give yourselves fully to the work of the Lord, because you know that your labor in the Lord is not in vain."

King Darius proceeded to punish those who had made the false accusation against Daniel. He then made a decree that "people must fear and reverence the God of Daniel" in his entire kingdom (Dan. 6:26). Darius proclaimed the following: "For he is the living God and he endures forever; his kingdom will not be destroyed, his dominion will never end. He rescues and he saves; he performs signs and wonders in the heavens and on the earth. He has rescued Daniel from the power of the lions" (Dan. 6:26-27). Daniel was fully vindicated!

Just as God rescued Daniel from the power of the lions and the scheme of his accusers, our rescuer is Jesus Christ! The Lord rescues us from the dangers of sin and the false accusations of Satan. Because of Jesus' death on the cross and his resurrection, we are not consumed. We are saved from our sin, and we are saved from our ultimate accuser. The Lord Jesus is our rescuer! He is our Savior! He saves us from the power of sin every day of our lives. As Daniel did, I encourage you to put your trust in God!

Daniel's life teaches us how to stand for God in an ungodly society. We need to use wisdom. We need to exercise tact. We need to be sensitive to the position of various people, including our supervisors at work. We learn from Daniel to live a life that ultimately gains favor from others, whether they are Christian or non-Christian. Ultimately, we learn that we must trust God and his Word. When others may be pressuring us or manipulating us to do wrong, we need to have the courage of conviction to stand for the Lord and be a leader in righteousness. We learn from Daniel that sometimes we need to stand alone for God's kingdom.

Memory Verse

Daniel 6:23 "The king was overjoyed and gave orders to lift Daniel out of the den. And when Daniel was lifted from the den, no wound was found on him, because he had trusted in his God."

SHADRACH, MESHACH, AND ABEDNEGO

Stand for God amid Peer Pressure

Daniel's contemporaries—Shadrach, Meshach, and Abednego—also had to stand for the Lord. Like Daniel, they are great examples to us of ones who trusted the Lord under extreme pressure.

Peer pressure is a very serious thing, particularly for young people. Peer pressure is pressure by one's peer group—friends, acquaintances, classmates, neighbors, and teammates—to do certain things, whether good or bad; however, it often has a negative connotation—pressure to do wrong things. I recall when I was in ninth grade, a neighborhood friend pressured me to smoke a cigarette. I told him no; I knew that it was wrong. Peers will often pressure their friends and try to impress them, often out of their own insecurity. They desire to carry others along into their wrongdoing.

In Daniel chapter 3, Shadrach, Meshach, and Abednego experienced serious peer pressure. In fact, they were pressured to deny God; they were pressured to deny their relationship with God. If they would not do so, they would experience a terrible death. It was the toughest peer pressure that anyone could experience.

Here's their story. King Nebuchadnezzar set up a huge gold image—an idol—that was ninety feet tall. He called all the government officials together. All these government officials were the peer group of Shadrach, Meshach, and Abednego. You see, these three young men were Israelites, God's chosen people, who were in captivity to King Nebuchadnezzar of Babylon. However, they had so distinguished themselves that they had entered the king's service and were government officials themselves, part of this group of administrators (Dan. 1:19).

Anyway, when all the government officials had come together to stand before this towering gold image, this is what the herald declared: "This is what you are commanded to do, O peoples, nations and men of every language: As soon as you hear the sound of the horn, flute, zither, lyre, harp, pipes and all kinds of music, you must fall down and worship the image of gold that King Nebuchadnezzar has set up. Whoever does not fall down and worship will immediately be thrown into a blazing furnace" (Dan. 3:4-6). Wow! What pressure! The pressure came in two fronts: pressure to submit in front of all of one's peers and pressure because of the threat of being burned alive in a fiery furnace!

Well, at the sound of all the instruments, everyone bowed down, except our three champions. The Bible says, "All the peoples, nations and men of every language fell down and worshiped the image of gold" (Dan. 3:7). Everyone, of course, except for Shadrach, Meshach, and Abednego! These three young men refused to bow down—they would not deny the one true God. They knew that bowing down to this idol would be in direct contradiction to obeying God.

Shadrach, Meshach, and Abednego were Israelites, God's chosen people. Of course, they had grown up learning God's Torah, including the Ten Commandments. The Ten Commandments give us guidance for living. Shadrach, Meshach, and Abednego knew that bowing down to this idol would be an act of clear disobedience to God's Ten Commandments:

> And God spoke all these words:
>
> "I am the Lord your God, who brought you out of Egypt, out of the land of slavery.
>
> "You shall have no other gods before me.
>
> "You shall not make for yourself an idol in the form of anything in heaven above or on the earth beneath or in the waters below. You shall not bow down to them or worship them; for I, the Lord your God, am a jealous God, punishing the children for the sin of the fathers to the third and fourth generation of those who hate me, but showing love to a thousand generations of those who love me and keep my commandments." (Exod. 20:1-6)

Shadrach, Meshach, and Abednego had committed themselves to worshiping and obeying the one true God. Young person, obeying God will inevitably cause you to come into conflict with this world system. Shadrach, Meshach, and Abednego did not bow down to the image of gold; they chose to serve God rather than to worship an idol, even at the threat of their lives.

When King Nebuchadnezzar heard about these ones' refusal to bow down to his image of gold, he became furious. He pressured them by questioning them: "Is it true, Shadrach, Meshach, and Abednego, that you do not serve my gods or worship the image of gold I have set up?" He gave them one more chance to bow down to worship his gold image and terribly warned them that if they didn't do so, he would throw them into the fiery furnace. He said, "Then what god will be able to rescue you from my hand?" (Dan. 3:14-15).

King Nebuchadnezzar tried to exert pressure on Shadrach, Meshach, and Abednego by interrogating them with questions. Being peppered with questions is one way that peers will try to pressure you. When your peers are doing wrong things, they might ask questions such as the following: "Why don't you go along with us? Who will ever know? What are you afraid of? You're just scared." And on and on it goes.

For young people and children, let me be clear. You need to answer your parents' questions; you need to answer your teachers' questions. But you don't need to answer all your peers' questions, especially when they are pressuring you to do things you know are wrong. Don't be intimidated when peers question you to do wrong things or persecute you for doing right things. Don't get defensive. When you're being pressured to do wrong, don't give in to it.

At the same time, when you're being pressured, don't just hope it goes away. Like Shadrach, Meshach, and Abednego, you need to look the person—the bully—in the eye and forthrightly tell him that you're committed to the Lord Jesus and are seeking to please him. After enduring the pressure of Nebuchadnezzar's questioning and threats, Shadrach, Meshach, and Abednego answered the following: "O Nebuchadnezzar, we do not need to defend ourselves before you in this matter. If we are thrown into the blazing furnace, the God we serve is able to save us from it, and he will rescue us from your hand, O king. But even if he does not, we want you to know, O king, that we will not serve your gods or worship the image of gold you have set up" (Dan. 3:16-18). These three champions had fully surrendered to the Lord. They communicated their conviction to the king. They were willing to die for their relationship with the Lord. Hebrews 11:34 alludes to the courage of these three champions: they "quenched the fury of the flames."

Shadrach, Meshach, and Abednego had the courage of their *convictions*. What is a conviction? A conviction is something that one is willing to die for. What are you willing to die for? If you believe in something strongly enough that you are willing to die for it, that is a conviction. Do you have any convictions that you are willing to die for? Hopefully you have a conviction about the Lord Jesus Christ, who died for us on the cross for our eternal salvation.

As champions for the Lord, we don't serve God just to be blessed. We obey and worship God because he is deserving of all our praise and devotion. He is the one true God, who created us, loves us, and paid the penalty of sin for us. Shadrach, Meshach, and Abednego stated that God was able to save them, but they made it clear that whether the Lord saved them or not, that was his choice. They said, "But even if he does not, we want you to know, O king, that we will not serve your gods or worship the image of gold you have set up" (Dan. 3:18).

Our worship of God is not dependent on whether God saves us from a certain outcome. Whether he saves us or not from a particular circumstance, God calls us to trust, serve, and obey him. Many young believers get disillusioned when God doesn't give them what they desire. We need to remember that the general reason bad things happen in this world is sin. Sin is what causes strife and destruction, not God. Romans 6:23 tells us, "For the wages of sin is death."

Also, perhaps the Lord is allowing a trial to come into our life so that we can grow and mature. James 1:2-4 reminds us, "Consider it pure joy, my brothers, whenever you face trials of many kinds, because you know that the testing of your faith develops perseverance. Perseverance must finish its work so that you may be mature and complete, not lacking anything." God may be using the trial to equip you to become the champion he is calling you to be. God wants us to be champions that love, obey, and serve him no matter what. That's a champion! We learn to trust and serve him through all of life whether he "blesses" us or not.

After Shadrach, Meshach, and Abednego declared their trust in God to King Nebuchadnezzar, his attitude turned for the worse. Furious Nebuchadnezzar made the fiery furnace "seven times hotter" (Dan. 3:19). The Bible says that "the king's command was so urgent and the furnace so hot that the flames of the fire killed the soldiers who took up Shadrach, Meshach and Abednego, and these three men, firmly tied, fell into the blazing furnace" (Dan. 3:22-23).

King Nebuchadnezzar was a bully. Young people, bullies will try to intimidate you—to persecute you for walking in righteousness—but stand for God. Keep your eyes on the Lord amid persecution. Don't yield to the pressure. As you honor God, he will honor you!

Well, even though the soldiers who threw them into the fiery furnace were killed from the flames themselves, Shadrach, Meshach, and Abednego were not. In fact, when a fourth man appeared with them in the furnace, King Nebuchadnezzar leaped to his feet in amazement. "He said, 'Look! I see four men walking around in the fire, unbound and unharmed, and the fourth looks like a son of the gods'" (Dan. 3:25). Nebuchadnezzar, a *pagan* believing in *false gods*, made this observation! While we don't know for sure whether the fourth person in the fiery furnace was the Lord or an angel, we can be sure that the Lord is with us when we face persecution for our faith!

Psalm 91:9-11, 14-16 reassures us with these words:

> If you make the Most High your dwelling—even the Lord, who is my refuge—then no harm will befall you, no disaster will come near your tent. For he will command his angels concerning you to guard you in all your ways. . . . "Because he loves me," says the Lord, "I will rescue him; I will protect him, for he acknowledges my name. He will call upon me, and I will answer him; I will be with him in trouble, I will deliver him and honor him. With long life will I satisfy him and show him my salvation."

After witnessing this miraculous salvation, King Nebuchadnezzar called out to these champions: "Shadrach, Meshach and Abednego, servants of the Most High God, come out! Come here!" (Dan. 3:26). These three young men were great witnesses for the one true God! When they exited the fiery furnace, there was not a hint of fire on them! Then Nebuchadnezzar praised the one true God and expressed the nature of their courageous stand:

> Praise be to the God of Shadrach, Meshach and Abednego, who has sent his angel and rescued his servants! They trusted in him and defied the king's command and were willing to give up their lives rather than serve or worship any god except their own God. (Dan. 3:28)

What courage by these three young men! What inspired them? They were inspired by their love and devotion to the Lord! Shadrach, Meshach, and Abednego stood the test, and the king promoted them. They stood on the courage of their convictions and honored the one true God! They would not deny their loving God.

Young person, I encourage you to stand for God amid peer pressure. When being persecuted for standing for God and for righteousness, keep your eyes on the Lord. Love the Lord, stand for him, be a champion!

Memory Passage

> Daniel 3:16-18 "Shadrach, Meshach and Abednego replied to the king, 'O Nebuchadnezzar, we do not need to defend ourselves before you in this matter. If we are thrown into the blazing furnace, the God we serve is able to save us from it, and he will rescue us from your hand, O king. But even if he does not, we want you to know, O king, that we will not serve your gods or worship the image of gold you have set up.'"

JONAH

Show God's Love by Sharing His Message

Have you ever played a tag game? Of course, when you play a tag game, you run away from the person trying to tag you. Playing tag can be a lot of fun. Experiencing the chase of a tag game can be invigorating. However, while running away is fine for tag games, you *never* should run away from your parents, and you *never* want to run away from God! A man named Jonah did just that. He ran away from God. From Jonah's experience, we can learn some very important lessons. When God calls us, we need to obey him the first time. Also, when God calls us, he wants us to help others. He calls us to show God's love by sharing God's message!

In Jonah 1:2, God called Jonah: "Go to the great city of Nineveh and preach against it, because its wickedness has come up before me." Historically this "great city" Nineveh was an important one. The ancient builder Nimrod had constructed it. It had been the capital of the world empire of Assyria. It also had become a great place of evil.

However, Jonah ran from God's call. In fact, he ran as far away as seemingly possible. He sought to go to what was known at that time as the end of the geographical world. He "sailed for Tarshish to flee from the Lord" (Jonah 1:3). If you look at a map of the Mediterranean Sea, Nineveh was inland on the east side of that great sea. Instead of obeying God and going to Nineveh in the East, Jonah went to the West. Boarding a ship headed in the opposite direction to the extreme west end of the Mediterranean Sea, he traveled to the city of Tarshish in Spain.

However, Jonah learned that no matter how much you try to run, you can't hide from God. Psalm 139 affirms this truth:

> Where can I go from your Spirit? Where can I flee from your presence? . . . If I rise on the wings of the dawn, if I settle on the far side of the sea, even there your hand will guide me, your right hand will hold me fast. If I say, "Surely the darkness will hide me and the light become night around me," even the darkness will not be dark to you; the night will shine like the day, for darkness is as light to you. (Ps. 139:7, 9-12)

Jonah found out that you can't run from God! As Jonah's ship sailed on the Mediterranean Sea, a terrible storm developed. Jonah 1:4 says, "Then the Lord sent a great wind on the sea, and such a violent storm arose that the ship threatened to break up." Indeed, we see here that the Lord controls nature—he controls the natural elements. He controls the wind, the waves, and the fish of the sea. In this story, we see that God is a miracle worker who controls all of creation.

With the ship in danger, all the sailors cried out in fear to their own pagan gods. However, during the storm, Jonah was sleeping soundly. Then the ship captain went to him, awoke him, and appealed to Jonah to call on his God. We see here that the captain cared more for the crew than Jonah did. Jonah was seemingly oblivious to their harrowing plight. While the captain was caring for the crew, Jonah was inattentive to the storm's effect on others.

Young person, when you follow the will of God, you will develop a love for people. God's will for you relates to others—in some way you will be helping others and caring for them. However, if you run away from God's will, the inevitable result will be that you will grow calloused toward others.

Well, often in ancient times, the method of using "lots" was used to determine who was at fault for a certain thing. For instance, a group of sticks might be put in a bag to see who would pick the largest stick. The shipmates cast lots to see who was responsible for this terrible storm, and God allowed the lot to fall to Jonah.

The other sailors questioned Jonah regarding his identity: "Tell us, who is responsible for making all this trouble for us? What do you do? Where do you come from? What is your country? From what people are you?" (Jonah 1:8). Notice that their questions focused on Jonah's identity. Jonah was running from his identity as a child of the God of Israel and his purpose as God's messenger.

Young person, what is your identity? Are you a follower of God? Are you a believer in the Lord? If so, you are identified with Messiah. You are a Christian—a follower of the Lord. If you have received Jesus as your Savior and Lord, you are a child of God. Remember that you are part of the family of God. As a child of God, you are called to be a worshiper and servant of the Lord.

Jonah admitted to his identity: "I am a Hebrew and I worship the Lord, the God of heaven, who made the sea and the land" (Jonah 1:9). At that point, as he admitted to his identity as one who worships the God of creation, Jonah must have realized that he couldn't run away from God. The most miserable person is a Christian who is not living for God—one running away from God out of rebellion, out of fear, or out of a cold heart.

Note that even while fleeing God, Jonah was still being a witness for the Lord. Jonah had shared with the sailors that he was running from the Lord's purpose for him. Out of fear of Jonah's God, they were very afraid as they asked him, "What have you done?" (Jonah 1:10). Their rhetorical question was really an accusation for causing the consequence of this terrible storm. As the storm got worse and worse, they asked Jonah, "What should we do to you to make the sea calm down for us?" (Jonah 1:11).

Jonah knew that he was responsible for the storm. He answered them: "Pick me up and throw me into the sea and it will become calm. I know that it is my fault that this great storm has come upon you" (Jonah 1:12). Jonah knew that being thrown overboard would be a death sentence. At this point, Jonah was ready to die.

Young person, when you run from God's call, you can become so miserable that you just want to die. However, by living for God and fulfilling his purpose for your life, you will experience abundant life! As a Christian, you really have no choice but to be in God's purpose for you. Running away from God's purpose for you will make you miserable, but walking in God's plan will grant you a life-giving sense of purpose!

Well, these pagan sailors were more caring for others than was Jonah. In running from God's call to the Ninevites, Jonah showed a lack of compassion for others. In contrast, the sailors showed care for Jonah by rowing harder to try to get to land, but the storm grew worse. As the sailors showed care for Jonah by valuing his life, they put him to shame for his lack of compassion toward the Ninevites.

Young person, if we as believers who know the living God run from his purpose for us, even people of the world will put us to shame. These pagan sailors cried out to the one true God: "O Lord, please do not let us die for taking this man's life. Do not hold us accountable for killing an innocent man, for you, O Lord, have done as you pleased" (Jonah 1:14).

Jonah allowed the sailors to throw him overboard into the stormy waters. When the sailors threw him overboard, the sea grew calm. Even the crew marveled at God's power: "At this the men greatly feared the Lord, and they offered a sacrifice to the Lord and made vows to him" (Jonah 1:16). These pagan sailors recognized the God of creation as the one true God. He is the only one who brings salvation. One of the key messages of the entire book is expressed in Jonah 2:9: "Salvation comes from the Lord."

However, Jonah did not die. God, the Creator of the universe, of nature, and of all wonders, sent a great fish to swallow Jonah. We see in the context of this story that God is over all of creation. Nothing is too hard for him. If the wind and the waves obey him, certainly he can provide a fish to house Jonah. For three days and nights Jonah was in that fish!

Again, we see that God is supreme over all of the natural elements! Yes, God *can do* these miraculous things and *did do* them! Our Creator is a miracle-working God!

From inside the fish, Jonah cried out to God. In the midst of his sinking into the depths of the Mediterranean Sea, Jonah prayed to the Lord: "In my distress I called to the Lord, and he answered me. From the depths of the grave I called for help, and you listened to my cry" (Jonah 2:2). When you run from God's plan, you may come to the point of feeling you're drowning. Sometimes you may feel as if you're sinking. Psalm 118:5 says, "In my anguish I cried to the Lord, and he answered by setting me free."

Jonah repented and returned to the Lord: "I have been banished from your sight; yet I will look again toward your holy temple" (Jonah 2:4). As Jonah repented, he affirmed that he would return to the temple, the place of God's presence, the place of God's people. He would look to the Lord. Indeed, we return to God by looking to him!

Young person, as we look to the Lord in repentance, he will redeem our life: "To the roots of the mountains I sank down; the earth beneath barred me in forever. But you brought my life up from the pit, O Lord my God" (Jonah 2:6). When we turn back to God, he redeems our life from drowning in sin. He redeems our life from the pit of destruction!

When we run away from God, we can tend to forget him. When our life is being destroyed in the storms of life and we're experiencing the reaping of our wrong behavior, we need to remember the Lord. "When my life was ebbing away, I remembered you, Lord, and my prayer rose to you, to your holy temple" (Jonah 2:7). As we remember him, he will lift us up and restore us.

Also, when you remember the Lord, you are turning away from idolatry. Jonah said, "Those who cling to worthless idols forfeit the grace that could be theirs" (Jonah 2:8). Young person, when you play a sport, you don't want to forfeit the game. It's sad when a team has to forfeit a game because they don't have enough players or because they have negative attitudes and quit. A forfeit means that both teams don't get a chance to play the game.

Likewise, when we run from God's plan, we're forfeiting God's grace for us. You see, God gives us grace for whatever he calls us to. However, if we run from God, then we forfeit his grace. Don't lose God's grace by running from his purpose for you!

When we "cling to worthless idols," we're really putting other things, including ourselves, above God. That's idolatry. We might put sports, our cell phones, social media, or electronic games above God. Whatever it may be, if it becomes more important than God to us, that's an idol. And when we pursue idolatry—other things over the Lord—we forfeit God's grace. Instead of God's grace being operational in our lives, we're letting other things take the place of God's plan for us. Don't forfeit God's grace in your life; instead worship and serve the one true God. By doing so, God's grace will be abundant in your life!

From inside the fish, Jonah rededicated himself to the Lord: "But I, with a song of thanksgiving, will sacrifice to you. What I have vowed I will make good. Salvation comes from the Lord" (Jonah 2:9). With a heart of thanks, Jonah vowed to follow the Lord. He recognized that salvation is from the Lord. God proceeded to command the fish to vomit Jonah onto dry land.

Young person, if you do run from the Lord, remember to return to him quickly and wholeheartedly. He will restore you, put you on solid ground, and help you to get back to his purpose!

Well, Jonah fulfilled his vow to the Lord. Thank the Lord that he is a God of second chances! "The word of the Lord came to Jonah a second time" (Jonah 3:1). God called Jonah again to proclaim his message to Nineveh.

God commissioned Jonah to bring *his message* to the Ninevites. That's what God does. He will give you a message—a message from his heart for others. When you preach, God gives you a message to communicate to the people.

Well, this time Jonah obeyed God. When Jonah arrived to Nineveh, he proclaimed God's message: "Forty more days and Nineveh will be overturned" (Jonah 3:4). When the Ninevites heard the message, what did they do? Did they rebel against God? No! Lo and behold, they *believed* the message—the Ninevites believed God and repented! Symbolic of their repentance, "they declared a fast, and all of them, from the greatest to the least, put on sackcloth" (Jonah 3:5).

In fact, Nineveh's king made a decree that called upon the people to repent. As part of his decree, he proclaimed the following: "Let everyone call urgently on God. Let them give up their evil ways and their violence. Who knows? God may yet relent and with compassion turn from his fierce anger so that we will not perish" (Jonah 3:8-9). The king and his nobles directed the people to call on God and repent from their evil and violent behavior.

When God saw the Ninevites' repentance, he relented, had compassion, and did not destroy Nineveh. You would think that Jonah would be happy that the people were responding to his message. Right? Not so. Instead, Jonah became angry that God was not punishing this pagan people. He wanted God's favor to be reserved for his people, the Israelites. Here God had shown mercy to Jonah by giving him a second chance. And yet Jonah himself was unwilling to extend that mercy to others.

Young person, that is often the way it is with us. So often we want to "stick it" to others for their failings. At the same time, we hope that God forgives us for our failings. Jesus emphasized that we should pray the following: "Forgive us our debts as we also have forgiven our debtors" (Matt. 6:12). He added, "For if you forgive men when they sin against you, your heavenly Father will also forgive you. But if you do not forgive men their sins, your Father will not forgive your sins" (Matt. 6:14-15). We need to remember that since God has forgiven us greatly, we should also be willing to be merciful and to forgive others.

Unfortunately, Jonah did not share God's heart of compassion for the Ninevites. Jonah 4:2 expresses the reason that Jonah disobeyed God in the first place: "O Lord, is this not what I said when I was still at home? That is why I was so quick to flee to Tarshish. I knew that you are a gracious and compassionate God, slow to anger and abounding in love, a God who relents from sending calamity." Jonah wanted God's love, forgiveness, and mercy to be reserved for the children of Israel.

Jonah was very displeased that God's grace was being extended to these evil Gentiles. He said that he would rather die: "Now, O Lord, take away my life, for it is better for me to die than to live" (Jonah 4:3). Jonah expressed a poor attitude.

From Jonah's experience, we learn that God's forgiveness is for all people. God's grace, which is his favor toward us even though we don't deserve it, is not just for us Christians. We need to share God's grace with unbelievers. Romans 5:8 says, "But God demonstrates his own love for us in this: While we were still sinners, Christ died for us." 1 Timothy 1:15 says, "Here is a trustworthy saying that deserves full acceptance: Christ Jesus came into the world to save sinners."

In addition, God's church is for all peoples. Isaiah 56:7 expresses this truth: "My house will be called a house of prayer for all nations." Always remember that God's compassion is for all people; he wants all people to come to him for salvation. Let's share God's love and mercy with others!

When God didn't destroy the people of Nineveh, Jonah had a pity party for himself. Hoping to see Nineveh's destruction, he sat down outside the city. To comfort Jonah from the hot sun, God provided him with a vine for shade. But then a worm ate the vine, and the vine withered. After the vine withered, the sun beat down on Jonah. Without shade to shield him from the sun, Jonah again said that he wanted to die: "It would be better for me to die than to live" (Jonah 4:8).

However, God asked Jonah, "Do you have a right to be angry about the vine?" (Jonah 4:9).

In his insolence, Jonah responded, "I do. I am angry enough to die" (Jonah 4:9).

Responding to Jonah's lack of compassion for others, the Lord told him the following: "You have been concerned about this vine, though you did not tend it or make it grow. It sprang up overnight and died overnight. But Nineveh has more than a hundred and twenty thousand people who cannot tell their right hand from their left, and many cattle as well. Should I not be concerned about that great city?" (Jonah 4:10-11).

Young person, many people are in a spiritual state of death. They can't "tell their right hand from their left." Many people are mixed up. It's almost as if they're living in the Dark Ages. They need God's Kingdom in their lives. God's Kingdom brings righteousness, order, and blessing to people's lives and families. All people desperately need the Lord!

God wants all people to turn to him for salvation. Ezekiel 33:11 expresses God's heart: "As surely as I live, declares the Sovereign Lord, I take no pleasure in the death of the wicked, but rather that they turn from their ways and live. Turn! Turn from your evil ways!" The Lord desires all people to have a true relationship with him: "He is patient with you, not wanting anyone to perish, but everyone to come to repentance" (2 Pet. 3:9).

What is God's message to us through the book of Jonah? He wants us to know that he has compassion and mercy for the lost, often more than we do. We have been given the awesome grace of God—we've received his favor even though we don't deserve it! Shouldn't we extend that same grace to others as opposed to selfishly hoarding it? People need the Lord! Jesus, our example, is compassionate. Let's follow his example, be compassionate, and share God's grace with others! I encourage you to show God's love by sharing his message!

Memory Passage

> Jonah 2:7-9 "When my life was ebbing away, I remembered you, Lord, and my prayer rose to you, to your holy temple. Those who cling to worthless idols forfeit the grace that could be theirs. But I, with a song of thanksgiving, will sacrifice to you. What I have vowed I will make good. Salvation comes from the Lord."

JOSEPH AND MARY

Humbly Listen to and Obey the Lord's Will

The Bible tells us of two individuals betrothed to one another by a legally-binding engagement. An angel appeared to both of them on separate occasions and told them the surprising news that a baby was to be born to them who would become the Savior of the world. Of course, we are talking about the baby Jesus, and the two individuals were Joseph and Mary. While their plans were being drastically changed, Joseph and Mary humbly listened to God's messenger and obeyed the Lord's will for them.

Angels appeared to both Joseph and Mary—an angel appeared to Joseph in a dream, and the angel Gabriel visited Mary. First let's examine this Christmas story from the perspective of Joseph. God spoke to Joseph a number of times through dreams. In fact, five times in the first two chapters of the gospel of Matthew, God communicated important messages to Joseph and Mary through dreams.

In Matthew 1:20-21, the angel first spoke to Joseph in a dream. However, before that dream occurred, Joseph's world had been turned upside down because Mary, who was pledged to become his wife, was found to be pregnant. The Bible tells us that the virgin Mary was to have a child through the Holy Spirit; however, Joseph did not yet know that this was God's plan. I am sure that Joseph was very saddened when he first found out that his betrothed Mary was pregnant. What must Joseph have been going through? Matthew 1:19 shares of Joseph's character: "Because Joseph her husband was a righteous man and did not want to expose her to public disgrace, he had in mind to divorce her quietly."

Notice that the Bible says that Joseph was "righteous." Because of his righteousness, even though he must have been terribly disappointed over Mary's seeming immorality, he was determined to divorce her in a way that would not humiliate her. Joseph was not self-righteous but was considerate of others. His righteousness included mercy and compassion toward others. Joseph was the embodiment of Micah 6:8: "He has showed you, O man, what is good. And what does the Lord require of you? To act justly and to love mercy and to walk humbly with your God."

But then through a dream, an angel shared with Joseph exactly what was happening: "Joseph, son of David, do not be afraid to take Mary home as your wife, because what is conceived in her is from the Holy Spirit. She will give birth to a son, and you are to give him the name Jesus, because he will save his people from their sins" (Matt. 1:20-21). Wow! What a swing of emotion Joseph must have experienced! Here on one hand, he is thinking of quietly divorcing Mary because of unfaithfulness; now, he is being told that the child in her womb is going to be a Savior!

In the angel's address to Joseph, he referred to Joseph as the "son of David." This address referred to the fact that Joseph and the baby Jesus were in the kingly line of David. (Both Mary and Joseph were descendants of Israel's King David, a man after God's heart.) The angel proceeded to declare that the baby will be given the name *Jesus*, which is the Greek word for the name *Joshua*, meaning "The Lord saves" or "The Lord is salvation." In effect, Jesus would be the Savior of the world. What a turn of events for Joseph!

This baby would bless not only Joseph and Mary but also the entire world! Jesus would be the Savior of the world! But what would Jesus save us from? The angel told Joseph that "he will save his people from their sins" (Matt. 1:21).

The purpose of Jesus' coming to this earth was to save us from our sin. What does sin do? What does unconfessed sin do? What does a pattern, or a lifestyle, of sin do in our lives? Left unchecked, sin destroys our lives and our relationships. Hurtful habits and obsessive addictions result in unintended consequences, which can lead to two kinds of imprisonment. Some times that imprisonment is in the form of legal man-made prisons. However, often the imprisonment comes in the form of very real spiritual prisons of our own hearts and minds. That kind of bondage is the effect of unconfessed sin.

However, Jesus came to save us from that bondage—the spiritual imprisonment of sin and its terrible consequences. The Bible says that Jesus came as a Redeemer. You see, Jesus came to purchase us from bondage—from slavery. It's as if you were a slave and someone bought you and then immediately told you that you're no longer in slavery—you're free! That's what Jesus did for us. We were in slavery to sin. But Jesus our Redeemer came and purchased us and then set us free. He purchased us by dying on a cross and taking our penalty for sin. Then Jesus showed us his love by saying you can now go free! You're free! You are no longer enslaved to sin and its terrible consequences. You're free to live the life that God created you to live in the first place!

Jesus saves us. He frees us from sin and its bondage! Matthew 20:28 explains that Jesus gave "his life as a ransom for many." We were enslaved and imprisoned by sin. But through his dying on the cross, Jesus paid our ransom price and freed us from the prison of sin.

During Christmas, we celebrate the birth of Christ. There are many stories told at Christmas time, but the only true one is the greatest one of all—the story of Christ's birth! Matthew 1:22 and 23 declares, "All this took place to fulfill what the Lord had said through the prophet: 'The virgin will be with child and will give birth to a son, and they will call him Immanuel'—which means, 'God with us.'" The best proof of God and his Word is the birth of Christ! There are multiple instances of Jesus fulfilling detailed Old Testament prophecies proclaimed hundreds of years earlier. These prophetic fulfillments surrounding the birth of Christ prove the authority and authenticity of Scripture as God's Word.

For instance, the prophet Isaiah prophesied the following: "Therefore the Lord himself will give you a sign: The virgin will be with child and will give birth to a son, and will call him Immanuel" (Isa. 7:14). Immanuel means "God with us" Or "WITH US is God!"

How does Jesus save us? How does a lifeguard save a drowning swimmer? How does a paramedic save a person having a heart attack? How does anyone save us in any circumstance? The person saving us has to be *with* us! Well, Jesus saves us because he's with us!

Jesus is Immanuel—God *with* us! John 1:14 explains, "The Word became flesh and made his dwelling among us. We have seen his glory, the glory of the One and Only, who came from the Father, full of grace and truth." Jesus is with us; he's dwelling among us! And he's full of grace and truth to save us!

The basis of our faith is that Jesus Christ is with us! He was born into this world through the virgin Mary, lived a sinless life, died on a cross for our sin, and rose again; and if we receive him as our Lord and Savior, he is *with us* today through the Holy Spirit! That's faith in Messiah—faith that he is with us! Faith that he is true to his Word!

After Joseph woke up from his dream, he obeyed the Lord. He took Mary home to be his wife; and when the baby was born, he named him Jesus.

Now that we have shared the story from Joseph's perspective, let's look at it from Mary's standpoint. Many times in Scripture, godly champions were greeted with the following words: "The Lord is with you!" Well, that's exactly how the Angel Gabriel greeted Mary: "Greetings, you who are highly favored! The Lord is with you" (Luke 1:28).

Mary didn't know what to make of the angel's greeting. The angel Gabriel reassured her: "Do not be afraid, Mary, you have found favor with God. You will be with child and give birth to a son, and you are to give him the name Jesus. He will be great and will be called the Son of the Most High. The Lord God will give him the throne of his father David, and he will reign over the house of Jacob forever; his kingdom will never end" (Luke 1:30-33). God was establishing a kingdom through this baby that would never end! Jesus would be a different kind of King that people all over the world would embrace and willingly follow out of love.

Mary asked the angel, "How will this be since I am a virgin?" (Luke 1:34). She was admittedly at a loss about this development.

The angel explained to Mary the miracle of her conception: "The Holy Spirit will come upon you, and the power of the Most High will overshadow you. So the holy one to be born will be called the Son of God. . . . For nothing is impossible with God" (Luke 1:35, 37).

Mary responded with humble submission to the Lord's will for her life: "I am the Lord's servant. May it be to me as you have said" (Luke 1:38). Mary surrendered herself to the Lord.

Mary's willingness to obey the Lord made her a champion for God! When Mary visited her relative Elizabeth, Elizabeth commended her for her faith: "Blessed is she who has believed that what the Lord has said to her will be accomplished!" (Luke 1:45).

Indeed, as Mary and Joseph exemplified, it is nothing less than God-pleasing faith that causes us to listen to and obey the Lord's will for our lives. Young person, I encourage you to seek the Lord's will for your life. God has a plan for you! And it's a good plan! Seek the Lord with all your heart. Humbly listen to and obey the Lord's will for you. As Joseph and Mary did, be willing to submit to God's will for you. You cannot go wrong if you sell all for Christ! As Jesus did, be willing to say, "Yet not as I will, but as you will" (Matt. 26:39).

Jesus was called Immanuel—God with us! You can know that this Jesus is with you today! If you have never received Christ as your personal Savior and Lord, I encourage you to do so today!

Make Jesus Immanuel in your life—God with you! It's how Jesus saves us! We're saved when we have Jesus with us! As the prophet Isaiah shared many generations earlier: "For to us a child is born, to us a son is given, and the government will be on his shoulders. And he will be called Wonderful Counselor, Mighty God, Everlasting Father, Prince of Peace. Of the increase of his government and peace there will be no end. . . . The zeal of the Lord Almighty will accomplish this" (Isa. 9:6-7).

Memory Verse

Luke 1:38 "'I am the Lord's servant,' Mary answered. 'May it be to me as you have said.' Then the angel left her."

SIMEON AND ANNA

Be Pure in Heart to See God

When Jesus grew older, he shared *attitudes of blessing* called beatitudes. One beatitude declares, "Blessed are the pure in heart, for they will see God" (Matt. 5:8). The earthly parents of Jesus—Mary and Joseph—were pure in heart, and indeed *they saw God.* They were called upon by God to usher Yeshua into the world. In addition to Mary and Joseph, I would like to share with you about two others who were pure in heart, who *saw* the infant Jesus!

In Luke 2, Yeshua's parents, Mary and Joseph, took him to the Jerusalem temple to be consecrated to God. Two individuals had been waiting for a long time to see the Messiah. Who were these two individuals?

First, there was Simeon, a godly man. Devoted to God, he was "waiting for the consolation of Israel" (Luke 2:25). The word *consolation* means comfort. Simeon, along with countless others of God's people, were *waiting* to be comforted by the coming of their Messiah.

Many years before, the prophet Isaiah had declared, "The Lord will surely comfort Zion and will look with compassion on all her ruins; he will make her deserts like Eden, her wastelands like the garden of the Lord. Joy and gladness will be found in her, thanksgiving and the sound of singing" (Isaiah 51:3). Simeon had been waiting for God's comfort, for his comforting words, for his comforting presence. And now, his long wait was over; he was in the presence of the Lord—the baby Jesus!

Young person, sometimes it may seem we have to wait so long for something we desire. You may be praying for a certain breakthrough in your life. My encouragement to you is to focus on waiting for the Lord—waiting for his presence in your life. Wait patiently for Messiah, who came as a baby. Anticipate his coming; let him become your inspiration; let him become the love of your life!

Well, the Bible tells us that the Holy Spirit was upon Simeon. Led by the Holy Spirit, Simeon went to the temple, recognized Jesus as Lord, took this baby in his arms, and praised God! Pure in heart, Simeon saw his Messiah!

Simeon received a word from God for Messiah and his parents. He declared, "My eyes have seen your salvation" (Luke 2:30). Simeon, out of a pure heart, was declaring that *his eyes* had seen Yeshua, which means "The Lord saves," or salvation, in Hebrew. He continued to emphasize that God had prepared this salvation for "all people, a light for revelation to the Gentiles and for glory to your people Israel" (Luke 2:31-32). Through Simeon, God was clearly communicating that Jesus would be the Savior for all people: Jews and Gentiles.

The Bible says that Simeon blessed Joseph's family and spoke of Messiah's future: "This child is destined to cause the falling and rising of many in Israel, and to be a sign that will be spoken against, so that the thoughts of many hearts will be revealed. And a sword will pierce your own soul too" (Luke 2:34-35). Jesus had a clear calling: people would fall because of his life and message, and others would rise. He would be a sign spoken against and would reveal people's hearts. 1 Corinthians 1:22-25 explains,

> Jews demand miraculous signs and Greeks look for wisdom, but we preach Christ crucified: a stumbling block to Jews and foolishness to Gentiles, but to those whom God has called, both Jews and Greeks, Christ the power of God and the wisdom of God. For the foolishness of God is wiser than man's wisdom, and the weakness of God is stronger than man's strength.

Not everyone would accept Jesus; in fact, most would reject him. Many would reject Jesus and fall, but others would accept him and rise.

Young person, I trust that you will embrace Jesus and rise! Just as he had a destiny, you have one too. My parents taught me the truth that I have a destiny, as do you. In fact, the way my parents raised me was to be willing to live in such a way that people would speak against me. In other words, be willing to stand for God and his Word, regardless of others' criticisms. For me personally, God has called me to be willing to be a watchman on the wall for children and young people. The beatitudes in Matthew 5:10-12 encourage us to be unafraid of opposition when we stand for the Lord:

> Blessed are those who are persecuted because of righteousness, for theirs is the kingdom of heaven. Blessed are you when people insult you, persecute you and falsely say all kinds of evil against you because of me. Rejoice and be glad, because great is your reward in heaven, for in the same way they persecuted the prophets who were before you.

Like Simeon, another individual saw Yeshua because she was pure in heart. This person was a lady named Anna, whose name means "gracious." Anna was a prophetess. She was married for seven years and then was a widow for the remainder of her life. At the age of eighty-four, after waiting a lifetime, Anna saw Jesus!

The Bible tells us that this Anna worshiped, fasted, and prayed night and day in the temple. When she met Messiah with his parents, she thanked God and shared with others about this child. She shared how Jesus would redeem her people! Pure in heart, Anna saw Yeshua!

Young person, do you want to see Jesus? Be pure in heart—that's how you see him! You see, it's with the eyes of your heart that you're able to see Jesus; it's how you see his love for you! In addition, it's with your heart that you are able to hear Yeshua's words for you! It's a matter of your heart. *See* him with your heart; *hear* him with your heart.

Your heart is the center of your life. It's where you really live. Your heart expresses your utmost desires. Proverbs 4:23 emphasizes the importance of keeping your heart for the Lord: "Above all else, guard your heart, for it is the wellspring of life." Your heart tells you what is most important to you.

When you have a pure heart—a heart clean of sin—you are able to hear God as opposed to all the other voices of this world. When you have a pure heart, you are able to see God.

How can you have a pure heart that sees God? The most important thing is to keep your heart for the Messiah—a close relationship with him. God loves you so much that he gave his only Son for you (John 3:16). Respond to his love by expressing your love in praise and worship. The way you love God is to walk with him. You keep your heart free of the things of this world through devotion to God's anointed one, Yeshua.

The life message of Simeon and Anna is a simple one: Be pure in heart and see Jesus!

Memory Verse

Matthew 5:8 "Blessed are the pure in heart, for they will see God."

JESUS

Be like Jesus—Lead by Example

As believers, we love Jesus. We love him because he first loved us; we love him because he died on the cross for our sins; and we love him because he has saved us and given us new life. He took our penalty upon himself, giving us the opportunity to receive salvation and live eternally with him! There is much to admire about our Lord and Savior Jesus Christ. Out of all the characteristics to be thankful about Jesus, one of the things I admire the most is that he leads by example. We see this characteristic of Jesus leading by example over and over in the gospels. He just didn't tell his disciples what to do; he showed them how to live through his life. Jesus demonstrated qualities such as self-sacrifice, humility, and servanthood. Our challenge is to be like Jesus, who led others by example.

In Luke 2, we gain a glimpse into Jesus' life when he was twelve years old. Traveling with a large company, Jesus' family went to Jerusalem for the Passover Feast. After it was over, they left to travel back home; but after traveling for a day, they realized that Jesus was not with their group. Of course, they immediately returned to Jerusalem to search for him. After three days, they found Jesus sitting with the teachers. Jesus was conversing with the teachers and showing great insight. When Jesus' parents questioned him about how he could treat them this way and shared their concern about his being lost, Jesus responded by saying, "Why were you searching for me? Didn't you know I had to be in my Father's house?" (Luke 2:49). Although his parents didn't understand what was happening, Jesus, at the age of twelve, was starting to understand his Father God's purpose for him.

Jesus' life as a twelve-year-old is an excellent example for young people. He was fully interested in God's kingdom. He was growing as a student of God's Word. Asking his teachers probing questions, Jesus was becoming an excellent student. Understanding more why he was created, he was gaining a sense of his life's purpose. He knew that he needed to be in his "Father's house." He knew that he needed to be growing in that place of serving his Father—God himself.

While Jesus was more and more understanding his purpose, he maintained obedience toward his earthly parents. Luke 2:51 tells us that Jesus went with his parents "and was obedient to them." He had a strong relationship with his parents. While he was fully God, Jesus still chose to submit completely to his parents' authority.

Even though he was the Son of God, Jesus had to grow as all children need to. The Bible says that Jesus grew in four ways that are important for all of us: "And Jesus grew in wisdom and stature, and in favor with God and men" (Luke 2:52). As young people, God also calls you to grow in these ways. Let's explore these four areas.

First, Jesus grew in wisdom. Wisdom is applying the principles of God's Word to our lives. We all need to learn to make right decisions based on the principles of Scripture. Wisdom is the opposite of foolishness. Shunning foolish behavior, Jesus sought to please God with his actions and his words. This is a very important area for young people. Too often young people like to involve themselves in foolish, mocking behavior. God calls us to avoid foolishness. We should not participate in making fun of people and mocking authority. Instead, we should seek to walk in behavior that is pleasing to the Lord.

Second, Jesus grew in stature. The son of a carpenter, Jesus learned the carpenter's trade. He must have wielded tools, such as a hammer. In the process of good hard work, Jesus developed physically. As children and young people, you should be growing in good physical health. We should not live a sedentary life, just playing video games and sitting around the house. We should help our parents with work and chores, play active sports, and be growing in stature. As we work and play wholeheartedly, we will be growing physically.

Next, Jesus grew in favor with God. He grew in relationship with his Father God. He prayed to the Father. In the gospels we see that Jesus often communicated with his Father through prayer. Jesus said, "I do nothing on my own but speak just what the Father has taught me. The one who sent me is with me; he has not left me alone, for I always do what pleases him" (John 8:28-29). Instructed and counseled by the Father, Jesus had an abiding relationship with him. So we too need to follow Jesus' example and develop our relationship with our Father God.

Finally, as a twelve-year-old, Jesus was growing in favor with others. We need to be developing our desire to reach out to others, to learn how to have conversations, and to show compassion. We need to be "others-focused champions." Shunning a focus on ourselves, we need to learn to focus on others: greeting them warmly, showing care, and being interested in others' lives. We need to grow in our relational skills. Developing in this way will help us to share the good news of Messiah with others. We need to seek to have excellent relationships with the people in our lives: our parents, our teachers and coaches, our siblings, and our friends. In this way, we will gain much favor with other people.

To sum up, we should endeavor to be a leader like Jesus by growing excellently in these four areas: in wisdom, in stature, in our relationship with God, and in our relationships with others.

Later on in life, as Jesus was about to begin his ministry, he went to John the Baptist to be baptized. Now the Pharisees had also gone to John to find out what he was doing. In contrast to Jesus, the Pharisees were not leaders who led by example. John's baptism was a baptism of repentance—of change. However, John said that the Pharisees didn't have fruit showing repentance. Their lives didn't show that they had changed. They were strict at keeping the external law, but they often missed the heart of God's Word. In other words, they were hypocrites—they looked good to others on the outside, but God knew that their hearts weren't right with him.

As hypocrites, the Pharisees didn't have the fruit of the Spirit as shared in Galatians 5:22-23: "Love, joy, peace, patience, kindness, goodness, faithfulness, gentleness and self-control." The Bible says that "against such things there is no law" (Gal. 5:23). There is no law, for instance, against showing kindness to someone. And yet, the Pharisees would criticize people for showing kindness to someone on the Sabbath, a day of rest. The Pharisees would accuse people of "working" on the Sabbath. This example is just one in which the Pharisees failed to lead by example. They may have said the right words, but they didn't have the actions to back up their words.

Moreover, John the Baptist told the Pharisees that they couldn't just say that they had Abraham as their father. In other words, they couldn't depend on the righteous pedigree of their parents for their righteousness. Young person, just because your parents are Christians doesn't mean that you are. Also, just because you may be living a basically good life doesn't mean that you are a Christian. You have to have a true relationship with Jesus yourself. You have to show fruit of repentance. In other words, your life—your words and your actions—must show whether you have truly repented and come to Messiah. After becoming born again, eventually you will show the fruit of that relationship. You will see good fruit coming from your life.

John said, "The ax is already at the root of the trees, and every tree that does not produce good fruit will be cut down and thrown into the fire" (Matt. 3:10). If there is no fruit showing repentance, then that tree will be cut down. Conversely, if there *is* fruit of repentance—a *changed* life—that is a glorious testimony of God's grace in our lives! The fruit coming from our life shows Christ within us.

John said, "I baptize you with water for repentance. But after me will come one who is more powerful than I, whose sandals I am not fit to carry. He will baptize you with the Holy Spirit and with fire" (Matt. 3:11). Water baptism is symbolic of repentance; it declares a changed life for one who is committed to following the Lord. At the same time, we need the baptism of the Holy Spirit to empower us to lead by example. We need the Holy Spirit flowing within us to bring life to others.

When Jesus came to John to be baptized, John was taken aback. Matthew 3:14 tells us, "But John tried to deter him, saying, 'I need to be baptized by you, and do you come to me?'" Here we see an interesting dynamic between John and Jesus. John was Jesus' older cousin. And yet, John knew that Jesus was the Messiah, the Christ. John came before Jesus, but Jesus was to surpass John. In humility, John the Baptizer told Jesus that Jesus should baptize him, but Jesus also expressed humility in wanting to be baptized by John. Jesus is an example to all of us—even though he didn't need to repent for sin, he still had John baptize him.

Jesus led by example. His answer to John was the following: "Let it be so now; it is proper for us to do this to fulfill all righteousness" (Matt. 3:15). Jesus didn't need to repent; he didn't need to change. Jesus had lived a sinless life, but he wanted to set an example for us all. If it's good enough for Jesus to be baptized, it's certainly necessary for us.

John proceeded to baptize Jesus. When Jesus came out of the water, his Father God proclaimed, "This is my Son, whom I love; with him I am well pleased" (Matt. 3:17). Jesus had pleased his Father. And that should be our goal—to please our Father God!

As Jesus began his ministry, he called different disciples to follow him. Jesus taught and led them by example. One instance that stood out was when he washed his disciples' feet. Normally the job of a lowly servant, foot washing was a humble act of serving others. John 13:1 emphasizes Jesus' teaching of his disciples: "He now showed them the full extent of his love." After their evening meal together, Jesus "poured water into a basin and began to wash his disciples' feet, drying them with the towel that was wrapped around him" (John 13:5). Jesus showed his disciples how to love others through humble service.

Through washing his disciples' feet, Jesus demonstrated his life message. He led by example in this humble, serving act. After Jesus finished, he made his point: "Now that I, your Lord and Teacher, have washed your feet, you also should wash one another's feet. I have set you an example that you should do as I have done for you. I tell you the truth, no servant is greater than his master, nor is a messenger greater than the one who sent him" (John 13:14-16). Jesus was saying that if it's important for me to serve in this way, then it's also important for you to do the same. Jesus emphasized, "Now that you know these things, you will be blessed if you do them" (John 13:17). We will be blessed if we follow Jesus' example of serving others.

Jesus led by example. He set us an example to serve in the same way. He made a very important point: we are to serve others. We lead through serving. It's how we're to relate to one another.

A little later Jesus gave a new command for us to follow which emphasizes his life message: "A new command I give you: Love one another. As I have loved you, so you must love one another. By this all men will know that you are my disciples, if you love one another" (John 13:34-35). Jesus loved his disciples by laying down his life for them. His example teaches us how we're to love others.

Similarly, Jesus used another opportunity to teach his disciples what true greatness is. When the mother of two of Jesus' disciples asked Jesus for her sons to sit at his right and left in his kingdom, Jesus told the two disciples that they didn't know what they were asking for. He asked them if they could drink his cup—the cup of suffering. After the other disciples expressed anger over two of them asking Jesus for these high positions of honor, Jesus used it as a teachable moment. He gathered his disciples together and declared the following: "You know that the rulers of the Gentiles lord it over them, and their high officials exercise authority over them. Not so with you. Instead, whoever wants to become great among you must be your servant, and whoever wants to be first must be your slave—just as the Son of Man did not come to be served, but to serve, and to give his life as a ransom for many" (Matt. 20:25-28). Leading by example, Jesus defined true greatness as serving others.

Of course, Jesus did "give his life as a ransom for many" (Matt. 20:28). He led by example in making the ultimate sacrifice as he took our punishment through his death on the cross. He said to his disciples in Matthew 16:24: "If anyone would come after me, he must deny himself and take up his cross and follow me." We're to follow Jesus' example of taking up our cross.

Philippians 2:5-8 expresses how we're to imitate Messiah's attitude: "Your attitude should be the same as that of Christ Jesus: Who, being in very nature God, did not consider equality with God something to be grasped, but made himself nothing, taking the very nature of a servant, being made in human likeness. And being found in appearance as a man, he humbled himself and became obedient to death—even death on a cross!" This is the attitude we're to embrace! We're to take up our cross for others. We're to lose our life for Jesus. We're to go low just as he did! The Lord's example shows us that the lower we go, the higher we go. Because Jesus went to the lowest point, "God exalted him to the highest place" (Phil. 2:9).

I encourage you to be like Jesus in leading by example. Allow the Holy Spirit to empower you to follow him. Be one who leads through service. As we follow in Christ's footsteps, he is our example! As you walk in this way, you will grow into being a champion for the Lord, a servant leader! I challenge you to be like Jesus—Lead others by example!

Memory Passage

John 13:14-17 "Now that I, your Lord and Teacher, have washed your feet, you also should wash one another's feet. I have set you an example that you should do as I have done for you. I tell you the truth, no servant is greater than his master, nor is a messenger greater than the one who sent him. Now that you know these things, you will be blessed if you do them."

JOHN THE BAPTIST

Prepare the Way for the Lord

In the Bible, there was a certain champion who clearly understood his life purpose. In sharing about Jesus in the last chapter, we touched on his mission. His name was John the Baptist. John knew that his calling was to prepare the way for the Lord! He is an example to all of us of what it means to be a witness for Christ.

Matthew 3:2 tells us that John the Baptist preached the following message: "Repent, for the kingdom of heaven is near." He preached a message of repentance.

What is repentance? It's turning away from self to God. It's choosing to follow Jesus. It's turning from sin and making Messiah your Lord.

What does it mean to make Jesus your Lord? It means that he becomes King in your life. As John emphasized, God's kingdom "is near." Jesus' kingdom was about to begin. He was about to inaugurate a kingdom of a loving God taking rulership in the hearts of people. And he wants to set up that kingdom in your heart as well.

John the Baptist was a fulfillment of the prophecy spoken by Isaiah: "A voice of one calling: 'In the desert prepare the way for the Lord; make straight in the wilderness a highway for our God. Every valley shall be raised up, every mountain and hill made low; the rough ground shall become level, the rugged places a plain. And the glory of the Lord will be revealed, and all mankind together will see it. For the mouth of the Lord has spoken'" (Isa. 40:3-5). God used John the Baptist to make a highway for the Lord Jesus. He was paving the way for Jesus!

John 1:7-9 explains how John the Baptist prepared the way for the Lord: "He came as a witness to testify concerning that light, so that through him all men might believe. He himself was not the light; he came only as a witness to the light. The true light was coming into the world." John prepared the way for the Lord by being a witness who proclaimed his coming.

Just as John testified of Jesus, we're also called to testify of him. God is calling you, young person, to testify of Christ so that others may believe!

How do we testify? The way we testify is to share with others how God has worked in our life. We share how God has changed us, how he has changed our family. We share how the Lord has helped us and our family through challenges. We see the truth of Romans 8:28 operating in our life: "And we know that in all things God works for the good of those who love him, who have been called according to his purpose." We share how God has used tough challenges to help us to grow more like Christ. As we become more and more like Jesus, our very life—our example—becomes a testimony to others.

Matthew 3:4 describes John's lifestyle: "John's clothes were made of camel's hair, and he had a leather belt around his waist. His food was locusts and wild honey." As John followed the Lord, he chose not to indulge in the pleasures of this world.

And John's message mirrored his lifestyle. He led the people in a baptism of repentance. People desiring to get right with God turned from the ways of this world, confessed their sin, were forgiven, and were baptized.

However, when the self-righteous Pharisees came to judge what John was doing, he spoke directly to them: "You brood of vipers! Who warned you to flee from the coming wrath? Produce fruit in keeping with repentance" (Matt. 3:7-8). John was telling them that true repentance brings fruit. That fruit is the life of God in us that blesses others.

John continued to speak against the Pharisees: "And do not think you can say to yourselves, 'We have Abraham as our father.' I tell you that out of these stones God can raise up children for Abraham. The ax is already at the root of the trees, and every tree that does not produce good fruit will be cut down and thrown into the fire" (Matt. 3:9-10). John was saying that we cannot depend on our family to get into the kingdom of God. While many are God's children, there are no grandchildren in God's kingdom. We all must come to Christ. If you've grown up in a Christian family, you can't depend on that fact to be saved; you can't depend on your parents to become saved. We all must come to the Lord Jesus and choose to follow him.

By their fruit, the Pharisees and the Sadducees had not shown true repentance. John was saying that in order for a person to be baptized, that person needs to show fruit of repentance.

In addition to knowing his message, John understood his role. He knew that his purpose was to prepare the way for Jesus, who would do even greater things than he would. He said, "I baptize you with water for repentance. But after me will come one who is more powerful than I, whose sandals I am not fit to carry. He will baptize you with the Holy Spirit and with fire" (Matt. 3:11). John knew that Jesus, the light of the world, was coming and that Jesus would change the world. He knew that his role was to serve Jesus by preparing the way for him.

When Jesus went to John at the Jordan River to be baptized, John was taken aback. (It's interesting—John was Jesus' older cousin, almost like an older brother. At the same time, Jesus, his younger cousin, would become the Savior of the world!) You might wonder, "Who looked up to whom?" John didn't feel comfortable baptizing Jesus, saying, "I need to be baptized by you, and do you come to me?" (Matt. 3:14).

However, Jesus told John, "Let it be so now; it is proper for us to do this to fulfill all righteousness" (Matt. 3:15). Then John was willing to baptize Jesus.

Jesus wanted to be an example of the need to be water baptized. He didn't have to submit to a baptism of repentance, but he wanted to set an example for us in order "to fulfill all righteousness."

By allowing John to baptize him, Jesus was communicating to the world that he agreed with John's message—his message of embracing godliness and right standing with God.

In addition, with John's baptism of Jesus, God used John to publicly declare Jesus as the Messiah. Jesus' baptism marked the beginning of his ministry on earth.

After John baptized Jesus, we see that the Father was pleased. He said, "This is my Son, whom I love; with him I am well pleased" (Matt. 3:17). And so with us. When we obey the Lord by publicly declaring our allegiance to him through water baptism, he is pleased with us! Jesus said, "Whoever acknowledges me before men, I will also acknowledge him before my Father in heaven" (Matt. 10:32).

Because he gave his life to serve the Lord, John the Baptist was a champion. He served the purposes of God's kingdom by preparing the way—by paving a highway—for the Lord. Young person, that's what God calls you to do: to prepare the way of the Lord in others' lives—to live in such a way that you give testimony of *his work* in your life!

Memory Verse

> Matt. 3:11 "I baptize you with water for repentance. But after me will come one who is more powerful than I, whose sandals I am not fit to carry. He will baptize you with the Holy Spirit and with fire."

JESUS ENTERING JERUSALEM ON A DONKEY

Be Humble and Know Your Authority

Jesus was (and is) a different kind of King leading a different kind of kingdom. As part of his kingdom, we're called to be different kind of citizens.

In Matthew 21, we find that Jesus simultaneously displayed humility and exercised his authority. He told his disciples to go get a donkey with her colt. Jesus said, "If anyone says anything to you, tell him that the Lord needs them, and he will send them right away" (Matt. 21:3).

Why did Jesus choose to ride on a donkey as opposed to a horse? A horse would be much more impressive. Instead, Jesus entered Jerusalem on a colt—a young donkey. In fact, Luke 19:30 says that it was a colt that no one had ever ridden before. This colt was set aside for a special purpose—to announce a king. But not just any king—a different kind of King!

Jesus came not as a conquering king on a horse with chariots of war. He arrived on a donkey. The greatest leader of all time knew the importance of symbolism. The donkey was a symbol of humility as opposed to pride.

Another way that Jesus would be a different King was that he would give his life away for others. Ephesians 4:7-8 emphasizes the gift-giving nature of our King: "But to each one of us grace has been given as Christ apportioned it. This is why it says: 'When he ascended on high, he led captives in his train and gave gifts to men.'" In Roman times, a victorious king coming home from war would parade through the city and be showered with gifts. Conquering kings would be inundated with gifts from their adoring subjects.

But Jesus is a different kind of King. Instead of being showered with gifts, he comes giving gifts. In fact, God gives us equipping gifts. These gifts are meant to advance his kingdom. That's what Jesus the King does for us! "He led captives in his train and gave gifts to men" (Eph. 4:8). These gifts are grace gifts—charisma gifts to advance his kingdom of love!

Young person, you have been given grace gifts in order to advance God's kingdom. God has given you grace to become a champion! He will equip you for your calling.

Because we serve a different King, we're called to be different citizens. Young person, God calls you to be different from the citizens of this world. Instead of involving yourself in bullying, you're called to stand up for the weak. Instead of lying, you're called to speak the truth. Instead of complaining, you're called to have an attitude of gratitude. Instead of disobedience, you're called to walk in cheerful obedience to your parents. Instead of laziness, you're called to work wholeheartedly. Instead of quitting, you're called to persevere! King Jesus calls us to behave differently!

When Jesus entered Jerusalem on a donkey, it was the fulfillment of prophecy hundreds of years earlier:

> Rejoice greatly, O Daughter of Zion! Shout, Daughter of Jerusalem! See, your king comes to you, righteous and having salvation, gentle and riding on a donkey, on a colt, the foal of a donkey. I will *take away the chariots* from Ephraim and the *war-horses* from Jerusalem, and *the battle bow will be broken*. He will *proclaim peace to the nations*. His rule will extend from sea to sea and from the River to the ends of the earth. (Zech. 9:9-10, italics added)

What a King! What a leader! What a servant who inspires through self-sacrificing love!

We are called to imitate that King! We are called to please this different kind of King. How do we do that? We do that by walking with Jesus; we do that by touching his heart. In Matthew 11:28-30, Jesus said, "Come to me, all you who are weary and burdened, and I will give you rest. Take my yoke upon you and learn from me, for I am gentle and humble in heart, and you will find rest for your souls. For my yoke is easy and my burden is light." As we walk with Jesus, we learn of his heart—his gentle and humble nature. We understand his care for others.

As Jesus rode on the donkey, the people spread their cloaks on the road. They took palm branches and shouted three distinct exclamations of praise: "Hosanna to the Son of David!" "Blessed is he who comes in the name of the Lord!" and "Hosanna in the highest!" (Matt. 21:9). Indeed, Jesus' arrival was cause for rejoicing! But what does the word *hosanna* mean? It is an exclamation for "Save!" Save us! It's also an exclamation for "Help!" Help us!

Do you need help? Do you need to be saved? We need salvation for eternity. We also need the Lord's help every day of our lives. The Lord is ready and willing to help you—He can save you today!

As Jesus rode on the donkey, the crowds used the words from Psalm 118:25-26: "O Lord, save us; O Lord, grant us success. Blessed is he who comes in the name of the Lord."

Later Jesus used his authority to drive out those who were using the temple courts for greed and dishonesty. Make no mistake: humility is not weakness, and meekness doesn't equate with weakness. Meekness is strength under control.

Knowing his authority, Jesus exercised strength under control. He was decisive. He took righteous action.

The Temple was supposed to be the home for God. Unfortunately, the temple had gained a reputation of being a place of greed and dishonest dealing. Jesus was rightfully angry; he wanted to restore the temple to being a place of worshiping God. In Mark 11:17, Jesus emphasized that the temple was to be a place for all peoples to worship God: "Is it not written: 'My house will be called a house of prayer for all nations'? But you have made it 'a den of robbers.'" Quoting Scripture from Isaiah 56:7, Jesus was agreeing with his Father God that his house was to be a home for peoples from all nations! Jesus wanted it to be a welcoming place for people from all nations. Jesus, a man of humility, knew his authority! He took decisive action to restore the temple to what it should be.

Jesus proceeded to use his authority to heal people. As he did so, the children praised him. When the religious leaders wanted to silence the children (and thereby come against Jesus), they angrily questioned Jesus: "Do you hear what these children are saying?" (Matt. 21:16).

Jesus responded again with Scripture: "Yes, have you never read, 'From the lips of children and infants you have ordained praise'?" (Matt. 21:16).

Young people, we need to imitate Jesus' memorization of Scripture. It's how you answer the opposition of the enemy—with the Word of God! Ephesians 6:12 tells us, "For our struggle is not against flesh and blood, but against the rulers, against the authorities, against the powers of this dark world and against the spiritual forces of evil in the heavenly realms." We answer the lies and intimidation of the enemy with God's Word.

This different kind of King—Jesus—answered opposition by confessing Scripture! Jesus had memorized Psalm 8:1-2, from which he quoted when the religious leaders challenged him: "O Lord, our Lord, how majestic is your name in all the earth! You have set your glory above the heavens. From the lips of children and infants you *have ordained praise because of your enemies, to silence the foe and the avenger*" (italics added). Talk about authority! Jesus was showing us how we silence the enemy!

Why has God ordained praise from children? *To silence the enemy!* The devil is silenced when you praise the Lord! We have authority to silence the enemy through praising the Lord!

Parents, no matter what you are going through, if you're seeking to lead your family in following the Lord, all your trials are worth it when you see your children worshiping the Lord. Our main purpose is to raise up our children to become disciples of Messiah. When that objective is being advanced, the enemy is silenced! Satan cannot say anything when you see your child expressing a true relationship with God through praising him!

Children, why is it important to practice praising the Lord with all your heart! The best activity and the most important commitment to develop is that of worshiping the Lord! My encouragement to both parents and children is the following: Practice the strategy of taking authority through praising the Lord at home as a family!

After emphasizing the effect of children praising the Lord, Jesus continued to walk in his rightful authority. He spoke against a fruitless fig tree, and it withered. Jesus' words had authority; he knew the power of his words! In explaining this occurrence to his disciples, Jesus said, "I tell you the truth, if you have faith and do not doubt, not only can you do what was done to the fig tree, but also you can say to this mountain, 'Go, throw yourself into the sea,' and it will be done. If you believe, you will receive whatever you ask for in prayer" (Matt. 21:21-22).

Young person, God has given you a measure of faith. I know that we all sometimes have uncertainty. You can take heart; God understands. But when the Holy Spirit reveals his will to you, it inspires you to pray confidently. 1 John 5:14-15 says, "This is the confidence we have in approaching God: that if we ask anything according to his will, he hears us. And if we know that he hears us—whatever we ask—we know that we have what we asked of him." Let the Holy Spirit reveal his will to you. Then pray with confidence! Pray with authority!

Learn to seek God and walk with God in such a way that he increasingly makes his will known to you. And then pray according to his will! There have been key times in my life in which I sought the Lord for his will, whether it be God's direction in work, direction for a home, or his calling us to start a school. God wants to reveal his good, perfect, and pleasing will to you!

As you walk in authoritative faith, remember that faith comes by hearing and hearing by the Word of God (Rom. 10:17). My encouragement to you is to read and study God's Word each day, know his will, and speak the Word of God daily. As you do so, your faith in God will grow stronger!

When Jesus was teaching in the temple courts, the religious leaders again questioned him: "By what authority are you doing these things?" . . . "And who gave you this authority?" (Matt. 21:23). Jesus responded by asking the religious leaders a question: "John's baptism—where did it come from? Was it from heaven, or from men?" (Matt. 21:25). After consulting among themselves, the religious leaders decided not to answer Jesus' wise question. Jesus showed that these religious "authorities" didn't have any real authority at all compared to his true God-given authority.

Jesus was humble and knew his authority! And he gives us authority to do his work. As he commissioned his disciples to make more disciples, he said, "All authority in heaven and on earth has been given to me" (Matt. 28:18). He gives us the necessary authority to fulfill his plans. Just as the religious leaders tried to question Jesus, remember that the enemy—Satan himself—will try to question your authority. Don't fall prey to the manipulative questions of the enemy.

Don't allow the enemy to manipulate you with his words. Don't allow him to distract you!

Young person, stand in faith! Read and study the Word. Be a soldier who knows your authority in Messiah and skillfully wield the Sword of the Spirit, which is the Word of God!

Finally, let the Holy Spirit reveal his will to you. Pray according to his will; and as Jesus did, speak the Word of God with authority: "It is written!"

Memory Passage

Psalm 8:1-2 "O Lord, our Lord, how majestic is your name in all the earth! You have set your glory above the heavens. From the lips of children and infants you have ordained praise because of your enemies, to silence the foe and the avenger."

JESUS IN THE GARDEN

Submit Your Will to God's Will

In the Garden of Gethsemane, Jesus showed us a very important example: He submitted to the will of his Father. To submit is to yield, to surrender one's own desire, to give command over one's will to another. It's letting another take charge.

Imagine anticipating an agonizing trial over the course of years. That's what Jesus did in facing the cross. He knew that his purpose was to die on the cross for the sins of the world. Now in the Garden of Gethsemane, he came face to face with his trial—his cross—as he sought to prepare himself. Indeed, Jesus suffered on the cross, but he also suffered as he anticipated the cross. He had to prepare himself in the garden; he had to prepare himself with his Father in prayer.

In Matthew 26:31, referring to a prophetic word, Jesus tells his disciples that they will leave him in his time of trial: "I will strike the shepherd, and the sheep of the flock will be scattered."

All of Jesus' beloved disciples—those he poured his life into—deserted him. They left him all alone! Do you ever feel that way?

Matthew 26:36-37 tells us that three of Jesus' disciples went with him to Gethsemane as he faced the cross. He shared with them, "My soul is overwhelmed with sorrow to the point of death. Stay here and keep watch with me" (Matt. 26:38). Jesus asked his disciples to stand with him. In this dark hour, he needed their companionship.

"Going a little farther, he fell with his face to the ground and prayed, 'My Father, if it is possible, may this cup be taken from me. Yet not as I will, but as you will'" (Matt. 26:39). Jesus fell to the ground in prayer and asked the Father if this cup could be taken away from him. The cup was symbolic of suffering. Even his Father would turn away from him when he took the sin of the whole world upon himself. 2 Corinthians 5:21 tells us, "God made him who had no sin to be sin for us, so that in him we might become the righteousness of God." Jesus, who had not sinned, *became sin* so that we might be made God's righteousness! What a glorious work he did for us on the cross! Aren't you grateful?

When Jesus went back to his disciples, he saw that they had fallen asleep. He told them, "Watch and pray so that you will not fall into temptation" (Matt. 26:41). Although facing a terrible trial himself, Jesus was still others-focused. He expressed concern for his disciples and the trial that they themselves were about to face. He wanted them to be prepared.

Jesus said, "The spirit is willing, but the body is weak" (Matt. 26:41). In his compassion, Jesus was referring to their humanity. As a human himself, he could sympathize. He knew that his disciples needed to be prepared for their own severe trial. And he wants you to be prepared for the trials you will face also!

Jesus went off to pray a second time, "Father, if it is not possible for this cup to be taken away unless I drink it, may your will be done" (Matt. 26:42). Jesus recognized the fact that he had to face the cross. He was willing to submit his will to his Father's will.

We all must come to this point in our lives. Will we submit to the Father's will? Will we take up our own cross? Will we follow Christ?

We all must face the cross of Messiah. We all have to decide on the cross. We have to look at this Jesus on the cross and make a decision. Are we going to take up the cross and follow him and his will? Or are we going to turn away from the cross, look away from Jesus' loving gaze, and go our own way?

Jesus declared, "If anyone would come after me, he must deny himself and take up his cross daily and follow me. For whoever wants to save his life will lose it, but whoever loses his life for me will save it" (Luke 9:23-24). You see, when we choose to follow the Lord, we take up our cross and go his way instead of going our own selfish way. We choose to lose our life—give up our life—to follow him. In doing so, we find our life—the abundant life of Christ! Thanks be to God!

After praying a second time, Jesus went back to his disciples and found them sleeping again. He then went to his Father a third time, communicating the same prayer.

Sometimes when we are facing a difficult situation, we need to go multiple times to the Lord in prayer. Sometimes we don't come to that place of peace until we've wrestled with God a number of times. Three times Jesus prayed about this cup he was facing. In the process he submitted to his Father's will and came to a place of readiness.

When we submit to the Lord Jesus, we come to a place of personal peace. Resigning ourselves to his will, we surrender to him. In effect, we spiritually die. We die to ourselves—death to self, death to selfishness—and allow Christ to live in and through us!

Jesus returned to his disciples and found that they were still sleeping. He said, "Are you still sleeping and resting?" (Matt. 26:45). Jesus recognized that his disciples had lost their opportunity to be prepared for their own impending trial through prayer.

Jesus went on to say, "Look, the hour is near, and the Son of Man is betrayed into the hands of sinners" (Matt. 26:45). In Luke 22:53, Jesus said to his captors, "But this is your hour—when darkness reigns."

Sometimes "an hour of darkness" comes into our lives. Thank God we don't live a life of darkness, but we will have periods of darkness. During those times, we need to call out to God for help. Jesus did so and God helped him. In fact, "An angel from heaven appeared to him and strengthened him" (Luke 22:43). The Father provided an angel to strengthen Jesus.

Just as God sent Jesus what he needed for his trial, God will give you what you need for your trial! The Lord is our provider, and you can be assured that he will provide what you need for any trial. When the Apostle Paul prayed three times for the thorn in his flesh to be taken from him, God said, "My grace is sufficient for you, for my power is made perfect in weakness" (2 Cor. 12:9). When you call out to God for help in your trial, you can be assured that he will provide what you need!

Although his disciples squandered their opportunity to be ready for their trail through prayer, Jesus himself was now prepared. He told his disciples, "Rise, let us go! Here comes my betrayer!" (Matt. 26:46). In contrast to his disciples, Jesus was ready to face his trial; he was ready for his cup of suffering!

Jesus had exhorted his disciples to prepare for their own trial through prayer. He instructed them, "Pray that you will not fall into temptation" (Luke 22:40). As we have seen, in this terrible trial of the cross, Jesus turned to his relationship with his Father.

Likewise, in our lives, when everything and everyone else fails, one thing remains—our relationship with God! I encourage you, young person, to have a strong, daily relationship with our Father God. He is your solid Rock. He is that Rock that endures. I think of the chorus in a famous hymn: "On Christ, the solid Rock I stand; all other ground is sinking sand; all other ground is sinking sand." On Christ the solid Rock we stand!

As Jesus surrendered to his Father's will, I encourage you to come to that point in which you surrender to the Father! Let God's will be done in your life!

I can remember that point in my life. It was right before my sophomore year of college. I had endured a summer of suffering. I had worked as a security guard, but I wasn't very secure at all. In fact, I was very insecure. At the end of that summer, on the eve of my attending a Christian camp, I surrendered to God. In effect, I communicated to God: "I don't know if you can do anything with me, God. You see my weakness. You see my life. I don't have much to offer you, but here I am." I submitted my life to Christ. That week the Lord called me to my life calling to teach and encourage young disciples for him.

That next year—my sophomore year of college—was a year of intense suffering and trial. But looking back, it was the best year of my life. I made the decision to walk the streets of my college campus late at night in order to walk and talk with my Savior, praising him. The only thing that sustained me was my relationship with God—the One who remains when all else fails!

Through the process of that trial, I experienced the truth expressed in Romans 5:3-5: "Not only so, but we also rejoice in our sufferings, because we know that suffering produces perseverance; perseverance, character; and character, hope. And hope does not disappoint us, because God has poured out his love into our hearts by the Holy Spirit, whom he has given us."

During that year, as I faced into the trial with the Lord, I gradually could see *perseverance* and even a little *character* produced through my suffering. When I discovered that passage from Romans 5, I thought that I wasn't yet to the *hope* part, but it gave me hope just to know that *hope* was on the way! God sealed his call in my life through this process of trial and suffering with enduring motivation—motivation that still sustains me to this day!

Even as Jesus faced *his* trial of the cross, he exhorted his disciples to pray so that they would be ready for *their* trial. Jesus' example encourages us to have a relationship with the Father, in order to be prepared for *our* impending trial. To be ready for our own cross, we must prepare through prayer—calling out to God, communicating with him, wrestling with him, and growing in our relationship with him. I encourage you to come to the Father in prayer until you submit wholly to his will.

Having a relationship with our Heavenly Father prepares us for whatever trial we may have to face. Let us imitate Jesus in his relationship with the Father and in his willingness to submit to the Father: "Yet not my will, but yours be done" (Luke 22:42).

Memory Verse

Luke 22:42 "Father, if you are willing, take this cup from me; yet not my will, but yours be done."

JESUS

Trust Jesus to Win the Victory

As Christians, we know that Jesus won the victory. However, from all appearances, up until Jesus rose from the dead, it really didn't look as if Jesus had won the victory. In terms of worldly wealth, Jesus was a poor man. He was a man who brought together the unlearned or despised of society, Jews who were in captivity to Rome; and then those same disciples, in his moment of greatest need, all deserted him! He was a man who was falsely accused and tried as a criminal. He was beaten by scourging, was mocked, and was taken away to be punished; he endured the humiliation of a shameful death on a cross. A person dying on a cross would be considered an utter failure.

Isaiah prophesied of Jesus: "He grew up before him like a tender shoot, and like a root out of dry ground. He had no beauty or majesty to attract us to him, nothing in his appearance that we should desire him. He was despised and rejected by men, a man of sorrows, and familiar with suffering. Like one from whom men hide their faces he was despised, and we esteemed him not" (Isa. 53:2-3). This passage definitely doesn't seem to be a description of a winner, does it? The passage goes on to say that Jesus was thought of as "stricken," "smitten," and "afflicted" (Isa. 53:4). He was "pierced," "crushed," punished, and wounded (Isa. 53:5). Such a one certainly doesn't seem to be the victor. However, as we shall see, Jesus ultimately won the victory! And you can trust Jesus to win the victory in your life as well!

In Luke 23, the ruling council of Judaism, called the Sanhedrin, brought false accusations against Jesus before Pilate: "We have found this man subverting our nation. He opposes payment of taxes to Caesar and claims to be Christ, a king" (Luke 23:2). When Pilate asked Jesus whether he was king of the Jews, Jesus answered, "Yes, it is as you say" (Luke 23:3). However, Pilate found that Jesus had done nothing wrong: "I find no basis for a charge against this man" (Luke 23:4). This was the first time that the governing authority found that Jesus was innocent of wrongdoing. After the people continued to clamor that Jesus was causing harm through his teaching and when Pilate learned that Jesus was under Herod's jurisdiction, Pilate sent him to be tried by Herod.

When Jesus came before Herod, Herod showed some casual interest in him. However, Herod wasn't really interested in finding out the truth about Jesus. He simply wanted to be entertained; he wanted to see a miracle. Herod wasn't a true seeker of the truth. He made fun of Jesus in a mocking way. Jeremiah 29:13 says,

"You will seek me and find me when you seek me with all your heart." Herod wasn't willing to seek God with all his heart. He had no interest in knowing the truth of Jesus.

Young person, when you come to Christ, truth is involved. When you come to God, you are sincerely seeking to find the truth. What is the truth? Jesus said, "I am the way and the truth and the life. No one comes to the Father except through me" (John 14:6). Do you believe that Jesus Christ is the way, the truth, and the life? Do you believe that Messiah is the only way of salvation? Or do you believe there are multiple ways to heaven?

The argument cannot go both ways. One can't say that Jesus was simply a good man because Jesus testified that he was the Christ, the Messiah, the son of God, and that he was the only way to the Father. Either you believe what Jesus said about himself, or you must say that Jesus was a liar or that he was insane.

What do you believe about Jesus? Romans 10:9 says, "If you confess with your mouth, 'Jesus is Lord,' and believe in your heart that God raised him from the dead, you will be saved." Do you believe that Jesus is Lord? Are you willing to confess him as Lord? Do you believe that Jesus rose from the dead?

Don't be like Herod! Don't just be interested in Jesus to see what you can get out of him. Seek the truth of Jesus. Seek God with all your heart. Yearn for the truth! Know the one true God! Make him your Lord and Savior.

Herod asked Jesus many questions, but Jesus gave him no answer. Jesus didn't answer the questions of this Herod who had no real convictions. Herod is an example of a fool who mocks others. He had no real interest in knowing who Jesus really was.

Jesus continued to be falsely accused by the religious leaders. Indeed, Herod and his soldiers participated in the ridicule of Jesus. However, Herod could find no reason to declare Jesus guilty; therefore, he sent Jesus back to Pilate.

When Jesus was tried a second time before Pilate, Pilate again could find no basis for charges against him and asserted that Herod could find nothing wrong with Jesus either. Pilate said, "He has done nothing to deserve death. Therefore, I will punish him and then release him" (Luke 23:15-16). Even though Pilate declared Jesus' innocence, to appease the people, he chose to punish Jesus through a scourging, a terribly painful whipping that often would cause death.

Now occurring at this time was the Feast of Passover. It was traditional for the governor to release a prisoner to the people during this feast. Matthew 27:15-18 explains the choice that the governor Pilate gave to the people: "Now it was the governor's custom at the Feast to release a prisoner chosen by the crowd. At that time they had a notorious prisoner, called Barabbas. So when the crowd had gathered, Pilate asked them, 'Which one do you want me to release to you: Barabbas, or Jesus who is called Christ?' For he knew it was out of envy that they had handed Jesus over to him." Pilate offered the crowd a drastic choice: either

Jesus, whom he had found to be innocent of wrongdoing, or Barabbas, a terrorist who had caused a rebellion. A notorious murderer, Barabbas was a terrible person. Even knowing that an evil person would be released from prison—someone who definitely needed to be in prison, the people cried out, "Away with this man! Release Barabbas to us!" (Luke 23:18).

Pilate wanted to release Jesus, but the mob kept yelling for Jesus to be crucified: "Crucify him! Crucify him!" (Luke 23:21). Pilate tried once again to convince the people of Jesus' innocence: "Why? What crime has this man committed? I have found in him no grounds for the death penalty. Therefore I will have him punished and then release him" (Luke 23:22). This was the third time that Pilate declared that he found no basis for charges against Jesus.

However, Pilate was a weak leader. He surrendered to the crowd's demands: "But with loud shouts they insistently demanded that he be crucified, and their shouts prevailed. So Pilate decided to grant their demand" (Luke 23:23-24). Pilate gave up Jesus to the people's will to be crucified, and he released the murderer Barabbas from prison. Jesus was then led to the cross for his death sentence of crucifixion, even though Pilate had found him innocent of any wrongdoing. Jesus, who had led a life without any sin, was going to be punished by death on a cross!

Jesus was crucified between two other men. Even as Jesus was being crucified, he prayed regarding his persecutors: "Father, forgive them, for they do not know what they are doing" (Luke 23:34). As Jesus died an excruciating death on the cross, the rulers and the soldiers ridiculed him. Pilate, mocking the Jewish leaders, had Jesus' crime posted at the top of his cross: "THIS IS THE KING OF THE JEWS" (Luke 23:38).

When one of the criminals being crucified along with Jesus participated in the insults, the other criminal rebuked him: "Don't you fear God since you are under the same sentence? We are punished justly, for we are getting what our deeds deserve. But this man has done nothing wrong" (Luke 23:40-41). While dying on the cross alongside Jesus, this repentant criminal was saved from his sins. He said, "Jesus, remember me when you come into your kingdom" (Luke 23:42).

Responding to his request, Jesus welcomed the criminal into his kingdom: "I tell you the truth, today you will be with me in paradise" (Luke 23:43). This criminal who had deserved death by crucifixion because of his sin was saved by Jesus from his sin! And you too can be saved from your sin today if you will only yield to the Lord! Death on this earth is not the end—this truth is what gives Christians all over the world hope! Even when confronted by evil terrorists, Christians know that if we are killed for our faith, we will be with God for all eternity! That promise gives us faith-filled hope!

No matter what sin you may have committed, the Bible declares that if you will call on the name of the Lord, you will be saved. Acts 2:21 promises us, "And everyone who calls on the name of the Lord will be saved."

Well, as Jesus died on the cross, he took on himself the sin of the whole world—including your sin and my sin. What is sin? Sin is wrongdoing. It is doing wrong acts and saying wrong things. It is not obeying God and not obeying your parents. It is hurting your neighbor. Sin is breaking God's commandments. Because Jesus took our sin, God the Father had to look away from him. You see, Jesus died for the purpose of taking away your sin. He died for your sin; he died to save you from your sin!

In addition, as Jesus was dying, the temple's curtain separating the holy place from the most holy place was torn in two. This curtain blocked the way of the people into the very presence of God. This tearing of the curtain signified that we can all now come into God's presence at any time. In fact, we can live in the light of his presence!

As he was about to die, the Bible tells us that Jesus called out to his Father: "Father, into your hands I commit my spirit" (Luke 23:46). Then Jesus died. At that point, by all objective accounts, Jesus would be considered a loser.

After observing Jesus' death, the centurion, who was in charge of Jesus' crucifixion, could not help but be moved by what he had experienced. He noticed something different about this man who had just died. Praising God, the centurion declared, "Surely this was a righteous man" (Luke 23:47). The centurion was impressed with Jesus' righteousness. Again, Jesus had done nothing wrong; he had not sinned. Having lived a sinless life, Jesus was the perfect sacrifice for our sins.

After Jesus' death, a member of the Sanhedrin who had not agreed to their decision to kill Jesus—Joseph of Arimathea—took care of Jesus' body. He placed him in a tomb that had never been used. The women who had been following Jesus watched how Jesus' body was laid in the tomb, and they prepared spices and perfumes for his body. However, they rested the next day because it was the Sabbath.

On Sunday, the women took the spices for Jesus' body to the tomb. However, when they arrived, they discovered that the stone covering the entrance to the tomb had been moved and that Jesus' body was gone. It was no longer in the tomb! While the women were wondering about this, two angels appeared and reminded them what Jesus had said previously: "Why do you look for the living among the dead? He is not here; he has risen! Remember how he told you, while he was still with you in Galilee: 'The Son of Man must be delivered into the hands of sinful men, be crucified and on the third day be raised again'" (Luke 24:5-7).

Of course, the women reported all they had seen and heard to the disciples. Peter and John ran to the tomb—it was almost like a race between the two of them! John arrived to the tomb first and looked in. When Peter got there, he went inside the tomb. Then John went inside as well. John "saw and believed" (John 20:8).

Far from being a loser, Jesus had won the victory! Jesus even had conquered death—Jesus rose from the dead! Jesus actually had won the victory!

However, "they still did not understand from Scripture that Jesus had to rise from the dead" (John 20:9). They still didn't "understand." You see, you may not understand everything about Jesus and his Kingdom. That's ok. In your journey with Jesus, faith comes before understanding. Faith comes first. Even though you may not understand everything about Jesus and his Kingdom, I encourage you to trust him today! He will teach you as you embark on this wonderful adventure with him!

Later, Jesus helped his followers to understand what had happened: "Then he opened their minds so they could understand the Scriptures. He told them, 'This is what is written: The Christ will suffer and rise from the dead on the third day, and repentance and forgiveness of sins will be preached in his name to all nations, beginning at Jerusalem. You are witnesses of these things'" (Luke 24:45-48). Finally his disciples' minds were opened. More importantly, their hearts were opened! They believed Jesus, and now he was giving them understanding about what God had done!

Jesus won the victory! He defeated death, he conquered sin and Satan, and he made the way to the Father—the way of abundant and eternal life!

1 Corinthians 15:54-57 inspires us: "'Death has been swallowed up in victory.' 'Where, O death, is your victory? Where, O death, is your sting?' The sting of death is sin, and the power of sin is the law. But thanks be to God! He gives us the victory through our Lord Jesus Christ."

How do we trust Jesus to win the victory in our lives? You see, in the beginning, God created us in his image. However, sin came into the world and caused our downfall. Sin has a way of destroying people's lives and relationships. But through his victory on the cross, Jesus conquered sin—Jesus won the victory over sin! Jesus died for our sin, and then he conquered sin and death by rising from the grave! Because of Jesus' great victory, we no longer have to be mastered by sin. If we repent from sin and trust Jesus to save us, he gives us the victory. Instead of living in sin which ruins lives, we live for Christ, who teaches us to live the way he created us to live in the first place! I encourage you to trust the Lord today—He will win the victory in your life!

Memory Verse

> 1 Corinthians 15:54-57 "'Death has been swallowed up in victory.' 'Where, O death, is your victory? Where, O death, is your sting?' The sting of death is sin, and the power of sin is the law. But thanks be to God! He gives us the victory through our Lord Jesus Christ."

JESUS

Learn to Endure the Cross

The ultimate champion—Jesus himself—called his disciples, including us, to take up our cross daily and follow him. Jesus declared in Luke 9:23-24, "If anyone would come after me, he must deny himself and take up his cross daily and follow me. For whoever wants to save his life will lose it, but whoever loses his life for me will save it." As true disciples of Christ, we're called to imitate him in taking up the cross. Of course, the cross is a symbol of suffering and death. When we take up the Lord's cross, we embrace those things that cause suffering in our lives and allow God to use them to help us grow. As we take up our cross, we learn from Jesus who endured his cross.

Hebrews 12:1-3 speaks of Jesus enduring the cross:

> Therefore, since we are surrounded by such a great cloud of witnesses, let us throw off everything that hinders and the sin that so easily entangles, and let us run with perseverance the race marked out for us. Let us fix our eyes on Jesus, the author and perfecter of our faith, who for the joy set before him endured the cross, scorning its shame, and sat down at the right hand of the throne of God. Consider him who endured such opposition from sinful men, so that you will not grow weary and lose heart.

First, in learning to endure the cross, we are called to "run with perseverance the race marked out for us." As we run our race, we are cheered on by great champions of faith who have gone before us. I recall running the 800 meters in track, a two-lap sprint that tests one's courage, particularly in the second half of the second lap. At that point, I always had a choice: either coast to the finish line *or* give everything that I had, pushing my body to the limit and enduring much pain. I also recall running a marathon when I hit the infamous "wall" at mile sixteen and still had ten miles to go. When one runs a race—particularly a distance race—one has to persevere to continue running. It takes endurance! It's hard! One has to endure! There is pain and suffering involved; as you run, you become weary. However, what motivates you is looking forward to the joy you will experience once you finish the race, once you accomplish your goal. That was what motivated Jesus. As he faced the cross, he was able to endure that terrible experience by focusing on "the joy set before him."

It's the same motivation for us in our race as Jesus' disciples. We have to endure; we have to persevere. When we experience opposition and hardship, we can't quit. When the cross we are bearing causes us shame, we can't quit. When others gossip about us, we can't give up. (Remember that Jesus "scorned the shame" of the cross.) Thank God that Jesus didn't quit! And neither should we! We have to endure and persevere to finish the race, looking unto Jesus, who is our finish line—our goal. And as we embrace the cross, as we endure, as we learn what it means to die to self, we find the joy of resurrection life. We experience Christ's resurrection in our life!

Jesus knew that his purpose—the finish line of his race—was to die for the sins of the world! Jesus didn't simply perform a momentary act. He wasn't simply a hero who did something heroic on the spur of the moment. He was more than a hero. *Jesus was and is a champion!* He knew his purpose, he knew his cause, and he followed it through to completion!

The prophet Isaiah depicted Jesus as the suffering servant. This illustration shows us that we're to imitate Jesus in helping others even if such assistance contributes to our own suffering. In Isaiah chapter 53, Isaiah prophesied that we would not be attracted to Jesus by his appearance, that "he was despised and rejected by men, a man of sorrows, and familiar with suffering" (Isa. 53:3). Isaiah prophesied that Jesus would be led to his punishment "like a lamb to the slaughter, and as a sheep before her shearers is silent, so he did not open his mouth" (Isa. 53:7). Before his accusers, Jesus was silent. Through all of his ordeal, Jesus knew what was happening. He knew he would suffer and die for the sins of the world.

Isaiah 53:9 says, "He was assigned a grave with the wicked, and with the rich in his death, though he had done no violence, nor was any deceit in his mouth." Peter, in the New Testament, upholds Jesus' suffering as an example for us to follow: "But if you suffer for doing good and you endure it, this is commendable before God. To this you were called, because Christ suffered for you, leaving you an example, that you should follow in his steps. . . . When they hurled their insults at him, he did not retaliate; when he suffered, he made no threats. Instead, he entrusted himself to him who judges justly" (1 Pet. 2:20-23). The Bible clearly calls us to imitate Jesus in enduring the cross.

Once Jesus finished his race by dying on the cross for our sins, he gained a rightful sense of fulfillment: "After the suffering of his soul, he will see the light of life and be satisfied" (Isa. 53:11). Jesus was "satisfied"—he was fulfilled when he accomplished his life's purpose! And he felt joy in that satisfaction. Similarly, when we go through the process of enduring the cross, of dying to self, and of experiencing resurrection life, we are "satisfied." We experience the joy of the Lord! We are champions that are fulfilled as we live for the cause of Christ!

The gospel writer Matthew tells of Jesus "going up to Jerusalem" with his twelve disciples. Jesus told his disciples his purpose for going to Jerusalem: "We are going up to Jerusalem, and the Son of Man will be betrayed to the chief priests and teachers of the law. They will condemn him to death and will turn him over to the Gentiles to be mocked and flogged and crucified. On the third day he will be raised to life!" (Matt. 20:18-19). Jesus knew what was coming! Instead of fleeing *from* the place of his crucifixion, he traveled *to* the place of his intended suffering! He wasn't running away from it. He was moving toward his ultimate purpose: to die for the sins of the world! As he anticipated his suffering, he shared with his disciples what would happen! Jesus shows us that he was willing to endure the cross for our salvation.

As Jesus proceeded toward his ultimate purpose, the mother of James and John asked Jesus if her sons could sit at his right and left in his kingdom. Jesus replied to them by saying, "You don't know what you are asking. Can you drink the cup I am going to drink?" (Matt. 20:22). The expression "drink the cup" is a figure of speech meaning "undergo" or "experience." In Jesus' case, it refers to his cup of suffering. Jesus would undergo a tremendous ordeal of suffering. Jesus asked his disciples if they could drink that same cup.

When the other ten disciples caught wind of this request, they became angry with James and John. Jesus used the opportunity as a teachable moment. He gathered his disciples together and declared the following principle: "You know that the rulers of the Gentiles lord it over them, and their high officials exercise authority over them. Not so with you. Instead, whoever wants to become great among you must be your servant, and whoever wants to be first must be your slave—just as the Son of Man did not come to be served, but to serve, and to give his life as a ransom for many" (Matt. 20:25-28). Jesus knew his cup—he knew his purpose: to serve the world and to give his life as a ransom for many. Jesus would serve humanity by becoming the perfect sacrifice for sin. Whoever avails himself of Jesus' sacrifice can be saved, forgiven, and freed from the destructive bondage of sin!

I have often wondered how long Jesus knew his ultimate purpose. At what point in his life did he realize his life calling—to die on a cross for the sins of the world? What was it like for him to anticipate this goal? In Matthew 26:2, he said, "As you know, the Passover is two days away—and the Son of Man will be handed over to be crucified." Jesus knew that he was to be the perfect Passover Lamb—the perfect sacrifice for sin—once and for all!

As Jesus prepared for Passover, a woman came to him to anoint his hair with perfume. Jesus' disciples, who were concerned with the monetary waste, rebuked her; they argued that the money for the expensive perfume could have been used to help the poor. However, Jesus told his disciples the following: "Why are you bothering this woman? She has done a beautiful thing to me. The poor you will always have with you, but you will not always have me. When she poured this perfume on my body, she did it to prepare me for burial" (Matt. 26:10-12). You see, through this action, Jesus was symbolically being prepared to be buried. The Jewish custom was to anoint a dead body with perfume; however, this courtesy was not performed for criminals. Though Jesus had committed no sin, he was anticipating being crucified like a criminal.

After this preparation, Jesus led his disciples in the taking of "the last supper." Taking the cup, Jesus again spoke of his death: "This is my blood of the covenant, which is poured out for many for the forgiveness of sins" (Matt. 26:28).

As Jesus continued to prepare his soul for the cross, he took three close friends—Peter, James, and John—with him into the garden of Gethsemane. He wanted these friends to stay with him as "he began to be sorrowful and troubled" (Matt. 26:37). Jesus shared with his friends: "My soul is overwhelmed with sorrow to the point of death. Stay here and keep watch with me" (Matt. 26:38). Jesus was overwhelmed with the task ahead of him: that of dying on a cross for the sin of the whole world.

Jesus struggled with his "cup." However, he submitted to his Father's will. He prayed three times to his Father as he prepared to be crucified. In his prayers, he expressed his willingness to follow through with his purpose. Finally, in Matthew 26:45-46, Jesus expressed his readiness for the coming ordeal: "Look, the hour is near, and the Son of Man is betrayed into the hands of sinners. Rise, let us go! Here comes my betrayer!" After all of his anticipation, the hour of his suffering was finally at hand!

Jesus willingly took up his cross to die for the sins of the world. He could have called down legions of angels to save himself. Instead, he courageously faced into his life purpose and sacrificed his life for the sins of the world, including your sin and mine.

Oh, what great joy our Lord must have felt when he declared on the cross, "It is finished" (John 19:30)! What joy he must have experienced when he rose from the dead, realizing that his purpose of conquering sin, death, and Satan had been accomplished! Jesus had achieved his goal!

Young person, there will be seasons in your life that are difficult. Perhaps you are going through one of those times now. Jesus' life teaches us how to endure hard times. We learn to endure by viewing these difficulties as the cross of Christ and then taking up our cross to follow him. As we die to self, we experience his resurrection life.

Let me repeat the great passage of Hebrews 12:1-3, which teaches us how to endure the cross:

> Therefore, since we are surrounded by such a great cloud of witnesses, let us throw off everything that hinders and the sin that so easily entangles, and let us run with perseverance the race marked out for us. Let us fix our eyes on Jesus, the author and perfecter of our faith, who for the joy set before him endured the cross, scorning its shame, and sat down at the right hand of the throne of God. Consider him who endured such opposition from sinful men, so that you will not grow weary and lose heart.

I encourage you to fasten the eyes of your heart on Jesus, who brings *eternal* salvation to your soul and *daily* salvation to your life. As you do so, you will gain endurance for the journey!

Memory Verse

> Hebrews 12:2-3 "Let us fix our eyes on Jesus, the author and perfecter of our faith, who for the joy set before him endured the cross, scorning its shame, and sat down at the right hand of the throne of God. Consider him who endured such opposition from sinful men, so that you will not grow weary and lose heart."

PETER

Get Back Up After Failure

Peter was one of Jesus' twelve disciples. In fact, he was a leader among the disciples. A fisherman accustomed to physical labor, Peter was a very strong man and a natural leader of men. However, Peter was strong in himself. He needed to be "sifted"—sifted of self. He needed to learn the secret of being strong in Christ, as opposed to being strong in himself.

In Matthew chapter 26, Jesus was having a meal with his disciples. After having this "last supper" together, Jesus went with his disciples to the Mount of Olives. While there, Jesus told his disciples that they would all fall away when Jesus was persecuted. However, Peter declared the following: "Even if all fall away on account of you, I never will" (Matt. 26:33). Jesus proceeded to tell Peter that he would deny him three times before the rooster crows. However, Peter still expressed self-confidence: "Even if I have to die with you, I will never disown you" (Matt. 26:35). Peter's expression shows that he was strong in himself; he was confident that he would stand with Jesus until the end—even to the death if need be!

Next Jesus took his disciples to a place called Gethsemane to prepare in prayer. Then he went aside with three of his particularly close disciples—Peter, James, and John. Jesus chose these ones to be with him as he prayed. Jesus shared his heart with them: "My soul is overwhelmed with sorrow to the point of death. Stay here and keep watch with me" (Matt. 26:38). Jesus needed his friends—his close disciples—to stand with him in prayer as he faced the greatest challenge of his life: going to the cross to die for the sins of the world!

When Jesus came back to Peter, James, and John after praying, they were sleeping. Specifically addressing Peter, Jesus challenged them: "'Could you men not keep watch with me for one hour?' he asked Peter" (Matt. 26:40). Jesus advised them, "Watch and pray so that you will not fall into temptation. The spirit is willing, but the body is weak" (Matt. 26:41). In addition to his own preparation, Jesus knew that his disciples also needed to prepare for the coming ordeal.

Filled with extreme sorrow, Jesus went away three times to pray. Each time when Jesus returned, he found his disciples sleeping. When he finished praying and returned to his disciples the third time, Jesus said, "Are you still sleeping and resting? Look, the hour is near, and the Son of Man is betrayed into the hands of sinners. Rise, let us go! Here comes my betrayer!" (Matt. 26:45-46). Because Jesus had spent time with his Father in prayer, he was prepared for his trial; however, his disciples, including Peter, were not.

When a large and hostile crowd arrived with swords and clubs to arrest Jesus, one of Jesus' disciples—Judas—betrayed Jesus with a kiss. Jesus said to Judas, "Friend, do what you came for" (Matt. 26:50). After the men seized Jesus, Peter took his sword and cut off the ear of one of Jesus' arresters. John 18:10 tells us that this person was Malchus, the high priest's servant. "Jesus commanded Peter, 'Put your sword away! Shall I not drink the cup the Father has given me?'" (John 18:11). He rebuked Peter: "Put your sword back in its place, for all who draw the sword will die by the sword" (Matt. 26:52).

Jesus was not a military leader; he was not a conquering dictator; he was not an earthly king. Jesus set up a different kind of kingdom—one that would last forever in the hearts of men and women and boys and girls all over the world! Jesus proceeded to heal Malchus's ear (Luke 22:51).

Far from being forced against his will, Jesus had prepared himself to fulfill his life's purpose. He willingly died on the cross for the sins of the world! He was not forced! He told Peter, "Do you think I cannot call on my Father, and he will at once put at my disposal more than twelve legions of angels? But how then would the Scriptures be fulfilled that say it must happen in this way?" (Matt. 26:53-54).

As Jesus was being arrested, all of his disciples, including Peter, fled. However, Peter proceeded to follow Jesus and his captors at a distance to see what would happen to him. Peter was able to hear the false accusations made against Jesus. We see that Peter truly cared for Jesus and wanted to be with him. Because Peter was able to observe Jesus' trial, he could see how badly Jesus was treated: "Then they spit in his face and struck him with their fists. Others slapped him and said, 'Prophesy to us, Christ. Who hit you?'" (Matt. 26:67-68).

After sitting in the high priest's courtyard to see what was happening to Jesus, Peter was noticed by a servant girl. She said to Peter that he was with Jesus, but Peter "denied it before them all. 'I don't know what you're talking about'" (Matt. 26:70). After another girl declared that Peter was with Jesus, Peter made a stronger denial, this time with an oath: "I don't know the man!" (Matt. 26:72). And then, after Peter was accused of being one of Jesus' group because of his accent, Peter made his strongest denial as he cursed himself and exclaimed, "I don't know the man!" (Matt. 26:74).

As soon as Peter made his third denial, the rooster crowed. At that point, Peter remembered Jesus' words; and weeping bitterly, he left that place. Peter had done exactly what Jesus had predicted—denied him three times before the rooster crowed. Now Peter was no longer strong in himself.

Peter had to be "sifted" of his own strength. The dross of self had to be sifted from him so that Christ could work through him. In Luke 22:31, Jesus referred to this sifting process as he encouraged Peter, who was also called Simon: "Simon,

Simon, Satan has asked to sift you as wheat. But I have prayed for you, Simon, that your faith may not fail. And when you have turned back, strengthen your brothers." Jesus' prayer would be answered! Even though Peter had failed miserably, eventually his faith would become steadfast and he would turn back to the Lord. Jesus would restore him so that he could "strengthen your brothers."

Peter felt great sorrow about failing Jesus. He still loved Jesus, but he hadn't been able to stand for Jesus and defend him as he had wanted. Another disciple, Judas, who had betrayed Jesus, also felt sorrow, but he didn't turn back to Jesus. He didn't get back up after failing. Instead, Judas hanged himself. When we fail, if we simply make a decision to repent and turn back to Jesus, God is ready to forgive us. His loving mercy is there for us as Peter would find out.

Proverbs 24:16 declares, "For though a righteous man falls seven times, he rises again." Peter had fallen. He had failed Jesus. But Peter would discover the great extent of Jesus' love as Jesus would help him get back up.

After Jesus died on the cross and rose from the dead, we see in John 21 how Jesus restored Peter. As Peter sat with some of the disciples, he suddenly said, "I'm going out to fish" (John 21:3). As we have seen, Peter was a natural leader, and the other disciples followed him to go fishing. However, they had no success fishing that night; they caught no fish.

Early that next morning, Jesus came to the shore near where they were fishing, but the disciples didn't recognize him. Calling them "friends," Jesus advised them to put their net on the boat's right side. Lo and behold! After they put their net on the other side of the boat, they caught a multitude of large fish!

Then, when John told Peter that the man on the beach was Jesus, Peter put on his outer garment and jumped into the water to go see him. In this spontaneous act, we see Peter's love for Jesus; he was so eager to see Jesus again. Peter was more than ready to turn back to Jesus!

After greeting Jesus, Peter went back to the boat and helped the others bring in the net. (It was full of 153 large fish.) When they got to the beach, Jesus proceeded to feed them. By doing so, Jesus showed the disciples a very important example—that of serving others by feeding them. After the disciples hadn't been able to catch any fish—any food—on their own, Jesus gave them more than enough fish and prepared breakfast for them.

When Jesus had finished feeding his disciples, he asked Peter, "Simon son of John, do you truly love me more than these?" (John 21:15). (Compare Jesus' question to Peter's earlier declaration before Jesus was arrested in Matthew 26:33: "Even if all fall away on account of you, I never will.") Jesus was harkening back to that moment when Peter declared that he would not fall away. Now that Peter had been "sifted" of his own strength, Jesus asked Peter if he truly loved him more than the other disciples did.

Now humbled, Peter responded by saying, "Yes, Lord, you know that I love you" (John 21:15). Jesus continued to ask Peter two more times if he loved him. As Peter answered Jesus' three questions, Jesus was preparing to make a point. He proceeded to emphasize the need for Peter to care for Jesus' sheep. Jesus said to Peter, "Feed my sheep" (John 21:17). As Jesus was an example in feeding his disciples, he emphasized the need for Peter to be a servant through feeding his sheep.

Jesus gave Peter a clear call: "Follow me!" (John 21:19). Jesus called Peter to follow him by feeding his sheep. Young person, what is your call? Seeking God's call will give you enduring purpose for your life!

Jesus helped Peter get back up after his failure. Jesus restored Peter. Peter became a leader in God's kingdom and was used by God tremendously. Once when Peter and John were going to the temple to pray, a crippled man begged them for money. After Peter got the man's attention, he said to him, "Silver or gold I do not have, but what I have I give you. In the name of Jesus Christ of Nazareth, walk" (Acts 3:6). Peter took him by his hand and lifted him up. Just as Jesus had helped Peter get up after his failure, Peter helped this crippled man to get up. The man proceeded to praise God exuberantly!

Of course, Peter also gave the Lord glory for this miracle. Peter was a changed man now. He was changed from pride to humility, from strength in self to strength in God. He now gave God all the praise!

In this account of Jesus with Peter, we see that Jesus prayed three times in Gethsemane, that Peter denied Jesus three times, and that Jesus asked Peter "Do you love me?" three times. Jesus helped Peter to get back up after his failure and totally restored him. Through this experience, Peter learned to depend humbly on the Lord as opposed to being strong in himself.

Young person, just like Peter, there will be times in life when you will fail. When you fail, I encourage you not to despair. The Lord Jesus is right there to pick you back up. When you fail—when you sin—learn to repent quickly. Look up to Jesus and let him lift you up; confess your sin and receive his forgiveness. He will lovingly restore you and help you to get back on the path of following him. He will make you an others-focused champion who feeds others in his kingdom. He will help you to depend on his strength as opposed to depending on yourself.

Memory Verse

Proverbs 24:16a "For though a righteous man falls seven times, he rises again."

STEPHEN

Share the Gospel Boldly, No Matter the Consequences

The gospel is the good news of Jesus Christ's victory on the cross over sin and death! We're called to share this victorious message boldly—to open our mouth and share the truth of Messiah. For people to come to the Lord Jesus, they must hear the message: "Faith comes from hearing the message, and the message is heard through the word of Christ" (Rom. 10:17). In order for others to hear, we must share the gospel. And we must do this task, regardless of the consequences.

I've had the experience of sharing the Lord in our church's neighborhood and enduring some boys' mockery. Although it is never pleasant to be ridiculed, it's important to know that if people mock us as we share the Lord, they are really insulting him. Jesus encourages us in Matthew 5:11-12: "Blessed are you when people insult you, persecute you and falsely say all kinds of evil against you because of me. Rejoice and be glad, because great is your reward in heaven, for in the same way they persecuted the prophets who were before you."

One man in the Bible who underwent persecution was Stephen. Full of faith and the Holy Spirit, Stephen was bold in sharing the Lord with others. He was a man who desired to serve God.

In Acts 6 we are told that the early church had relational issues. There was a dispute between the Grecian widows and the Hebrew widows over the distribution of food. The apostles resolved this manner in a loving and forthright manner. They appointed certain men as deacons to distribute the food to the widows in an equitable manner. Stephen was one of the deacons that was used by God to serve in this way.

Stephen illustrates the Biblical principle of being faithful in small things before being faithful in larger things. In addition to having an attitude of servanthood, Stephen was "full of God's grace and power" (Acts 6:8). By the power of the Holy Spirit, Stephen was used by God to work miracles!

In addition, Stephen was a very wise, logical debater. When different ones started to argue and oppose Stephen, they could not match his wisdom as he was led by the Holy Spirit. Stephen illustrates the need for young people to learn Biblical wisdom as well as to gain a Biblical world view to help them defend the faith.

When the ones opposing Stephen could not win by honest debate, they falsely accused him of speaking against Moses. Stephen was brought before the ruling council of Judaism, known as the Sanhedrin. Amid the false witnesses, Stephen kept his focus on the Lord Jesus: "All who were sitting in the Sanhedrin looked intently at Stephen, and they saw that his face was like the face of an angel" (Acts 6:15). Through his trial, Stephen knew that Christ was with him!

When Stephen was questioned by the high priest of the Sanhedrin, Stephen responded with a speech detailing God's work among his people. He shared the history of the nation of Israel. He recalled how God's people often rejected his offers of salvation, climaxing with the council's rejection of Jesus the Messiah—the same council persecuting Stephen!

How did Stephen know God's Word and Biblical history so well? He knew God's Word because he had studied it. As the Word says, he had studied to show himself "approved unto God" (2 Tim. 2:15). Likewise, it's important for young people to know God, to study God's Word, and to know history from a Biblical perspective.

Well, when Stephen accused the Sanhedrin of resisting the Holy Spirit, of murdering Jesus, and of receiving the law of Moses without obeying it, they were outraged: "When they heard this, they were furious and gnashed their teeth at him" (Acts 7:54). Stephen proclaimed the Word of God boldly, but those who heard it didn't like what they heard.

However, through their fury, Stephen stayed focused on the Lord: "But Stephen, full of the Holy Spirit, looked up to heaven and saw the glory of God, and Jesus standing at the right hand of God. 'Look,' he said, 'I see heaven open and the Son of Man standing at the right hand of God'" (Acts 7:55-56). Stephen focused on Jesus amid opposition. When he told the council that he saw Jesus standing at the right hand of God, they became exceedingly angry at Stephen. Then they forcefully took him out of the city and stoned him. For proclaiming the Word of God faithfully and boldly, Stephen became the church's first *martyr*, one who dies for standing for the Lord!

The word *martyr* is the Greek for "witness"—those willing to die for Christ. A witness shares the good news with others, whether or not they receive it. He is willing to suffer any consequences for teaching the truth of God's Word.

Stephen shared the gospel boldly, no matter the consequences. He wasn't focused on his own life. He was focused on Jesus; he was even willing to die for the Lord. He wasn't worried about the consequences. As he was being stoned to death, Stephen fixed his eyes on Jesus! God was with him!

Whenever I have had the opportunity to share Jesus with others, I have noticed that the Lord gives me the witness of the Holy Spirit in my being. I sense the power of the Holy Spirit to enable me to share Christ boldly with that person. 2 Timothy 1:6-7 reminds us to allow the Holy Spirit within us to make us bold: "I remind you to fan into flame the gift of God, which is in you through the laying on of hands. For God did not give us a spirit of timidity, but a spirit of power, of love and of self-discipline." The gift of God is from the Holy Spirit, and the Holy Spirit enables us to share with others boldly and powerfully! When we share the Lord with others, God's Spirit within us gives us a great sense of his presence! The Holy Spirit makes us bold for him!

As they were stoning him, Stephen committed himself to the Lord. "Stephen prayed, 'Lord Jesus, receive my spirit'" (Acts 7:59). Falling on his knees, Stephen called to the Lord: "Lord, do not hold this sin against them" (Acts 7:60). Even as he was murdered, Stephen forgave his persecutors. His action was reminiscent of Jesus' request on the cross: "Father, forgive them, for they do not know what they are doing" (Luke 23:34). Stephen faithfully proclaimed the Lord Jesus, who was crucified for the sin of the whole world and raised to new life!

As Stephen was martyred for the faith, Saul was watching. "Saul was there, giving approval to his death" (Acts 8:1). Even though Saul wasn't converted at this time, surely Stephen served as a witness to him. Later Saul had a life-changing conversion, receiving a new name and becoming the great Apostle Paul. God used Paul to spread Christianity and to write much of the New Testament.

Young person, there will be times when others will not receive your sharing of God's Word. In fact, they might outright reject you. Even so, God still calls us to share the gospel as the Holy Spirit leads us. God will be with you as you open your mouth to share Jesus! He will give you the words to speak. Share the good news that Jesus loves us so much that he took our punishment—that he died in our place. Share the greatness of coming into God's Kingdom—that we learn to live the way God created us to live! And that includes living boldly for Christ!

Often it takes a person as many as five, six, or seven encounters with the gospel before he responds and becomes saved. The Apostle Paul shared this dynamic of planting seeds in 1 Corinthians 3:6-9: "I planted the seed, Apollos watered it, but God made it grow. So neither he who plants nor he who waters is anything, but only God, who makes things grow. The man who plants and the man who waters have one purpose, and each will be rewarded according to his own labor. For we are God's fellow workers; you are God's field, God's building." We are all called to be working in God's harvest field. Some of us plant seeds, others of us water those seeds, and God makes those seeds grow. The one who makes those seeds grow is the Lord of the harvest!

The Lord of the harvest calls us to be planting seeds by sharing the gospel. If you lead someone to Jesus, you may be reaping the result of someone else's seed planting. One thing is for sure: if we're going to reap a harvest, we need to be involved in planting seed. And people are ripe for the harvest, as Jesus emphasized in Matthew 9:37-38: "The harvest is plentiful but the workers are few. Ask the Lord of the harvest, therefore, to send out workers into his harvest field."

Even though Stephen didn't change the hearts of the Sanhedrin and even though Saul wasn't converted at that time, with Stephen's death the gospel spread as a great persecution broke out against the church. As Christians were dispersed in different directions because of the persecution, "those who had been scattered preached the word wherever they went" (Acts 8:4). Stephen's martyrdom and the church's persecution resulted in God's kingdom advancing!

Young person, I challenge you to let God use you to advance his kingdom. Be faithful to share Jesus, by your example and your words, regardless of the consequences! Recognize that we all need to be planting seeds. People have gone before us, just as Stephen did, to plant seeds. We need to plant seeds that others will reap after us. As we are faithful to plant seeds, we will eventually reap a good harvest. Be confident that Jesus' sacrificial love for others is real. Be confident that God's message is powerful to change lives. Be bold to share the GOOD NEWS with others!

Memory Verse

Acts 4:29 "Now, Lord, consider their threats and enable your servants to speak your word with great boldness."

PHILIP

Be Led by the Holy Spirit!

In Acts chapter 6, Philip was one of seven responsible deacons chosen along with Stephen to care for widows after a complaint of unfairness was registered in the allocation of the food. These seven deacons were chosen for their responsibility and for their being "full of the Spirit and wisdom" (Acts 6:3). Because of these seven faithful and responsible servants, God's kingdom was able to advance.

After Stephen boldly proclaimed the truth of Jesus and was martyred, a great persecution broke out against the church. As Christians scattered because of the persecution, God's Word spread. As we have seen throughout history, Stephen's martyrdom actually caused God's kingdom to advance. History has taught us that when persecution comes against the church, Christians' hearts grow stronger, their faith gets firmer, and their love for the Lord grows deeper. That is exactly what happened in the early church.

As disciples scattered everywhere, the good news of the gospel also spread. Philip, one of the seven responsible deacons, was among those being scattered. In the process, Philip became an evangelist who was led by the Holy Spirit to share the gospel!

When Philip preached Christ to a Samarian city, the people listened attentively to him because of his preaching and miracles. In fact, many people were healed through his ministry. Philip's life teaches us the principle that he who is faithful in smaller things will be entrusted to be faithful with larger things (Matt. 25:21). While Philip demonstrated faithfulness waiting on tables and serving widows, God prepared him for larger tasks for his kingdom.

Young person, this is an important principle of the kingdom. Whatever your parents, teachers, coaches, employers, and pastors give you to do, I encourage you to do it faithfully, wholeheartedly, and cheerfully. As you do so, the Lord will see your attitude, and he will promote you. Who is the one person who sees all things? It's God, of course. I have seen this principle operate in my life: as I was faithful in one area, such as my employment, God promoted me in the church; as I was faithful in the church, God also helped me to grow in taking larger responsibilities in my work field.

God sees your faithfulness in whatever you do. As you are faithful in one area, he might promote you in another area. Remember this very important principle: promotion is from the Lord, who sees all things. He sees us when no one else can. Even when it seems that others don't notice your work and faithfulness, God always does. As you are faithful in the little things, the Lord will give you larger and larger responsibilities for his kingdom!

The Lord uses all things to prepare us for our future. When I was in high school, I played the trumpet in the band. However, the way that I earned the respect of my band director was my setting up the chairs for the performances. He knew that he could count on me to do this task. This experience, in turn, prepared me for later in life as I was responsible to set up for worship services. I have seen that the Lord uses all things in our lives—no matter how mundane—to prepare us for our calling, his ultimate plan for us!

As Philip was led by the Holy Spirit to share the good news, "there was great joy in that city" (Acts 8:8). However, in Samaria there was a man named Simon who was enthralled by Philip's signs and miracles. Simon practiced sorcery, which is the use of evil to practice magic arts.

Young person, you want to be sure to not get involved in evil magic arts. Doing so would make you vulnerable to the devil. You want to be sure to follow Jesus and not the devices of the enemy, Satan himself. Don't get involved in activities such as "Dungeons and Dragons," Ouija boards, fortune telling, crystal balls, palm readings, mediums, and horoscopes. Your peers may try to entice you with these types of activities, but stay clear of them. Delving into them would open you up to the enemy's plans. If you have involved yourself in these kinds of things, talk with your parents and your pastor, repent of this sin, and claim the blood of Christ over your life. Then you will be completely free of the work of the enemy.

Well, the apostles Peter and John went to Samaria to check on the work of the Lord there. They laid hands on the Christians to receive the baptism of the Holy Spirit. Previously the believers there had been born again and water baptized; now they were being baptized in the Holy Spirit. Acts 8:17 explains, "Then Peter and John placed their hands on them, and they received the Holy Spirit."

Young person, there are three foundational experiences that we all need to embrace. In Acts 2:38-39, Peter summarized them: "Repent and be baptized, every one of you, in the name of Jesus Christ for the forgiveness of your sins. And you will receive the gift of the Holy Spirit. The promise is for you and your children and for all who are far off—for all whom the Lord our God will call."

The first foundational experience we need is to be born again through repentance and faith in Jesus. We're born again by repenting of our sin and turning to the Lord in faith to receive Jesus as our Lord and Savior. Romans 10:9 declares, "That if you confess with your mouth, 'Jesus is Lord,' and believe in your heart that God raised him from the dead, you will be saved." The Bible says, "Everyone who calls on the name of the Lord will be saved" (Acts 2:21).

The second foundational experience is to be water baptized. When we are baptized in water, we are identifying with the Lord in his death, burial, and resurrection. When we go under the water, that symbolizes his death; when we are under the water, that symbolizes his burial; and when we come up out of the water, that symbolizes his resurrection. In addition, when you are water baptized, it is done publicly—you are making a public declaration that you are Jesus' disciple. You are declaring that you will follow Jesus the rest of your life!

The third foundational experience is to be baptized in the Holy Spirit. Jesus said, "Which of you fathers, if your son asks for a fish, will give him a snake instead? Or if he asks for an egg, will give him a scorpion? If you then, though you are evil, know how to give good gifts to your children, how much more will your Father in heaven give the Holy Spirit to those who ask him!" (Luke 11:11-13). To receive the gift of the Holy Spirit, all we need to do is ask God! Often, by the leading of the Holy Spirit, this gift was given in prayer through the laying on of hands.

As a young man, I received the baptism of the Holy Spirit at a retreat. A group of men laid their hands on me as I asked for and received the baptism of the Holy Spirit. Afterward, a great desire to worship God came over me. I recall worshiping God with all my heart as I washed dishes at my restaurant job. As I was getting wet *outwardly* while washing dishes, streams of living water were flowing *inside* me through the Holy Spirit! Jesus declared, "If anyone is thirsty, let him come to me and drink. Whoever believes in me, as the Scripture has said, streams of living water will flow from within him. By this he meant the Spirit, whom those who believed in him were later to receive" (John 7:37-39).

Ever since I was baptized in the Holy Spirit, I love to worship the Lord! When God empowers you by the Holy Spirit, he infuses you with his abundant love, and you receive a great desire to worship and serve him. The Apostle Paul encouraged Timothy with these words: "For this reason I remind you to fan into flame the gift of God, which is in you through the laying on of my hands. For God did not give us a spirit of timidity, but a spirit of power, of love and of self-discipline" (2 Tim. 1:6-7). The gift of the Holy Spirit enables us to love and serve God with power, with love, and with the self-discipline that maximizes our testimony!

Well, once Simon saw the apostles giving the Holy Spirit through the laying on of their hands, he tried to *buy* the power of the Holy Spirit with *money*! Peter rebuked Simon, told him that he had no part in this ministry, and called on him to repent of his evil. With the apostles' leadership and the saints' inspiration, the kingdom of God spread.

As Philip continued to be led by the Holy Spirit, an angel told him to go south on the desert road from Jerusalem to Gaza. Empowered by the Spirit, Philip started out on this trip of some fifty miles. As he was traveling, Philip met an Ethiopian in charge of the Ethiopian queen's treasury. "This man had gone to Jerusalem to worship" (Acts 8:27). It's important to understand that Philip left an outreach involving many people to be led by the Holy Spirit to minister to just one person. Young person, remember that the Holy Spirit will lead you to care for people as individuals.

Well, the Ethiopian had been reading from the Bible, specifically from the book of Isaiah. (When we read his Word, God works in our hearts and minds by the Holy Spirit.) Meanwhile Philip continued to be directed by the Holy Spirit: "The Spirit told Philip, 'Go to that chariot and stay near it'" (Acts 8:29). Philip was in touch with the Holy Spirit—he followed the Spirit's leading to do this or to do that! He listened to the voice of the Lord.

God calls us to be led by the Holy Spirit. It is more important to be led by the Holy Spirit than to do what is perceived by others to be the right thing. This quality helps us to focus on pleasing God instead of pleasing man. As the Apostle Paul emphasized, "Am I now trying to win the approval of men, or of God? Or am I trying to please men? If I were still trying to please men, I would not be a servant of Christ" (Gal. 1:10). Proverbs 29:25 counsels, "Fear of man will prove to be a snare, but whoever trusts in the Lord is kept safe." In the decisions that we make, we cannot be afraid of what people think of us or be swayed by their criticisms. Instead, our focus needs to be on allowing the Holy Spirit to guide us. Otherwise, our decisions will be out of balance and cause problems. In order to please God, we need to have that moment-by-moment, day-by-day leading of the Holy Spirit in our lives.

As the Holy Spirit spurred Philip on, Philip was inspired to run! Indeed, Philip was a fast runner! Acts 8:30 says, "Then Philip ran up to the chariot and heard the man reading Isaiah the prophet. 'Do you understand what you are reading?' Philip asked." When Philip overheard the Ethiopian reading from the book of Isaiah, Philip asked him if he understood its meaning.

The Ethiopian asked Philip to explain the passage to him. It was Isaiah 53:7-8, which describes Jesus as he approached the cross: "He was led like a sheep to the slaughter, and as a lamb before the shearer is silent, so he did not open his mouth. In his humiliation he was deprived of justice. Who can speak of his descendants? For his life was taken from the earth." The Ethiopian asked Philip whom the prophet Isaiah was talking about. Philip seized the opportunity to use that Old Testament passage to share the gospel.

What is the gospel? What is the meaning of the word *gospel*? The word is from the old English *godspel*, meaning "good story" or "good news." Indeed, the gospel is the good news about Jesus—his taking our punishment for sin through his death and his rising from the dead so that we can receive eternal life!

Philip was ready to share the good news about Jesus! He wore the spiritual sandals "fitted with the readiness that comes from the gospel of peace" (Eph. 6:15). He was ready to be led by the Holy Spirit. Indeed, we all need to be prepared to listen to the Holy Spirit when he is prodding us to share the gospel with someone! Allow the Holy Spirit to lead you to share the Lord with others!

When they came to a body of water, the Ethiopian asked to be baptized; and Philip baptized him. Then something amazing happened: "When they came up out of the water, the Spirit of the Lord suddenly took Philip away" (Acts 8:39). Philip disappeared from the Ethiopian's presence, and the Ethiopian rejoiced over his changed life!

Philip continued to preach Christ to the multitudes. And God's kingdom advanced as Philip and many other disciples were led by the Holy Spirit to spread the gospel!

Young person, I encourage you to be led by the Holy Spirit. Rather than being led by evil influences in this world, be sure that you are being led by the Spirit of God! If you are a Christian, that means that the Holy Spirit abides in you to guide you every day of your life and in every area of your life. Moreover, whether you are ministering to hundreds or to just one person, know that the Lord is leading you. That one person is important to God! I encourage you to grow in letting the Holy Spirit lead you to share the good news of Jesus Christ with others!

Memory Verse

Galatians 5:25 "Since we live by the Spirit, let us keep in step with the Spirit."

BARNABAS

Encourage Others by Lifting Them Up When They Are Down!

In the book of Acts, we learn of a man who possessed the gift of encouragement. In fact, his name means "encourager." This champion of God was Barnabas; he was called the "son of encouragement." Barnabas truly lived up to his name.

Many people have the gift of encouragement. Romans 12:8 says that if a person's gift "is encouraging, let him encourage." In fact, we can all cultivate this excellent practice of encouraging others. When you look at the word *en-courage*, you can see that the word means to *put courage into* another person. You literally give that person courage—you give that person strength to get back up, strength to keep on going, and strength to face into any challenge that person may be facing!

In our lives, it's very important to have people around us that encourage us. For instance, my wife Silvia encourages me. After I lead a meeting, she'll give me input regarding how I did well and how I can improve. Our son Nehemiah has the gift of encouragement. When he was younger, he would tell his mommy that she's the best mommy in the whole world! He also encourages her and expresses gratitude for the meals that she makes us. In addition, my son Joshua will often encourage others. I especially appreciate it when he encourages me after soccer practice; he'll say, "Good practice, Daddy." We all need to practice the discipline of encouraging others.

About the early church, the Bible speaks of how believers were encouraged through the gift of giving:

> All the believers were one in heart and mind. No one claimed that any of his possessions was his own, but they shared everything they had. With great power the apostles continued to testify to the resurrection of the Lord Jesus, and much grace was upon them all. There were no needy persons among them. For from time to time those who owned lands or houses sold them, brought the money from the sales and put it at the apostles' feet, and it was distributed to anyone as he had need. (Acts 4:32-35)

One of those disciples who gave of his possessions to encourage others was a man named Barnabas. He sold his field and gave the money to the apostles to distribute as they saw fit. In our church, we have a certain fund named after this disciple. It's called the "Barnabas Fund," and its purpose is to help people in dire need. When we help people in a financial hardship, we encourage them.

Some people use this passage about the selling of one's possessions and giving them to the leaders for the poor as advocating "Christian Communism." However, this assessment is erroneous. With communism, the government *forces* you to give up ownership of what you possess. Here, the disciple is in control of how he uses the resources God has given him. As Jesus' disciples, we're called to cheerfully and willingly *give* unto the Lord. One decides in his own heart to give; it's not decided for him. As 2 Corinthians 9:7-8 says, "Each man should give what he has decided in his heart to give, not reluctantly or under compulsion, for God loves a cheerful giver. And God is able to make all grace abound to you, so that in all things at all times, having all that you need, you will abound in every good work."

This dynamic was in operation in Barnabas's life. Because he gave, he encouraged others. Giving to the church results in encouragement and in thanksgiving to God. 2 Corinthians 9:12-15 explains the thanksgiving and encouragement that occurs when we practice generosity:

> This service that you perform is not only supplying the needs of God's people but is also overflowing in many expressions of thanks to God. Because of the service by which you have proved yourselves, men will praise God for the obedience that accompanies your confession of the gospel of Christ, and for your generosity in sharing with them and with everyone else. And in their prayers for you their hearts will go out to you, because of the surpassing grace God has given you. Thanks be to God for his indescribable gift!

What an encouraging circle of gratitude! The grace of giving results in thanksgiving resulting in praising God resulting in prayer for the giver! The Lord is thanked for "his indescribable gift!" When you give to meet a need, you are encouraging others and causing much thanksgiving!

Before the Apostle Paul became arguably the most important leader of the early church, he was known as Saul, the persecutor of the church. Having been a terrible persecutor of Christians, Saul underwent a dramatic conversion while traveling on the road to Damascus. During his conversion, he became blinded by a light sent from God. God chose to use a zealous persecutor of the church to become a zealous leader of the church. What a turnaround!

However, Saul would have to go through a process before he became accepted as a leader. Because of Saul's blindness, the Lord told the disciple Ananias, whose name means "the Lord shows grace," to pray for Saul that his sight would be restored. However, Ananias was concerned: "Lord, I have heard many reports about this man and all the harm he has done to your saints in Jerusalem. And he has come here with authority from the chief priests to arrest all who call on your name" (Acts 9:13-14).

But God told Ananias: "Go! This man is my chosen instrument to carry my name before the Gentiles and their kings and before the people of Israel. I will show him how much he must suffer for my name" (Acts 9:15-16).

As Ananias was obedient to the Lord's leading, God used him to show grace to Saul. He went to Saul, laid praying hands on him, and spoke words of encouragement over him! Saul regained his sight and was baptized.

If we are going to be an encourager like Ananias, we must be obedient to the voice of the Holy Spirit. I have learned to recognize God's voice when he is telling me to go out of my way to encourage someone. The Lord will lead you through the voice of the Holy Spirit to encourage this person or that person. Allow the Holy Spirit to *encourage you to encourage others!*

Sometimes people have a perspective of keeping a person down or making that person "prove" himself after he has committed a certain sin. They might even say that the person has to be "fired" from his position because of his mistake. As you are getting older and becoming leaders yourselves, I encourage you to remember that God is a merciful God. Unless the person is "a wolf in sheep's clothing"—one seeking to sabotage God's work or hurt God's people, the Lord wants us to keep encouraging that disciple.

Saul was in a precarious position—in the middle between two sides. The Jews were conspiring to kill him; at the same time, he had not earned the trust of the disciples because of their fear of him. "When [Saul] came to Jerusalem, he tried to join the disciples, but they were all afraid of him, not believing that he really was a disciple" (Acts 9:26).

In one respect, we can understand the disciples' mistrust of Saul—he had been a serious persecutor of Christians. At the same time, we see the great effect of encouragement that a fellow disciple can have on someone like Saul.

The encourager Barnabas became just that person for Saul. He chose to take Saul to the apostles and personally vouch for him: "But Barnabas took him and brought him to the apostles. He told them how Saul on his journey had seen the Lord and that the Lord had spoken to him, and how in Damascus he had preached fearlessly in the name of Jesus" (Acts 9:27). The only one who chose to speak up for Saul was Barnabas. He put his reputation on the line for Saul. If things turned out badly with Saul, who had been the church's persecutor, Barnabas would be responsible. As a result of Barnabas's encouragement and standing up for Saul, the disciples received Saul into their company.

Young person, people need encouragement. They need people to believe in them. When they "mess up," even repeatedly, they need people to still believe in what the Lord is doing in them! Barnabas encouraged Saul by his words and by his actions.

Saul was now a changed man. Whereas he previously had zealously stirred up persecution against Christians, now he zealously stirred up things for God's kingdom! As much as Saul worked against the church, now Saul was working even more for the church—and with much vigor! The Bible says that Saul spoke "boldly in the name of the Lord" (Acts 9:28). He "debated with the Grecian Jews, but they tried to kill him" (Acts 9:29).

Saul was so on fire for the Lord that he stirred things up in the church! Zealous brothers and sisters like Saul may make mistakes out of their zeal, but we need to keep working with them as the Lord refines them for his good purpose!

Well, the brothers sent Saul to Tarsus and things settled down for the church. When Saul was "sent off" to Tarsus, the church "enjoyed a time of peace" (Acts 9:31). Saul had to go away for a while. The Lord had to help Saul to mature.

Just like Saul, we also have to go through that process of growth, of maturation, of refinement. Malachi 3:3 says of the Lord: "He will sit as a refiner and purifier of silver; he will purify the Levites and refine them like gold and silver." With gold and silver, the refiner's fire is used to get rid of the impurities. Similarly, like gold and silver we have to go through that process of refinement for the Lord's use!

As Saul went away for a season of growth, the church was encouraged by the Holy Spirit: "Then the church throughout Judea, Galilee and Samaria enjoyed a time of peace. It was strengthened; and encouraged by the Holy Spirit, it grew in numbers, living in the fear of the Lord" (Acts 9:31). The people of the church were "encouraged by the Holy Spirit"! The Holy Spirit works inside us to encourage others!

Through the leading of the Holy Spirit, the church continued to grow, even amid persecution! Acts 11:20 tells of evangelists going to Antioch to share the good news with Greeks. "The Lord's hand was with them, and a great number of people believed and turned to the Lord" (Acts 11:21). The news reached the Jerusalem church, and they sent Barnabas to Antioch. Barnabas joyfully encouraged the Christians at Antioch: "When he arrived and saw the evidence of the grace of God, he was glad and encouraged them all to remain true to the Lord with all their hearts" (Acts 11:23).

The application that we can receive from the life of Barnabas is that of being a constant encouragement to others. I challenge you to faithfully encourage your peers to be strong in the Lord! Barnabas lived the life of an encourager. He embodied encouragement! The description of Barnabas in Acts 11:24 is very similar to that of the martyr Stephen: "He was a good man, full of the Holy Spirit and faith, and a great number of people were brought to the Lord." What a legacy of living for the Lord!

Barnabas continued his ministry of encouragement. Going out of his way, Barnabas again pursued Saul. "Then Barnabas went to Tarsus to look for Saul" (Acts 11:25). He found him and brought him back to Antioch. Barnabas sought to get Saul involved in God's work and to disciple him. He encouraged Saul. He got him "back in the game," so to speak!

Again, Barnabas *went looking* for Saul. That is an act of an encourager, one who seeks out someone to encourage. An encourager sees the worth in the other person and invests in that person!

Barnabas brought Saul to the church at Antioch and discipled him. Barnabas got Saul serving in the local church there. That year they taught in the church together, and Saul became a leader in the Antioch church. The Bible says that "the disciples were called Christians first at Antioch" (Acts 11:26).

Young person, it's important to allow the Holy Spirit to lead you to encourage people by lifting them up when they are down. See the gold inside people; see their value in God's eyes! Perhaps they may be rough around the edges, but see what the Lord wants to do in that person's life. Don't give up on him. This is what Barnabas did in going after Saul and getting him involved in serving the Lord!

In Acts 15, we have another example of Barnabas using his gift of encouragement. The disciple John Mark had previously deserted Saul and Barnabas as they traveled in ministry: "Barnabas wanted to take John, also called Mark, with them, but Paul did not think it wise to take him, because he had deserted them in Pamphylia and had not continued with them in the work" (Acts 15:37-38). (Saul's name had been changed to Paul.) Because of this failure on Mark's part, Paul didn't want Mark to continue with them in the ministry. However, Barnabas advocated for Mark and wanted to give him a second chance. But Paul didn't agree. Therefore, Barnabas and Paul decided to part company.

Whereas Paul decided that Mark was not deserving of ministering with them, Barnabas had the encouraging perspective of still involving Mark in the ministry. While Paul went with Silas to the churches in Syria and Cilicia, Barnabas took Mark with him to Cyprus. Even though Mark had failed in ministry, Barnabas was willing to keep working with Mark for his continued growth in the ministry.

Young people, as you become servant leaders in your churches, I want to encourage you to be ones that give people a second chance when they have failed. When you do so, you encourage that person and communicate God's grace to him. Sometimes, true disciples will be up and down in their life and ministry—I encourage you to keep working with them. If you discern that they have a sincere desire to follow God, keep encouraging them and involving them in serving God.

Years later, the Apostle Paul himself—in his last days on earth—came to a much different perspective about Mark. Paul advocated for Mark that he was helpful to him in the ministry. He wrote, "Get Mark and bring him with you, because he is helpful to me in my ministry" (2 Tim. 4:11). So over time, Mark proved himself even to Paul, who came to view Mark as valuable to him in the ministry.

Young person, Hebrews 3:12-14 gives us good advice when it comes to encouraging our friends: "See to it, brothers, that none of you has a sinful, unbelieving heart that turns away from the living God. But encourage one another daily, as long as it is called Today, so that none of you may be hardened by sin's deceitfulness. We have come to share in Christ if we hold firmly till the end the confidence we had at first." As Barnabas did, I challenge you to encourage your brothers and sisters in Christ to remain true to the Lord. Reach out to them when they are down, even when they may have fallen into sin. I encourage you to pursue friends who have sinned. Don't let them be hardened by sin's deceitfulness. Encourage them to return wholeheartedly to the Lord. Go after them and encourage them so that they don't get a hard heart. Encourage them to "keep on keeping on" in this journey with the Lord! It's important for us to believe in what God is doing in people. Encourage them that the Lord will complete his good work in them! Like Barnabas, be an encourager of others!

Memory Verse

> Hebrews 3:13 "But encourage one another daily, as long as it is called Today, so that none of you may be hardened by sin's deceitfulness."

APOSTLE PAUL

Learn to Rely on the Lord

One of the greatest leaders of all time—one of the greatest Christians of all time—was the Apostle Paul. However, before becoming a believer, Paul was the epitome of self-righteousness. A religious Jew through and through, Paul knew his righteous pedigree: "Circumcised on the eighth day, of the people of Israel, of the tribe of Benjamin, a Hebrew of Hebrews; in regard to the law, a Pharisee; as for zeal, persecuting the church; as for legalistic righteousness, faultless" (Phil. 3:4-6). However, as he came to Christ, Paul learned to put no confidence in his own righteousness. He learned to rely completely on the Lord!

Paul had been a persecutor of the church. However, after he was blinded by God's light, he made a radical decision. Giving up all the commendations of this world, he decided to put all his dependence on Jesus. He radically gave up all worldly honors—even religious prestige—for the Lord! Instead of relying on himself, he learned to rely on God. Instead of finding strength in his self-righteousness, Paul learned to walk in Jesus' righteousness.

The Apostle Paul said the following about his past accomplishments:

> But whatever was to my profit I now consider loss for the sake of Christ. What is more, I consider everything a loss compared to the surpassing greatness of knowing Christ Jesus my Lord, for whose sake I have lost all things. I consider them rubbish, that I may gain Christ and be found in him, not having a righteousness of my own that comes from the law, but that which is through faith in Christ—the righteousness that comes from God and is by faith. I want to know Christ and the power of his resurrection and the fellowship of sharing in his sufferings, becoming like him in his death, and so, somehow, to attain to the resurrection from the dead. (Phil. 3:7-11)

Paul no longer put confidence in himself; his confidence was now in the Lord. He said of Jesus, "In him we live and move and have our being" (Acts 17:28). When we come to Christ, we have everything that we need in him alone!

We all have weaknesses. The Bible tells us that the Apostle Paul did as well. In fact, Paul asked God three times for a "thorn in my flesh" to be removed from him. This thorn was an affliction causing some kind of pain. He referred to it as "a messenger of Satan, to torment me" (2 Cor. 12:7). This statement is reminiscent of Satan's torment of Job: "So Satan went out from the presence of the Lord and afflicted Job with painful sores from the soles of his feet to the top of his head" (Job 2:7). In that trial, Job didn't know that God was allowing Satan to test him.

As we grow as disciples, we come to understand that we will experience tests to help us to learn to depend on God as opposed to ourselves. Understanding God's Word in areas such as this one is an example of what is called growing in the meat of the Word as opposed to simply living on the milk of the Word. Hebrews 5:14 says, "But solid food is for the mature, who by constant use have trained themselves to distinguish good from evil." As disciples, we need to be ever learning God's Word, a quality which helps us to grow stronger in our relationship with Jesus.

Well, the Apostle Paul was experiencing a thorn. A thorn hurts us. It makes us feel our weakness. It causes us to need help. This thorn was causing Paul pain. However, when Paul asked God for the thorn to be removed from him, God denied his request. As God's children, it's important for us to remember that when we are making requests of him, that we are asking our *Father* God. Our Father teaches us through our asking. While fathers love to bless their children, a good father won't grant his child's every request.

Let me give you a simple example. When our son Joshua was a young boy, one day he had been eating donuts for breakfast. After eating donuts, he then asked for dessert. Now mind you, it was breakfast time. Joshua had been eating donuts for breakfast, and now he was asking for dessert! We told him no, of course.

Through the asking process, children are taught life lessons. Sometimes the answer doesn't come right away and sometimes the answer will be "no." Just as our parents seek to do what is best for us, how much more will our Father God do what is best for us! God's answer to Paul's pleadings for the thorn to be removed was that it would not be removed. God didn't grant Paul's request. He knew what was best for Paul. He knew that it was best for Paul to learn to rely on him through this thorn. Doing so would allow him to grow as a servant of the Lord.

The Apostle Paul realized that God had a good reason for the thorn: "To keep me from becoming conceited because of these surpassingly great revelations, there was given me a thorn in my flesh, a messenger of Satan, to torment me" (2 Cor. 12:7). God didn't want Paul to become prideful because of the supernatural revelations God gave him. God wanted Paul to stay humble and dependent on him. Although Paul begged God three times to take away the thorn, God's answer was clear: "My grace is sufficient for you, for my power is made perfect in weakness" (2 Cor. 12:9).

After that answer from the Lord, Paul determined to "boast all the more gladly about my weaknesses, so that Christ's power may rest on me" (2 Cor. 12:9). He said, "That is why, for Christ's sake, I delight in weaknesses, in insults, in hardships, in persecutions, in difficulties. For when I am weak, then I am strong" (2 Cor. 12:10). Instead of being self-sufficient, Paul learned to be Christ-sufficient.

In Philippians 4:13, Paul emphasized this point about God's strength in his weakness: "I can do everything through him who gives me strength."

What does it mean to boast in our weaknesses? It means that we use our weaknesses to trust God and God alone for our strength. It's remembering to give the Lord all the glory for his working in our lives. It means that we recognize that any success—any good—comes from Christ alone! It's relying on the Lord to be able to serve him! "And so we know and rely on the love God has for us" (1 John 4:16).

As the Lord's disciple, what do you resolve to do? Paul declared, "For I resolved to know nothing while I was with you except Jesus Christ and him crucified" (1 Cor. 2:2). Young people, I challenge you to resolve to know the Lord Jesus. And don't desire to know him just because of the good things he can do for you. Resolve to know this man Jesus who went to the cross in our place and now calls us to take up *our* cross and follow him!

In Luke 9:23-24, Jesus said the following about being his disciple: "If anyone would come after me, he must deny himself and take up his cross daily and follow me. For whoever wants to save his life will lose it, but whoever loses his life for me will save it." When we die to ourselves—our self, our selfishness, and our desires, something amazing happens in our lives! Jesus' life—his abundant, eternal, resurrection life—flows from us!

What does it mean to take up our cross daily? Well, first we must "take up" our cross. A cross is something that causes pain and ultimately death. What are some of those tough things in your life? What are your hardships? What are your trials? Your cross can take many forms: difficult work assignments, tough subjects, an ornery teacher, hard homework, challenging projects, a bullying student, hard family situations, chronic illnesses, and even things such as cancer treatments. When we embrace the cross—embrace the hard things in our life, that posture changes our perspective about these trials. We see with the Apostle Paul that these things can cause us to learn what it means to rely totally on God.

Taking up our cross daily enables us to see everything in our life in a positive, freeing light! The Apostle Paul declared, "For to me, to live is Christ and to die is gain" (Phil. 1:21). Paul made this declaration while he was imprisoned for the gospel! He viewed his whole life as Christ—even the hard things of life. He had many hardships, yet he viewed his life as Messiah. When we can embrace the hard things of our life as Christ, it changes our perspective. It enables us to be a champion for the Lord through the difficulties. What's more, we learn the truth of Romans 8:28: "We know that in all things God works for the good of those who love him, who have been called according to his purpose."

I encourage you to *live Christ* as Paul did! See your life—even the tough things—as *Christ*. In the process, you will become more and more Christlike, and you will enjoy the sweet presence of the Lord. You will enjoy sweet fellowship with God himself, no matter the external matter!

In light of this life message from Paul, how can we know the Lord so much so that we truly rely on him? First, start your day with him. Start your day by communicating with him through prayer and reading his Word. I encourage you to use the disciples' prayer given in Matthew 6:9-13 as an outline for your growing prayer life. Purposefully take up your cross, die to self, and invite Jesus' resurrected presence into your life.

Second, after establishing God's presence in your life, make it your goal to walk with him throughout the day. Stay in his presence throughout the day; don't let anything disturb you from his presence.

Third, commit all your ways to the Lord; he will guide you during your day and throughout your life. He will help you to make right decisions. In this way, you will learn to completely depend on the Lord.

Memory Verse

2 Corinthians 12:9 "My grace is sufficient for you, for my power is made perfect in weakness."

PAUL AND TIMOTHY

Be Confident to Share Jesus with Others

In my personal family history, my great grandfather had twelve children. Sometime between the time of child number five and child number six, my Great Grandpa James Melvin Switzer turned to the Lord and began to regularly take his children to church. In hindsight, our family can see a clear demarcation between the first group of children and the second group of children of my great grandfather. The first group generally did not follow the Lord; however, after my great grandfather committed himself to the Lord, the children in the second group did follow the Lord. I am very thankful that the first child of the second group was *my grandfather*—James Clark Switzer. My great grandfather's Christian faith was passed on to my grandfather, who passed his faith to my father, who then passed his faith on to me and my brothers.

In the Bible we see a similar transfer of sincere Christian faith in Timothy's life. Timothy didn't have a dramatic conversion such as Paul who was blinded by the light on the road to Damascus. However, Paul commended Timothy for his "sincere faith" which first lived in his grandmother and then in his mother (2 Tim. 1:5). Timothy was a lot like many of us; he grew up in a godly home. He grew up with a godly grandmother and mother. Undoubtedly, their faith impacted Timothy's upbringing. It's important for all of us to realize that our decision for Jesus impacts not only our life but also our future children and grandchildren—and those beyond in our future family line!

Timothy had a "sincere faith." He had received Jesus as his personal Savior and Lord. As he grew up, he eventually became a co-laborer with the Apostle Paul in sharing the gospel. He became a close friend to Paul.

In 2 Timothy 1:2, Paul referred to Timothy as "my dear son." The word used is the Greek word *agapatos*, which means "dearly loved." It connotes a depth of affection. Timothy wasn't Paul's physical son, but his spiritual son, a son in the faith. Paul encouraged Timothy with the following: "You then, my son, be strong in the grace that is in Christ Jesus. And the things you have heard me say in the presence of many witnesses entrust to reliable men who will also be qualified to teach others" (2 Tim. 2:1-2). Here we see Paul referring to four generations: first Paul, second Timothy, third reliable men, and fourth others. Both with our physical children and our spiritual children, our faith can impact many generations down the line—even people that we may never see until we meet them in heaven!

In 2 Timothy 1:4, Paul remembered Timothy's "tears." Paul had a heartfelt connection with Timothy as a father and son do. He said, "I have been reminded of your sincere faith, which first lived in your grandmother Lois and in your mother Eunice and, I am persuaded, now lives in you also" (2 Tim. 1:5). Paul was reminding and encouraging Timothy that his faith was real—that there was a generational transfer of faith that is a good thing. As parents, it's important for us to take to heart that we can take nothing with us to heaven except for our children. Because of this fact, we need to be all the more motivated to teach our children God's Word and lead them to Messiah.

In addition, the Apostle Paul encouraged Timothy to "fan into flame the gift of God, which is in you through the laying on of my hands" (2 Tim. 1:6). Timothy had received a special gift for the work of the ministry. Indeed, all of us have been given gifts from the Lord to help us serve him. How do we "fan into flame" those gifts?

First of all we need to identify our gift. Perhaps we have the gift of teaching, the gift of leadership, the gift of encouragement, or the gift of giving. Once you identify the gift that the Lord has granted you, you fan it into flame by using it. We need to remember to use the gifts God has given us.

Paul exhorted Timothy with the following: "Timothy, my dear son, I give you this instruction in keeping with the prophecies once made about you, so that by following them you may fight the good fight, holding on to faith and a good conscience" (1 Tim. 1:18-19). I recall the Word that was prophesied over me many times as a child which helped me to "hold on" to faith: "'For I know the plans I have for you,' declares the Lord, 'plans to prosper you and not to harm you, plans to give you hope and a future'" (Jer. 29:11). This word of encouragement instilled in me a sense that God had a plan—a purpose—for my life. As your parents and your pastors speak words over you, remember those words of edification. They will give you a strong sense of purpose and help you to be confident in God's plan for your life!

The Apostle Paul gave Timothy great advice. This advice holds true for all of us as we grow to maturity, and it is particularly helpful for young Christians:

> Command and teach these things. Don't let anyone look down on you because you are young, but set an example for the believers in speech, in life, in love, in faith and in purity. Until I come, devote yourself to the public reading of Scripture, to preaching and to teaching. Do not neglect your gift, which was given you through a prophetic message when the body of elders laid their hands on you. (1 Tim. 4:11-14)

What great advice! Young person, the Lord calls you to be an example with your speech, your life, your love, your faith, and your purity! That's what it's all about! If you're living this way, you have nothing to be ashamed about. It doesn't matter how young you are. By being a godly example in these ways, you are being a leader worth emulating!

Young person, I encourage you to be confident in the Lord. Lead by being a godly example. If God has called you to serve and to lead in some area, serve with confidence. As you grow older, the elders of your church may even "lay hands" on you to commission you to lead a ministry. As you prove faithful in the small things, you will be given larger responsibilities. Whatever God gives you to do, serve him with all your heart. That is the way you grow!

And then the Apostle Paul gave Timothy this key exhortation: "For God did not give us a spirit of timidity, but a spirit of power, of love and of self-discipline" (2 Tim. 1:7). We are called not to be timid—to be shy—about sharing Christ; rather, by the grace of God we are called to share confidently because we know that God's Spirit is with us. We boldly share with love and with the self-discipline that maximizes our effectiveness.

In 1 Corinthians 16:10 Paul said, "If Timothy comes, see to it that he has nothing to fear while he is with you, for he is carrying on the work of the Lord, just as I am." As we participate in God's work, we have "nothing to fear." Jesus gives us his confidence to share with others! I encourage you, young person, to step out in faith to use the gift God has given you. Through the Holy Spirit, you will be given his enabling power, love, and self-discipline to use your gift to bless others!

In 2 Timothy 1:8-9, Paul exhorted Timothy to not hold back: "So do not be ashamed to testify about our Lord, or ashamed of me his prisoner. But join with me in suffering for the gospel, by the power of God, who has saved us and called us to a holy life—not because of anything we have done but because of his own purpose and grace." Because of the Lord's great salvation and out of love for him, we should not be shy about sharing him with others. We should not be ashamed. In fact, it's an honor to suffer for the cause of Christ.

Paul called his "dear son" Timothy to total commitment to Jesus, so much so that Timothy would even be willing to undergo persecution. To endure suffering is not a typical parent's desire for one's child, but Paul knew that to suffer for the cause of Christ is more than worth it. Paul proclaimed this statement about his life: "For to me, to live is Christ and to die is gain" (Phil. 1:21). Paul's life was *Christ*, and he exhorted Timothy to join with him in suffering for God's cause.

Parents, what do you want for your children? The "American dream"? Success, a good career, prosperity? Or do you desire that your young person would surrender to the Lord and be poured out in service to him? To give all for the cause of Christ is worth it!

What about our lives? Are we totally committed to Jesus? Do we love the Lord with all our heart? Are we willing to sell all for Christ? Paul said, "I am not ashamed of the gospel, because it is the power of God for the salvation of everyone who believes" (Rom. 1:16). It's an honor to suffer for God's cause. Of course, this view of suffering is not typical in our society today.

Because the Lord has given us so great a salvation, Paul was called to be "a herald and an apostle and a teacher" (2 Tim. 1:11). About his call, Paul explained, "That is why I am suffering as I am. Yet I am not ashamed, because I know whom I have believed, and am convinced that he is able to guard what I have entrusted to him for that day" (2 Tim. 1:12). Paul *knew* the Lord; he knew that God is faithful—he had experienced God's faithfulness! He had confidence in the Lord! Because of this confidence, he was not ashamed and did all he could to share the good news of our loving Savior! Moreover, Paul was convinced that the Lord was able to guard his salvation, his work, and his investment in reaching people. In fact, he entrusted *everything* to God's care!

Paul provided a sound pattern—a blueprint for godly living—both to Timothy and to us. He exhorted Timothy to give sound teaching "with faith and love in Christ Jesus" (2 Tim. 1:13). He called Timothy to "guard the good deposit that was entrusted to you—guard it with the help of the Holy Spirit who lives in us" (2 Tim. 1:14).

Young person, we can take to heart Paul's same exhortations to Timothy for us: to guard the good deposit that the Lord has placed in us, to follow God's Word and sound teaching for our lives, to use our gifts to share the gospel with others, and to allow the Holy Spirit to raise us up to be champions for his use! Remember that you have the help of the Holy Spirit inside you to guard your salvation and to inspire you in being a Christ-like disciple—one who reaches out with Jesus' love! Be confident to share the Lord with others!

Memory Passage

> 2 Timothy 1:5-7 "I have been reminded of your sincere faith, which first lived in your grandmother Lois and in your mother Eunice and, I am persuaded, now lives in you also. For this reason I remind you to fan into flame the gift of God, which is in you through the laying on of my hands. For God did not give us a spirit of timidity, but a spirit of power, of love and of self-discipline."

CONCLUSION

The Courage Challenge is the call to be a champion for God. It's a personal challenge: Will you stand up for God? Will you stand up for righteousness? Will you be willing to stand alone if need be? It's a call to respond courageously to life's challenges. It's a call to help others—to be an "others-focused champion."

At the same time, the Courage Challenge is not a call to be strong in yourself. It's a call to depend on the Lord Jesus. God's challenge to Joshua as he was about to lead the people to take the promised land expresses the heart of the Courage Challenge: "Have I not commanded you? Be strong and courageous. Do not be terrified; do not be discouraged, *for the Lord your God will be with you wherever you go*" (Joshua 1:9, italics added). If you are confident that the Lord is with you, then that focus gives you the courage you need.

The only way to know that God is with you is to become born again. Romans 10:9 shares how we can become saved: "If you confess with your mouth, 'Jesus is Lord,' and believe in your heart that God raised him from the dead, you will be saved." John 1:12-13 affirms the truth of salvation: "Yet to all who received him, to those who believed in his name, he gave the right to become children of God—children born not of natural descent, nor of human decision or a husband's will, but born of God." If you receive Jesus as Lord, then you can be confident that he is with you! Being conscious of God's presence gives you the courage to be a champion!

This life takes courage! To stand for God in this society takes courage! If you seek the Lord with all your heart, he will reveal his plans for you. I encourage you to be a courageous champion by focusing on God's presence! Always remember: The Lord is with you!

BIBLIOGRAPHY

Barton, David. *Benjamin Rush: Signer of the Declaration of Independence*. Aledo, Texas: WallBuilder Press, 1999.

Fugate, J. R. *What the Bible Says about . . . Child Training*. 2nd ed. Tempe, AZ: Foundation for Biblical Research, 1996.

Josephus. *Antiquities*.

King James Version of the Holy Bible (KJV).

Lewis, C. S. *The Abolition of Man*. United Kingdom: Oxford University Press, 1943.

Printed in the United States
By Bookmasters